TEXT BOOK OF RESEARCH METHODOLOGY & IPR

DR.GAMPA VIJAYA KUMAR | DR.AKKALADEVI MURALIDHAR RAO

Made with ♥ on the Notion Press Platform
www.notionpress.com

Contents

Preface

The importance of research methodology and intellectual property rights (IPR) in the field of pharmaceutical sciences cannot be overstated. As educators and researchers, we have observed the challenges students face in finding comprehensive and reliable resources that cover these critical areas. To address this gap, we havc authored the "Text Book of Research Methodology & IPR," aiming to provide a thorough and accessible guide for students pursuing pharmaceutical chemistry.

This book is born out of our collective experience and dedication to fostering academic excellence. Dr. Gampa Vijaya Kumar, Professor & Principal at the Department of Pharmacy, KGRITM, Hyderabad, and Dr. Akkaladevi Muralidhar Rao, Principal at St. Mary's College of Pharmacy, Secunderabad, bring together a wealth of knowledge and practical insights. Our goal is to make complex concepts in research methodology and IPR more digestible, ensuring students have all the necessary tools and information at their fingertips.

The textbook is structured to cover the entire spectrum of research methodology, from understanding and formulating research problems to conducting effective literature reviews and adhering to ethical standards. Additionally, it delves into the realm of IPR, elucidating the nuances of patents, trademarks, copyrights, and geographical indications. By including detailed explanations, real-world examples, and case studies, we aim to bridge the gap between theoretical knowledge and practical application.

We have meticulously designed this book to align with the syllabus requirements of Jawaharlal Nehru Technological University Hyderabad (JNTUH), ensuring it serves as a comprehensive reference for M.Pharm students. Each chapter is crafted to provide in-depth knowledge and foster critical thinking, enabling students to navigate the intricacies of research and innovation effectively.

We are confident that this textbook will become an essential resource for students, educators, and researchers in the pharmaceutical field. It is our hope that it will inspire and equip the next generation of pharmaceutical scientists to achieve excellence in their academic and professional endeavors.

We extend our gratitude to our colleagues, students, and the academic community for their continuous support and encouragement. Together, let us advance the frontiers of pharmaceutical research and innovation.

Sincerely,

Dr. Gampa Vijaya Kumar
Professor & Principal, Dept. of Pharmacy, KGRITM, Hyderabad

Dr. Akkaladevi Muralidhar Rao
Principal, St. Mary's College of Pharmacy, Secunderabad

Text Book Of Research Methodology & Ipr

Dr. GAMPA VIJAYA KUMAR

Professor & Principal, Dept. of Pharmacy, KGRITM, Hyderabad

&

Dr. AKKALADEVI MURALIDHAR RAO

Principal, St. Mary's College of Pharmacy, Secunderabad

Published by Notion Press

Notion Press, Inc.
800, West EI Camino Real #180,
California USA 94040

Notion Press Media Pvt Ltd,
#7, Red Cross Road,
Egmore, Chennai, Tamil Nadu 600008

Email ID: publish@notionpress.com

Phone Number: +91 44 46315631

CHAPTER ONE

UNDERSTANDING RESEARCH PROBLEMS

1.1 Introduction to Research Problems

1.1.1 Definition and Importance

Definition of a Research Problem

A research problem is a clear, concise statement about an area of concern, a condition to be improved, a difficulty to be eliminated, or a troubling question that exists in scholarly literature, in theory, or in practice that points to the need for meaningful understanding and deliberate investigation. In the context of scientific inquiry, identifying a research problem is the first step in a systematic study. It serves as the foundation on which the entire framework of the research project is built. By clearly defining what needs to be studied and providing a clear question or statement, the research problem sets the stage for hypothesis formulation and subsequent research design.

Importance in Guiding Research Direction and Focus

The significance of a well-defined research problem extends beyond mere academic interest; it is pivotal in guiding the research direction and sharpening its focus. When a research problem is specified, it aids researchers in delineating their study's boundaries, focusing on relevant data, and avoiding areas that are not pertinent to the immediate goals of the study. This focus ensures that resources such as time, effort, and finance are utilized efficiently and that the research does not deviate from its intended objectives.

Moreover, a well-articulated research problem is essential for guiding the choice of research methods, determining the research design, and selecting the appropriate analytical tools and techniques. It helps in formulating research questions and/or hypotheses that are specific, measurable, attainable, relevant, and time-bound (SMART). Such clarity increases the likelihood of producing valid and reliable results that can contribute effectively to the body of knowledge in the field.

Additionally, the clarity of a research problem facilitates peer understanding and critique, which are crucial for scholarly communication. It enables other researchers to understand the scope and scale of the research, thus allowing for better evaluation of its applicability and generalizability. This clarity and focus driven by a well-defined research problem enhance the impact and relevance of the research outcomes, potentially leading to significant advancements in the field and informing future research directions.

1.1.2 Types of Research Problems

Theoretical vs. Applied Problems

Theoretical Problems Theoretical research problems focus on expanding and refining existing knowledge or theories. They are concerned with understanding the fundamental aspects of a concept or phenomenon, often driven by curiosity and the pursuit of knowledge for its own sake. Theoretical problems may not have immediate practical applications but are vital for the continuous development of a discipline. They help in building, testing, and refining the theories that ultimately form the basis for applied research. Researchers tackling theoretical problems typically engage in extensive literature review and conceptual analysis to identify gaps or inconsistencies in existing theories that need further exploration.

Applied Problems In contrast, applied research problems are directly related to solving real-world issues. These problems are designed to address specific, practical questions that affect individuals, organizations, or societies. The primary goal of research addressing applied problems is to produce findings that can be implemented to improve conditions or resolve issues within a specific context. For example, developing a new pharmaceutical treatment for a disease or optimizing a manufacturing process are types of applied research problems. This kind of research is often valued by funding bodies because of its potential to lead to tangible benefits and immediate solutions.

Descriptive vs. Causal Problems

Descriptive Problems Descriptive research problems are concerned with describing characteristics of a phenomenon or the state of a situation as accurately as possible. The aim is to paint a clear picture of what is occurring or to map out the dimensions of a phenomenon without delving into what causes it. Questions like "What is the current rate of medication adherence among patients with chronic illnesses?" or "How do consumers perceive a new product?" are examples of descriptive research problems. This type of research is often preliminary and can serve as a stepping-stone to more complex studies.

Causal Problems Causal research problems, on the other hand, are interested in determining cause-and-effect relationships between variables. The focus is on understanding whether, how, and under what circumstances one variable affects another. This type of research problem is crucial for developing knowledge that can predict how changes in one variable might influence another, thereby allowing for interventions. For example, a causal study might investigate whether a new teaching method improves student learning outcomes compared to traditional methods. Causal research is more complex as it requires rigorous experimental designs or statistical methods to ensure that the observed effects are due to the variables being studied and not external factors.

1.2 Sources of Research Problems

1.2.1 Academic Literature

Identifying Gaps in Existing Research

One of the most fruitful sources for identifying research problems is through academic literature. Reviewing existing studies provides a critical insight into what has been explored and what remains under-investigated. Gaps can manifest as unexplored areas, insufficient data, conflicting results, or limited scopes of previous studies. Researchers scrutinize literature to pinpoint these deficiencies, which often highlight the need for further investigation. Identifying such gaps not only contributes to the continuity of scholarly work but also ensures the progressive build-up of knowledge in a specific field. For instance, if previous studies on a medication's effectiveness have been limited to certain populations, a gap might exist in understanding its impact on different demographic groups, thus warranting further study.

Building on Previous Studies

Building on previous studies is another significant method through which research problems are derived from academic literature. This approach involves extending the research by adding new dimensions, using different methodologies, or exploring new populations. By building on the foundations laid by prior work, researchers can deepen and broaden the understanding of a subject. For example, if earlier research provided a basic model of consumer behavior, subsequent studies might explore how cultural differences modify these behaviors. This approach not only helps in validating previous findings but also in refining and expanding theoretical frameworks. It encourages a cumulative progression of knowledge that is essential for the advancement of any scientific or academic discipline.

Each of these methods of sourcing problems from academic literature serves to strengthen the interconnected network of research, encouraging a systematic exploration that continuously evolves and expands the boundaries of knowledge.

1.2.2 Practical Observations

Problems Identified in Professional Practice

Practical observations in professional settings often reveal research problems that are directly relevant to the field. These problems typically emerge from the day-to-day experiences of professionals who encounter inefficiencies, unmet needs, or unexpected challenges. For instance, in healthcare, doctors might notice that a certain treatment is less effective in a specific subgroup of patients, prompting research into alternative therapies or tailored treatment plans. Similarly, engineers might identify durability issues in materials used in construction, leading to studies aimed at developing more resilient materials. Identifying research problems through professional practice not only ensures that the research is grounded in real-world relevance but also enhances the potential for practical applications of the research findings.

Issues Observed in Real-World Settings

Research problems can also originate from issues observed in broader real-world settings beyond professional practices. These problems often involve complex social, economic, or environmental issues that affect communities, regions, or even global populations. For example, urban planners observing traffic congestion in major cities might initiate research into more efficient public transportation systems. Environmental scientists might study changes in local biodiversity due to urban expansion to develop strategies for conservation. Research stemming from real-world observations is crucial as it addresses immediate and tangible issues, offering solutions that can significantly impact people's lives and well-being.

Both sources of research problems from practical observations—whether in professional practice or wider real-world settings—highlight the essential link between observation and inquiry. They underscore the importance of research in solving practical problems and advancing our ability to manage and improve various aspects of professional and everyday life.

1.2.3 Societal Needs and Trends

Emerging Societal Issues

Research problems often arise from emerging societal issues that reflect the changing dynamics of populations, cultures, or economic conditions. These issues are identified through the observation of social trends, public health data, policy changes, and demographic shifts, among other indicators. For instance, aging populations in many countries pose new challenges in healthcare, pension systems, and social services, prompting a range of studies aimed at addressing these challenges. Similarly, the increasing awareness of mental health issues has led to research focused on better diagnostic tools, treatment programs, and public health strategies. Addressing these emerging societal issues through research is crucial as it helps societies adapt to changes and improve the quality of life for their populations.

Technological Advancements and Their Implications

Technological advancements are a significant driver of new research problems. As technology evolves, it continuously reshapes industries, lifestyles, and the very fabric of society, often outpacing the existing regulatory and ethical frameworks. Researchers investigate the implications of these advancements to understand their impacts fully and to guide their development in beneficial directions. For example, the rise of artificial intelligence (AI) invites studies into its ethical use, its effects on employment, and its potential biases. Similarly, advancements in genetic engineering prompt research into bioethical issues, regulatory needs, and social acceptance. The rapid pace of technological change makes it a particularly rich area for research, as scholars seek to forecast future trends and prepare for their implications.

These two sources from societal needs and trends—emerging societal issues and technological advancements—underscore the responsive nature of research. They highlight how research is not only a tool for understanding but also for intervention, shaping societal structures and responses to ensure progress and mitigate adverse impacts.

1.2.4 Personal Interests and Experiences

Drawing from Personal Expertise and Curiosity

Personal interests and experiences of researchers often serve as a deep wellspring for identifying unique and compelling research problems. When researchers draw on their own expertise and areas of curiosity, they bring a passionate and insightful perspective to their work. This personal connection can lead to the exploration of niche areas that might otherwise be overlooked in broader academic or practical contexts. For instance, a researcher with a background in folk medicine might choose to investigate the scientific underpinnings of traditional remedies, potentially uncovering new applications for contemporary medicine. Personal curiosity not only fuels the persistence required for extensive research but also guides the researcher to ask distinctive questions that can lead to innovative discoveries and contributions to knowledge.

Leveraging Unique Perspectives

Leveraging unique personal perspectives in research allows for the exploration of problems that reflect diverse experiences and backgrounds. This approach can significantly enrich the research field by introducing new viewpoints and methodologies. For example, a researcher from a minority background might explore health disparities affecting their community, which are often underrepresented in mainstream research. By bringing personal insights into the research process, these unique perspectives can help address gaps in understanding and provide solutions that are culturally sensitive and broadly inclusive. Furthermore, leveraging personal experiences can help tailor research outcomes to serve specific populations better, enhancing the applicability and impact of the research.

Both personal expertise and unique perspectives highlight the value of individuality in research. They remind us that behind every scientific inquiry and exploration lies a human element, which when effectively harnessed, can lead to profound insights and meaningful change.

1.3 Criteria for a Good Research Problem

1.3.1 Clarity and Specificity

Defining the Problem Clearly

A good research problem must be defined with utmost clarity to ensure that it is understandable and manageable. Clarity in defining a research problem involves articulating it in a way that is precise and easy to comprehend. This clarity helps in setting the direction for the research and in communicating the purpose and objectives to others, including peers, academic advisors, and potential funding bodies. A clearly defined problem leaves no ambiguity about what the researcher intends to investigate, which facilitates the development of a coherent research strategy. For example, instead of a broad topic like "health effects of pollution," a clearer problem would be "examining the respiratory health effects of particulate matter exposure among children in urban areas." This specificity not only sharpens the focus of the research but also enhances the formulation of research questions and hypotheses.

Narrowing Down the Focus

Narrowing down the focus of a research problem is essential to make the research feasible and focused. A well-narrowed problem allows the researcher to delve deeply into a specific aspect of a broader topic, making the study more manageable and the findings more profound. This specificity aids in concentrating resources and efforts on a particular issue, enhancing the overall quality and depth of the research. It also helps in defining the scope of the study, which is crucial for maintaining a clear boundary of what the study will cover and what it will not. For instance, focusing on "the impact of interactive digital learning tools on mathematics achievement in middle school students" rather than a vague, broad investigation into "technology in education" allows for a more detailed study that can yield actionable insights specific to the chosen focus.

In summary, clarity and specificity are foundational to crafting a good research problem. They ensure that the research is directed and insightful, providing a solid basis for the entire research process, from methodology selection to data analysis and reporting of findings.

1.3.2 Relevance and Significance

Importance to the Field and Society

For a research problem to be considered good, it must hold significant relevance to both the academic field and society at large. This relevance is measured by the problem's potential to address a pressing issue, fill a critical gap in the existing literature, or provide solutions to societal challenges. A research problem that resonates with current needs and aligns with societal goals tends to attract more interest, funding, and support from both academic and non-academic sectors. For example, research into renewable energy technologies gains importance due to the global push for sustainable development and the urgent need to reduce reliance on fossil fuels. Similarly, studies focused on improving online privacy protections become increasingly relevant in the digital age, reflecting societal concerns about data security and personal privacy. The importance of a research problem to the field and society ensures that the findings are likely to be utilized and valued, thereby maximizing the impact of the research.

Potential to Contribute New Knowledge

Another crucial criterion for a good research problem is its potential to contribute new knowledge or insights to the field. This involves not only discovering new facts or data but also developing new theories, refining existing models, or providing a new understanding of established concepts. The potential for a research problem to expand the boundaries of knowledge is a key driver of academic inquiry, fostering innovation and intellectual growth within the discipline. For instance, a study investigating the underlying mechanisms of Alzheimer's disease could potentially revolutionize treatments and preventive strategies, contributing significantly to medical science. Additionally, research that challenges conventional wisdom or explores uncharted territories can lead to paradigm shifts and open up new avenues for further investigation. The capability of a research problem to add to the knowledge pool is essential for the continual evolution of any field, making it a fundamental aspect of a good research problem.

1.3.3 Feasibility and Manageability

Availability of Resources and Data

A critical aspect of a good research problem is its feasibility, which largely depends on the availability of necessary resources and data. The resources in question can include a wide range of elements, from funding and equipment to skilled personnel. Similarly, data availability is crucial for conducting thorough and meaningful research. Researchers must consider whether they can access the required data, whether through existing databases, through primary data collection, or via collaborations with other institutions. For example, a research problem investigating the effects of a new drug might require access to clinical trial facilities, patient groups for testing, and funding to cover these activities. If these resources and data are not reasonably accessible, the research problem may need to be adjusted to reflect what is realistically achievable, ensuring that the project can be completed successfully and within reasonable timeframes.

Practicality of the Research Scope

The scope of the research problem must also be practical. This means that the problem should be neither too broad nor too narrow, but instead appropriately scaled to match the researcher's time frame, expertise, and resource availability. A practical scope ensures that the research can be managed effectively and that the objectives can be realistically achieved. For instance, a study aiming to analyze the global economic impact of climate change over the next century might be too broad and ambitious for a single research team to handle without extensive support and collaboration. Conversely, a study examining the preferences for coffee brands in a small town might be too narrow to warrant extensive resources. Researchers must balance ambition with practicality, ensuring that the scope of their research problem allows for a thorough investigation that can be completed efficiently and effectively.

Both the availability of resources and data and the practicality of the research scope are essential for ensuring that a research problem is feasible and manageable. These considerations help prevent projects from being stalled or failing due to overambition or underestimation of the necessary logistical arrangements.

1.3.4 Originality and Innovation

Novelty of the Problem

Originality in a research problem is essential for contributing fresh perspectives and new insights to the field. A novel research problem explores areas that are either completely unexamined or have only been superficially addressed in previous studies. The novelty of a research problem can stem from a variety of sources, such as new phenomena, recent technological advancements, or evolving societal trends that have not yet been thoroughly investigated. For example, researching the impact of virtual reality on rehabilitation therapies for stroke patients could be considered novel if previous studies have not extensively explored this intersection. The introduction of a novel problem not only fills knowledge gaps but also stimulates further research and discussion within the academic community, thereby enriching the field.

Potential for Innovative Solutions

Alongside originality, the potential for innovative solutions is a critical attribute of a good research problem. This involves looking at existing problems through new lenses or applying new methodologies and technologies to solve old challenges. Innovative solutions are particularly valued because they can lead to breakthroughs that significantly advance the field, offering more effective, efficient, or sustainable outcomes. For instance, a research problem that investigates the use of artificial intelligence to optimize traffic flow in urban centers has the potential to yield innovative solutions that could transform urban planning and management. Innovation in research often requires creative thinking and a willingness to take risks, venturing into untested or speculative areas that, if successful, could deliver substantial rewards.

Originality and innovation are closely linked in defining the quality and impact of a research problem. They ensure that the research does not merely replicate what is already known but pushes the boundaries of knowledge and application. This drive towards original and innovative research fosters a dynamic academic environment and contributes significantly to technological and societal advancements.

1.4 Errors in Selecting Research Problems

1.4.1 Common Pitfalls

Selecting Overly Broad or Vague Problems

One of the most common pitfalls in selecting research problems is opting for topics that are too broad or vague. Such problems often lack a clear focus, making it difficult to formulate precise research questions and hypotheses. When a problem is too broad, it can lead to a dispersal of efforts and resources, making it challenging to achieve any significant depth in the research findings. For instance, a research problem like "studying the effects of climate change" is immensely broad, encompassing myriad variables and potential effects across the globe. Narrowing this problem to a specific aspect, such as "the impact of rising sea levels on coastal urban infrastructure," would provide a more manageable scope and clearer direction for systematic investigation.

Choosing Problems with Limited Data Availability

Another significant error is selecting a research problem without ensuring the availability of necessary data. This can stall the research process if data are inaccessible, too costly to obtain, or non-existent. Before committing to a research problem, it is crucial to conduct a preliminary review to ascertain the availability of data or the feasibility of collecting new data. Failing to do so can lead to significant delays and might even require a complete redefinition of the research problem midway through the project. For example, if a researcher intends to study the long-term health outcomes of a new drug, but clinical trial data are proprietary or incomplete, the research would face substantial obstacles right from the start. Checking data availability and considering alternative sources or methods of data collection are essential steps in the selection of a viable research problem.

These pitfalls highlight the importance of careful and thoughtful selection of research problems. Avoiding these common errors by ensuring clarity, focus, and data availability can greatly enhance the effectiveness and efficiency of the research process.

1.4.2 How to Avoid Them

Conducting Thorough Preliminary Research

To avoid the pitfalls of selecting an inappropriate research problem, it is crucial to conduct thorough preliminary research. This step involves extensive literature reviews to understand the current state of research in the intended area of study. By doing so, researchers can identify what has been done, which areas are oversaturated, and where significant gaps exist. This groundwork helps in formulating a research problem that is both original and achievable. Additionally, preliminary research can reveal the availability of data and resources, which are critical for the feasibility of the project. It also allows the researcher to gauge the scope and complexity of the problem, ensuring that it is neither too broad nor too narrow.

Consulting with Experts and Peers

Consultation with experts and peers in the field is another effective strategy to avoid common pitfalls in selecting research problems. Feedback from experienced researchers can provide invaluable insights into the relevance and viability of the proposed problem. Experts can offer advice on refining the problem statement, potential methodological approaches, and pitfalls to avoid. Peer consultation, especially during conferences, workshops, or seminars, can also expose the researcher to different perspectives and constructive criticism that can strengthen the research proposal. These interactions help in building a robust network and can lead to collaborations that enhance the quality and scope of the research.

Refining the Problem Statement Iteratively

Refining the research problem statement iteratively is a critical process that can significantly mitigate the risk of selecting an unsuitable problem. This involves continuously sharpening and focusing the research question based on feedback from preliminary research and consultations, as well as ongoing analysis of literature and data. Each iteration should aim to clarify the purpose, enhance the specificity, and align the problem with available resources and methods. This iterative process helps in developing a well-defined, targeted research problem that is deeply rooted in the current needs and gaps of the field. It ensures that the research problem remains relevant and feasible throughout the study, adapting as necessary to new findings and insights.

By employing these strategies—conducting thorough preliminary research, consulting with experts and peers, and refining the problem statement iteratively—researchers can effectively avoid common pitfalls in selecting research problems and set a solid foundation for a successful research project.

1.5 Scope and Objectives

1.5.1 Defining the Scope of Research

Determining the Boundaries of the Study

Defining the scope of research is crucial for setting clear boundaries that determine what the study will cover and what it will exclude. This delineation helps to focus the research efforts and ensures that the project remains manageable and within reasonable limits. It involves specifying the geographical area, the time frame, the population, and the aspects of the phenomenon that will be examined. For example, a study on the impact of educational interventions on student performance might limit its scope to middle school students within a particular city over one academic year. By clearly defining these boundaries, researchers can concentrate their resources and methods on a targeted set of data, enhancing the study's effectiveness and relevance.

Identifying Key Variables and Parameters

Another critical aspect of defining the research scope is identifying the key variables and parameters that will be investigated. This step involves deciding which variables are essential for understanding the phenomenon and determining how they will be measured. Variables can include independent variables (which are manipulated), dependent variables (which are observed), and controlling variables (which are held constant to prevent external influence on the outcomes). Properly identifying and defining these variables ensure that the research can systematically address the research problem. For example, in a study examining the effects of a specific dietary intervention on blood pressure, key variables would include the type of diet (independent variable), blood pressure levels (dependent variable), and factors like age and baseline health status (control variables). Identifying these variables is crucial for designing the study's methodology and for ensuring that the data collected will be relevant and adequate to answer the research questions.

By thoughtfully determining the boundaries of the study and identifying key variables and parameters, researchers can effectively define the scope of their research. This definition plays a fundamental role in guiding all subsequent stages of the research process, from the design and implementation of the study to the analysis and interpretation of results.

1.5.2 Setting Clear and Achievable Objectives

Formulating Specific Research Questions

Setting clear and achievable objectives begins with formulating specific research questions. These questions should be directly derived from the research problem and must be precise enough to guide the investigation. A well-crafted research question focuses the study on particular aspects of the topic and delineates the scope of inquiry. This specificity helps in designing the methodology and in aligning the research with its intended outcomes. For example, instead of a general question like "How does technology affect learning?", a more specific question would be "What is the impact of interactive digital tools on the math achievement of high school students in rural areas?" This level of specificity not only narrows down the focus but also sets a clear direction for the study, making it easier to determine which data to collect and which analytical approaches to use.

Establishing Measurable Goals and Outcomes

Along with specific research questions, setting measurable goals and outcomes is essential for successful research. These goals should be clearly defined, quantifiable, and achievable within the scope and resources of the project. They serve as benchmarks for assessing the progress and success of the research. Measurable goals require clear criteria for evaluation, which might include statistical evidence, qualitative analysis, or specific performance metrics. For instance, a measurable goal for a public health study might be to "reduce the incidence of smoking among teenagers by 20% over the next two years through targeted educational programs." This goal is not only specific and aligned with the research question but also quantifiable and time-bound, providing a clear target against which the effectiveness of the intervention can be measured.

Setting clear and achievable objectives through specific research questions and measurable goals ensures that the research is structured, focused, and oriented towards obtaining meaningful and valuable results. These objectives guide the entire research process, providing a roadmap for what the study aims to achieve and how it plans to achieve it.

1.5.3 Aligning Objectives with Research Goals

Ensuring Objectives Support the Overall Research Aim

Aligning the specific objectives of a study with its overarching research goals is crucial for ensuring coherence and relevance in the research process. Each objective should directly contribute to fulfilling the broader aim of the research, effectively acting as stepping stones towards achieving the main goal. This alignment guarantees that every component of the research is purposeful and that resources are utilized efficiently. For instance, if the overall aim of a research project is to evaluate the effectiveness of a new educational curriculum, the objectives might include assessing student engagement, comparing test scores before and after implementation, and analyzing teacher feedback. Each of these objectives should be crafted to directly feed into the overarching aim, providing clear evidence and insights related to the curriculum's effectiveness.

Prioritizing Objectives Based on Importance and Feasibility

Prioritizing research objectives involves evaluating them based on their importance to the research aim and their feasibility given the available resources and constraints. This prioritization helps in managing the research process, particularly when resources are limited or when objectives may be competing for attention. Important objectives that directly impact the research outcome should be prioritized higher and given more attention in terms of time and resources. Feasibility is also a critical consideration; objectives that are more realistic to achieve with the available resources and within the timeframe of the project should be prioritized to ensure that the research can be completed successfully. For example, if a project involves multiple complex objectives, a researcher might prioritize a pivotal experiment that tests the main hypothesis over a supplementary survey that provides additional but less critical information.

By ensuring that objectives support the overall research aim and prioritizing them based on importance and feasibility, researchers can create a focused and efficient research plan. This alignment not only enhances the integrity and impact of the research but also maximizes the chances of achieving meaningful results that contribute significantly to the field.

1.6 Investigative Approaches

1.6.1 Methods for Investigating Research Problems

Qualitative Methods: Interviews, Focus Groups, Case Studies

Qualitative research methods are invaluable for gaining deep insights into phenomena, particularly those involving complex human behaviors, feelings, and interactions. These methods allow researchers to explore the nuances of a research problem in a detailed and exploratory manner.

- **Interviews** are a fundamental qualitative technique where researchers conduct one-on-one conversations with participants to gather in-depth information. This method is particularly effective for exploring personal experiences, opinions, and motivations, allowing for a deep dive into individual perspectives.
- **Focus Groups** involve guided discussions with a small group of people. This method is excellent for generating a broad range of ideas, gauging consensus, and understanding the diversity of perspectives within a target population. Focus groups are particularly useful when the interaction among participants can illuminate new aspects of a topic.
- **Case Studies** are a comprehensive approach to studying particular instances (individuals, groups, organizations, events) in depth and within their real-life context. Case studies are particularly effective in providing detailed insights into complex issues, and they can be used to illustrate broader trends and draw specific, contextually rich conclusions.

Quantitative Methods: Surveys, Experiments, Statistical Analysis

Quantitative research methods are designed to quantify the problem by way of generating numerical data or data that can be transformed into usable statistics. They are useful for quantifying attitudes, opinions, behaviors, and other defined variables and generalizing results from a larger sample population.

- **Surveys** are a common quantitative method that involves asking people a set of standardized questions. This approach can reach a large number of people relatively quickly and economically, making it ideal for studies that require broad data collection.
- **Experiments** provide a way to perform controlled tests to determine the cause-and-effect relationships between variables. This method is fundamental in fields like psychology, medicine, and the natural sciences, where isolating and testing variables can directly inform policy and practice.
- **Statistical Analysis** is used to analyze the data collected through various quantitative methods. It involves applying mathematical theories and formulas to quantify relationships, test hypotheses, and make

predictions. Statistical techniques can range from simple descriptive statistics that summarize data to complex inferential statistics that draw conclusions about a larger population based on a sample.

Both qualitative and quantitative methods have their distinct strengths and can often be used complementarily to provide a comprehensive understanding of a research problem. Choosing the right investigative approach depends on the nature of the research question, the specific objectives of the study, and the type of data required to answer those questions effectively.

1.6.2 Data Collection Techniques

Primary Data Collection: Observations, Experiments, Surveys

Primary data collection involves gathering new data first-hand for the specific purpose of addressing the research question. This data is original and collected at the source, providing a direct measurement of the variables of interest.

- **Observations** are a fundamental method of primary data collection where researchers systematically record behavior, processes, or physical aspects of a situation as they naturally occur in real-time, without manipulating the environment. This method is particularly useful in fields like anthropology, sociology, and education.
- **Experiments** involve manipulating one variable to determine if changes in one variable cause changes in another variable. This method allows researchers to establish cause-and-effect relationships between variables under controlled conditions, typically within a laboratory setting or structured field environments.
- **Surveys** are used to collect data from a predefined group of respondents. They are designed to gather large amounts of data in a standardized form, allowing for efficient analysis across a broad population. Surveys can be administered in various formats, such as online questionnaires, telephone interviews, or paper forms distributed to respondents.

Secondary Data Collection: Literature Review, Existing Datasets

Secondary data collection involves using data that has already been collected by other researchers or organizations. This type of data is accessible through various sources and can be reanalyzed or used as a basis for comparison with primary data.

- **Literature Review** is a systematic method of collecting data from existing research published in books, articles, and online databases. The purpose of a literature review is to summarize, analyze, and synthesize the published material to provide a foundation of knowledge on which current research can build.
- **Existing Datasets** can be obtained from numerous sources, including government agencies, non-governmental organizations, and previous research studies. These datasets may provide extensive data that can be used for statistical analysis without the need for time-consuming and expensive data collection efforts. Researchers can use these datasets to validate findings from primary data or to identify trends and patterns that are not observable in smaller, primary data sets.

Both primary and secondary data collection techniques are crucial in the research process. They each have specific roles and can complement each other, providing a richer and more comprehensive analysis when combined effectively. Choosing the appropriate data collection technique depends on the research objectives, the nature of the data needed, and the resources available to the research project.

1.6.3 Data Analysis and Interpretation

Qualitative Data Analysis: Coding, Thematic Analysis

Qualitative data analysis involves processing non-numerical data (e.g., text, video, or audio) to identify patterns, themes, or insights. This form of analysis is interpretative, aiming to understand the deeper significance and implications of the data collected.

- **Coding** is one of the primary steps in qualitative data analysis. It involves categorizing the collected data into segments that are tagged with a label that accurately describes the essence of those segments. This process helps to systematically organize the data and prepare it for deeper analysis. For example, interviews might be coded to identify common responses or feelings among participants.
- **Thematic Analysis** is a method used for identifying, analyzing, and reporting patterns (themes) within data. It minimally organizes and describes your data set in rich detail. However, frequently it goes further than this and interprets various aspects of the research topic. For instance, in exploring the experiences of participants using a new healthcare service, thematic analysis might reveal themes such as

"accessibility issues" and "perceived benefits," which provide insights into the service's impact and areas for improvement.

Quantitative Data Analysis: Descriptive Statistics, Inferential Statistics

Quantitative data analysis involves numerical data to quantify patterns and draw conclusions based on statistical significance.

- **Descriptive Statistics** provide a way to summarize and describe the features of a collection of data effectively. This can include measures of central tendency like the mean, median, and mode, which provide information on the typical values of a dataset, and measures of dispersion like standard deviation and variance, which tell how spread out the values are.
- **Inferential Statistics** involve techniques that allow the drawing of conclusions and the making of predictions about a population based on a sample. This form of analysis is used to infer properties of an underlying distribution of data. Common methods include hypothesis testing, regression analysis, and ANOVA, which help determine if the observed effects are statistically significant, or if they might have occurred by chance.

Both qualitative and quantitative analysis methods play crucial roles in the interpretation of collected data. Qualitative analysis allows for a detailed and nuanced understanding of the data, uncovering deeper insights into participants' attitudes, behaviors, and experiences. Quantitative analysis provides the means to quantify these insights and apply them to larger populations, making it possible to generalize findings and apply them in practical settings. Together, these methods provide a comprehensive toolkit for researchers to analyze and interpret their data effectively.

1.6.4 Necessary Instrumentation and Tools

Laboratory Equipment and Software for Data Collection

Effective data collection in research often relies on the availability and use of specific laboratory equipment and software. The type of equipment required depends on the nature of the study but commonly includes instruments for measuring, recording, and controlling experimental conditions.

- **Laboratory Equipment**: This can range from basic items like microscopes and spectrometers to more specialized apparatus like chromatography systems for chemical analysis or electrophoresis units for DNA and protein studies. For example, in a biology research lab, centrifuges, incubators, and PCR (polymerase chain reaction) machines are fundamental for conducting experiments.
- **Software for Data Collection**: Various types of software are also essential for the efficient collection and initial processing of data. This might include software for experimental design, data logging, or more specialized applications tailored to specific research needs, such as statistical software for clinical trials or simulation software for engineering experiments.

Analytical Tools for Data Processing and Visualization

Once data is collected, it must be processed and analyzed to extract meaningful information. This stage of research uses various analytical tools and software to handle, analyze, and visualize data.

- **Data Processing Software**: Tools like MATLAB, Python (with libraries such as Pandas, NumPy), or R are crucial for processing large sets of data. These tools can perform complex calculations, statistical analyses, and data transformation processes needed to prepare data for final analysis.
- **Data Visualization Tools**: Effective visualization helps in understanding and communicating the results of the research. Tools such as Tableau, Microsoft Excel, or Python's Matplotlib and Seaborn libraries provide powerful capabilities for creating a wide range of visual representations of data, including graphs, charts, and heat maps. These tools are invaluable not just for the analysis phase but also for presenting findings in a way that is accessible to stakeholders or the academic community.

Integration and Compatibility: It's essential that all these instruments and tools are compatible with each other and can integrate smoothly to facilitate a seamless flow of data from collection through to analysis. For example, data collected via laboratory instruments should be easily importable into statistical software without significant conversion.

The choice of instrumentation and tools is crucial for the efficiency and accuracy of both data collection and analysis processes in research. They must be selected carefully based on the specific needs and constraints of the research project to ensure they provide the necessary functionality and are within budgetary limits.

CHAPTER TWO

LITERATURE REVIEW AND RESEARCH ETHICS

2.1 Conducting Effective Literature Studies

2.1.1 Approaches to Literature Review

Systematic Reviews

Systematic reviews are a highly structured form of literature review that aim to collate all empirical evidence fitting pre-specified eligibility criteria in order to answer a specific research question. They are characterized by a rigorous and methodical approach: defining a clear set of objectives with predefined criteria for selecting studies, extensive search strategies that encompass multiple databases to identify all relevant studies, and systematic presentation and synthesis of the findings. This approach minimizes bias and allows for comprehensive coverage of the literature related to a particular research question, making systematic reviews a fundamental tool in evidence-based practice.

Narrative Reviews

Narrative reviews, often less structured, provide a broad overview of existing literature on a specific topic or field. Unlike systematic reviews, they do not typically follow a strict methodological framework and are more subjective in nature. Narrative reviews are useful for gaining a general understanding of a complex subject, identifying key theories, methods, and conclusions in the field. They often serve to identify gaps in research that have not been addressed thoroughly, providing a more exploratory and interpretative analysis of the topic.

Meta-analyses

Meta-analyses are a form of statistical technique used to combine the results of multiple studies that address a set of related research hypotheses. This method is particularly useful in quantifying the effect of a treatment or intervention across several studies and is often an integral part of systematic reviews. By aggregating data from several studies, meta-analyses can provide more precise estimates of the effects of studied interventions than any individual study. This is particularly valuable in fields where research studies may have small sample sizes or when results from individual studies vary widely.

Each of these approaches serves a different purpose and can be chosen based on the specific needs of the research question, the nature of the field of study, and the overall objectives of the researcher. They provide a systematic way to critically analyze and synthesize the vast amount of literature available, ensuring that research findings are based on a comprehensive understanding of existing knowledge.

2.1.2 Identifying Credible Sources

Identifying and utilizing credible sources is crucial for conducting effective literature studies. Credible sources provide reliable and valid data that can support research findings. The most reputable sources typically include peer-reviewed journals, academic books, and well-regarded databases and online resources.

Peer-reviewed Journals

Peer-reviewed journals are considered the gold standard for research credibility. Articles submitted to these journals undergo a rigorous review process by experts in the field before they are published. This process ensures that the research is original, significant, methodologically sound, and that the conclusions are justified by the data. Researchers rely on peer-reviewed journals to obtain up-to-date and accurate information that reflects current trends and innovations in their field.

Academic Books

Academic books published by reputable publishers are another crucial source of credible information. These books are often written by experts and are meticulously reviewed before publication. While they may not be as current as journal articles due to longer publication timelines, academic books can provide comprehensive coverage and in-depth analysis of a topic. They are particularly valuable for gaining a thorough understanding of theoretical frameworks and historical contexts.

Reputable Databases and Online Resources

Reputable databases and online resources are indispensable for accessing a wide range of academic materials. Databases such as PubMed, JSTOR, and Scopus offer access to a large volume of peer-reviewed articles, books, and conference papers across various disciplines. These platforms typically have rigorous selection criteria for the materials they include, ensuring that only credible and authoritative sources are available to researchers. Additionally, reputable online resources such as government publications, reports by recognized institutions, and academic repositories like Google Scholar also provide reliable information that can support a wide range of research activities.

Utilizing these credible sources ensures that the literature review is built on a solid foundation of reliable and authoritative information, crucial for establishing the validity of the research findings. Researchers must be diligent in verifying the credibility of their sources, especially when venturing into new subject areas or reviewing materials from less familiar publications or databases.

2.1.3 Synthesizing Information

Summarizing Key Findings

The first step in synthesizing information from a literature review is to summarize the key findings from the various sources reviewed. This involves distilling the essential points, results, and conclusions from each source into a concise format. Effective summarization allows researchers to understand the core insights and contributions of each work, setting the stage for deeper analysis. This process helps in highlighting significant advancements in the field, areas of agreement or disagreement among researchers, and potential gaps in the existing knowledge.

Identifying Patterns and Trends

Once the key findings are summarized, the next step involves identifying patterns and trends across the literature. This analysis can reveal common themes, methodologies, or results that appear repeatedly in different studies. Recognizing these patterns is crucial for understanding the direction of research in the field and the consensus or divergence among scholars. For instance, in medical research, identifying a trend in successful treatment methods across multiple studies can lead to recommendations for clinical practice or further research.

Developing a Theoretical Framework

The final step in synthesizing information is to develop a theoretical framework based on the patterns and insights identified. This framework serves as a conceptual structure that ties together the existing research and guides the future direction of the study. It provides a basis for formulating hypotheses, designing research methodology, and interpreting subsequent findings. A well-developed theoretical framework integrates the review's findings into a broader scholarly context, offering explanations that extend beyond the data from individual studies. This framework not only helps in contextualizing the research within the field but also in identifying where further inquiry is necessary, thus setting a purposeful path for continuing exploration and contribution to the academic discourse.

Through summarizing key findings, identifying patterns and trends, and developing a theoretical framework, researchers can effectively synthesize information from a comprehensive literature review. This synthesis not only enhances the depth and breadth of understanding of the subject area but also ensures that new research is grounded in a thorough appreciation of existing academic work.

2.2 Understanding Plagiarism

2.2.1 Definition and Types of Plagiarism

Direct Plagiarism

Direct plagiarism occurs when a person copies text verbatim from a source without proper attribution and presents it as their own work. This type of plagiarism is a serious ethical violation in the academic and professional world. It involves the deliberate copying of language, ideas, or expressions from another author and claiming them as original. This can include copying entire papers, paragraphs, or even a few lines without enclosing the copied text in quotation marks or without acknowledging the source through proper citation.

Direct plagiarism is often easily detectable through various software and tools designed to identify unoriginal content. Educational and research institutions strictly prohibit this practice and impose penalties ranging from failing grades to more severe academic sanctions. It undermines the integrity of academic work, devalues the original author's contributions, and can significantly harm the plagiarist's reputation and credibility.

Self-plagiarism

Self-plagiarism occurs when an individual reuses significant portions of their own previously published work without proper attribution or without indicating that the current work is a reiteration or expansion of earlier materials. This practice can mislead readers about the novelty of the content, as it presents previously disseminated information as new research, which can skew the perceived contribution to the field.

Self-plagiarism is problematic because it violates the publishing ethics that demand originality and transparency in scholarly communication. It can also infringe upon copyright if the previous work has been transferred to a publisher. In academic settings, self-plagiarism can lead to complications such as duplicate publication, which can dilute the research's apparent impact and distort the academic record.

To avoid self-plagiarism, researchers should always strive to be transparent about the origins of their content. This involves citing previous works and clearly indicating any recycled data, methods, or text, even if it is their own. When publishing or presenting, authors should disclose any overlaps with previously published works to editors, reviewers, and audiences to maintain integrity and trust in the scholarly communication process.

Mosaic Plagiarism

Mosaic plagiarism, also known as patchwriting, occurs when a person borrows phrases from a source without using quotation marks or finds synonyms for the author's language while keeping the original structure and meaning of the source. It involves piecing together ideas and expressions from various sources and presenting them as original work, often by slightly altering the words or superficially reordering them. This type of plagiarism can be deceptive because it may not be immediately evident and can give the impression of originality if not closely examined.

Mosaic plagiarism is considered unethical because it represents a form of intellectual theft, even though it may not be as overt as direct plagiarism. It undermines the essence of academic and professional integrity by presenting a false facade of originality. Detecting this form of plagiarism can be more challenging because it requires a thorough comparison of suspected texts against potential source materials to identify subtle similarities in structure and content.

To combat mosaic plagiarism, writers and researchers should ensure they fully understand the material they are citing and present their synthesis or interpretation in their own words. Proper citation and a clear demarcation between original and borrowed content are essential. Additionally, educational and professional settings can use plagiarism detection tools that highlight not only exact matches but also similar structures and patterns to safeguard against this deceptive practice.

Accidental Plagiarism

Accidental plagiarism occurs when an individual unknowingly fails to cite a source, improperly quotes their sources, or paraphrases without giving due credit due to misunderstanding, carelessness, or a lack of knowledge about citation and referencing practices. This type of plagiarism is not intentional but can still have serious consequences, such as loss of credibility and academic penalties, similar to those for intentional plagiarism.

The common causes of accidental plagiarism include:

- **Misunderstanding citation requirements**: Sometimes, individuals might be unaware of the need to cite all sources of information, including data, images, and ideas that have influenced their work.
- **Poor note-taking**: Mixing personal notes with copied text without marking the difference can lead to unintentional plagiarism when these notes are used to compose a final document.
- **Inadequate paraphrasing**: Simply changing a few words in a sentence from a source without altering the structure or summarizing the idea in one's own words can result in plagiarism.

To prevent accidental plagiarism, it is important to:

- **Educate on citation practices**: Proper training in the use of citations and references should be a fundamental aspect of academic instruction.
- **Use plagiarism detection software**: These tools can help identify areas where citations are missing or where paraphrasing is too close to the original text.
- **Review and proofread work**: Before final submission, reviewing work to ensure all sources are properly acknowledged can prevent accidental plagiarism.

Understanding and adhering to proper citation and referencing guidelines are crucial in academic writing and research to maintain integrity and uphold the standards of scholarly communication.

2.2.2 Consequences of Plagiarism

Academic Penalties

Plagiarism can lead to severe academic penalties, which vary depending on the policies of the educational institution and the severity of the offense. These penalties are implemented to uphold academic integrity and discourage dishonest practices. Some common academic penalties for plagiarism include:

- **Failing the Assignment**: Often, the immediate consequence of being caught plagiarizing is receiving a failing grade on the specific assignment. This penalty is usually applied in cases of first-time or minor plagiarism infractions.
- **Failing the Course**: More severe or repeated instances of plagiarism may result in failing the course entirely. This consequence reflects the seriousness with which academic institutions treat integrity and originality in student work.
- **Academic Probation**: Students caught plagiarizing might be placed on academic probation for a period. During probation, the student's academic behavior is closely monitored, and any further violations could lead to more severe consequences.
- **Suspension or Expulsion from the Institution**: In cases of severe or repeated plagiarism, a student may be suspended or expelled from the institution. Suspension involves temporarily banning the student from attending classes for a certain period, while expulsion is a permanent dismissal.
- **Revocation of Degrees**: In particularly egregious cases, degrees already awarded can be revoked if plagiarism is discovered in key components of the work submitted for the degree, such as a thesis or dissertation.

These penalties not only affect a student's academic record but can also have long-term repercussions on their future educational and career opportunities. The stigma of being caught plagiarizing can tarnish a student's reputation and integrity, making it difficult to gain trust from peers, professors, and potential employers. Therefore, understanding the consequences of plagiarism underscores the importance of maintaining academic honesty and the diligent use of proper citation and referencing in all scholarly work.

Legal Repercussions

Beyond the academic consequences, plagiarism can also lead to legal repercussions, particularly when it involves copyright infringement. Copyright laws protect the rights of creators by giving them exclusive rights to reproduce, distribute, and display their work. When someone plagiarizes, they may be violating these rights if the copied material is protected by copyright. Here are some potential legal repercussions of plagiarism:

- **Copyright Infringement Lawsuits**: If the plagiarized work is copyrighted, the original author has the right to file a lawsuit against the plagiarizer. Such lawsuits can result in the requirement to pay damages for the unauthorized use of the copyrighted material. The amount of damages can vary significantly but can be substantial, depending on the extent of the infringement and the commercial value of the copyrighted material.
- **Fines and Penalties**: Courts can impose fines and penalties on individuals who are found guilty of copyright infringement. These financial penalties are meant to compensate the copyright holder for the loss incurred due to the unauthorized use of their work.
- **Cease and Desist Orders**: The court may issue a cease and desist order, which legally forces the plagiarizer to stop the infringement activity. This might include removing the plagiarized material from publication or discontinuing its distribution.
- **Criminal Charges**: In severe cases, particularly where there is significant commercial gain from plagiarism, criminal charges may be pursued. This could result in more severe penalties, including jail time, especially in cases where the infringement is extensive and willfully deceptive.

It's important to note that while legal actions are more common in cases involving significant commercial interests, the potential for such actions adds a layer of serious consequence to plagiarism. Therefore, understanding the legal aspects of plagiarism emphasizes the importance of ethical writing and the need to adhere strictly to copyright laws.

Damage to Professional Reputation

One of the most enduring consequences of plagiarism is the damage it can inflict on an individual's professional reputation. This impact extends beyond the academic world and into one's professional life, where integrity and trustworthiness are paramount.

- **Loss of Credibility**: Being found guilty of plagiarism can tarnish a professional's credibility. In fields where integrity is critical, such as academia, journalism, and research, credibility is a fundamental asset. Once lost, it can be extremely difficult to regain.

- **Career Setbacks**: Professional opportunities may become limited following a plagiarism scandal. Potential employers or collaborators who perform background checks and discover a history of plagiarism might deem the individual unreliable or unethical, leading to diminished career prospects.
- **Legal and Financial Consequences**: Beyond the immediate legal repercussions, the long-term financial impact of plagiarism can be significant. This might include losing a job, being demoted, or facing challenges in securing future positions, especially in roles that require a high level of trust and ethical standards.
- **Public Humiliation**: In the age of digital media, cases of plagiarism can receive widespread publicity, compounding the damage to one's professional image. Once labeled a plagiarist, an individual may face public scrutiny and criticism that can persist long after the incident.
- **Strained Professional Relationships**: Plagiarism can lead to strained relationships with peers, mentors, and colleagues. It can erode trust, making collaborative work difficult and isolating professionals from their networks.

Rebuilding a professional reputation after an incident of plagiarism involves demonstrating a commitment to ethical practices over time. It requires transparency, ongoing education on intellectual property rights, and adherence to ethical standards in all professional undertakings. The damage to one's reputation serves as a powerful deterrent and a reminder of the importance of maintaining ethical integrity in all professional activities.

2.2.3 How to Avoid Plagiarism

Proper Citation and Referencing

One of the most effective ways to avoid plagiarism is through diligent and accurate citation and referencing of all sources used in any piece of written work. Proper citation and referencing not only give credit to the original authors but also lend credibility to the academic work by demonstrating a thorough engagement with the scholarly community. Here are key practices to ensure proper citation and referencing:

- **Understand Citation Styles**: Different academic disciplines prefer specific citation styles, such as APA, MLA, Chicago, or Harvard. Familiarize yourself with the citation style that is required for your work, and consistently apply it throughout your document.

- **Cite All Sources**: Include a citation for any information that is not your original idea, including theories, arguments, facts, statistics, or data. This applies even when you paraphrase or summarize information from another source.
- **Use Quotation Marks for Direct Quotes**: When using text verbatim from a source, enclose it in quotation marks and include a citation with the exact location of the source material. This clearly distinguishes the author's original words from your own.
- **Include a Comprehensive Bibliography**: At the end of your document, include a bibliography or reference list that details all the sources you consulted during your research. This should align with the in-text citations and provide sufficient information for readers to locate each source.
- **Utilize Reference Management Tools**: Tools such as EndNote, Zotero, or Mendeley can help manage citations and keep track of sources. These tools automatically format citations and bibliographies, which can reduce errors and simplify the referencing process.
- **Educate Yourself on Plagiarism**: Understanding what constitutes plagiarism and familiarizing yourself with the ethical guidelines of academic writing is crucial. Many institutions offer resources and training sessions on plagiarism and how to avoid it.

By adhering to these guidelines, you can safeguard your academic and professional integrity and contribute respectfully and ethically to the scholarly conversation. Proper citation and referencing are not merely procedural but are fundamental to the practice of responsible and credible academic writing.

Paraphrasing and Summarizing Techniques

Effective paraphrasing and summarizing are essential skills for avoiding plagiarism and for incorporating external sources into your writing while maintaining your own voice and perspective. These techniques allow you to convey information from sources with clarity and conciseness, adapting it to the context of your own work. Here's how to employ these techniques properly:

Paraphrasing

Paraphrasing involves rewording and rephrasing the content from a source in your own words. It is more detailed than summarizing and should reflect the same meaning as the original text without using the same words or structure.

- **Read Thoroughly**: Understand the complete message of the passage you intend to paraphrase. This deep understanding is necessary to accurately convey the information in a new form.
- **Use Your Own Words and Syntax**: Change the structure of the sentence and choose synonyms for the words used in the original text. However, be careful that the synonyms make sense in the context and keep the original meaning intact.
- **Include Key Details**: Ensure that essential facts or concepts are preserved in your paraphrasing. The goal is to be as accurate as the original text without copying it.
- **Cite the Source**: Even though you are using your own words, the idea came from another source. Provide a citation to acknowledge this.

Summarizing

Summarizing involves condensing the main ideas of a larger body of work into a brief overview. It focuses on the core concepts and eliminates most of the detail.

- **Identify the Main Ideas**: Read the source material to grasp the central themes or arguments. Look for topic sentences in paragraphs as they often highlight key points.
- **Write in Your Own Voice**: Express these ideas in your own words, creating a condensed version of the original content that reflects the overarching message or argument.
- **Keep it Brief**: A summary should be significantly shorter than the original text. It includes only the most crucial elements, leaving out examples, detailed evidence, and secondary points.
- **Always Cite the Source**: Like paraphrasing, summarizing also requires citation, as the ideas originated from another author.

Both paraphrasing and summarizing require practice to master. It's important to check your work against the original text to ensure you haven't accidentally copied phrases or structures. Regularly practicing these techniques can enhance your writing skills and help you present information in a clear, concise, and original manner while properly acknowledging the contributions of previous scholars.

Using Plagiarism Detection Tools

Plagiarism detection tools are valuable resources for identifying and preventing plagiarism in written work. These tools compare your text against a vast database of published materials, including books, academic papers, and online content, to check for similarities that might indicate plagiarism. Here's how to effectively use these tools:

- **Select a Reputable Plagiarism Checker**: Choose a well-regarded plagiarism detection tool that is trusted by academic institutions and professionals. Examples include Turnitin, Grammarly, Copyscape, and Plagscan. Each has different features, such as direct feedback on potential plagiarism, grammar suggestions, and citation assistance.
- **Regular Checks During Writing**: Use plagiarism detection software as a part of your writing process, not just as a final check. This can help you identify and rectify any inadvertent plagiarism that might occur as you compose and revise your document.
- **Understand the Results**: These tools often provide a percentage score indicating the amount of plagiarized content. They also highlight specific sections of your text that match other sources. Review these highlighted sections carefully to determine if they are properly cited, need paraphrasing, or require additional original input.
- **Use Reports to Improve Your Writing**: Some tools offer detailed reports that can help you understand how well you integrate source material. Use this feedback to improve your paraphrasing and summarizing skills, and ensure that you maintain academic integrity in your work.
- **Check for False Positives**: Sometimes, these tools may flag common phrases or technical terms as plagiarism. It's important to manually review these instances to determine whether they are indeed instances of plagiarism or merely necessary uses of standard language.
- **Incorporate into Best Practices**: Make plagiarism checking part of your regular writing habits. This not only helps prevent plagiarism but also ensures that your work maintains a high standard of academic integrity and professionalism.

By integrating these tools into your writing process, you can safeguard your work against plagiarism, uphold ethical standards, and contribute original thoughts and analyses to your field of study.

2.3 Research Ethics

2.3.1 Ethical Considerations in Research

Informed Consent

Informed consent is a foundational principle in research ethics, particularly in studies involving human participants. It ensures that all participants are fully aware of the nature of the research, the procedures they will undergo, potential risks, benefits, and their rights as participants before they agree to take part. Here's how informed consent plays a crucial role in upholding ethical standards in research:

- **Full Disclosure**: The researcher must provide all the necessary information about the study. This includes the purpose of the research, the procedures to be followed, the expected duration of the study, and any potential risks or discomforts that may occur.
- **Understanding**: It is not enough to merely provide information; researchers must also ensure that participants understand what has been explained. This may involve using simpler language, providing examples, or using visual aids, especially when dealing with participants with varying levels of education or comprehension.
- **Voluntariness**: Consent must be given voluntarily, without any form of coercion or undue influence. Participants should feel free to decline participation or withdraw from the study at any time without any negative consequences.
- **Documentation**: Informed consent is typically documented by means of a written, signed, and dated consent form. However, in certain cases, verbal consent may be appropriate and can be documented through audio or video recordings, especially in cultures where written consent is not the norm.
- **Special Considerations**: Additional considerations are necessary when dealing with vulnerable populations such as children, the elderly, or people with disabilities. In such cases, consent must also be obtained from legal guardians or caretakers, and the methods of obtaining consent should be tailored to meet the specific needs of these groups.
- **Continuous Process**: Informed consent is not a one-time event but a continuous process throughout the duration of the research. Participants should be updated about any new risks or findings that emerge during the study.

Informed consent protects participants by ensuring they are not exposed to research without their knowledge and consent, thereby respecting their autonomy and safeguarding their welfare. It also protects researchers by ensuring that they conduct their studies ethically, maintaining trust and integrity in the research process.

Confidentiality and Privacy

Confidentiality and privacy are critical ethical considerations in research, particularly when dealing with sensitive information or vulnerable populations. These principles ensure that personal information collected during a study is kept secure and is only used for the purposes agreed upon by the participants. Here's how confidentiality and privacy can be effectively maintained in research settings:

- **Data Protection**: Implement robust measures to protect the data collected from participants. This includes using secure servers, encrypted communications, and restricted access controls. Only authorized personnel should have access to sensitive data, and they should be trained on privacy protocols.
- **Anonymity and Pseudonymity**: Whenever possible, remove identifiers from the data to protect participants' identities. In cases where complete anonymity cannot be achieved, use pseudonyms or codes to identify data without directly exposing participants' identities.
- **Informed Consent**: As part of the informed consent process, clearly explain to participants how their data will be used, who will have access to it, and the steps taken to protect their privacy. Make sure they understand that their participation is confidential and what that means for them.
- **Minimize Data Collection**: Only collect data that is essential for the research objectives. Avoid gathering unnecessary information that could increase the risk of breaching confidentiality.
- **Legal Compliance**: Adhere to all relevant laws and regulations regarding data protection. This includes understanding and implementing guidelines specified under laws such as the General Data Protection Regulation (GDPR) in Europe or the Health Insurance Portability and Accountability Act (HIPAA) in the United States.
- **Data Disposal**: Establish clear protocols for the secure disposal of data once it is no longer needed for research purposes or after the legally mandated retention period has expired. This includes proper methods

for deleting electronic data and destroying physical records.

- **Handling Breaches**: Have a plan in place for responding to any breaches of confidentiality. This should include steps to mitigate damage, such as notifying affected individuals and regulatory bodies, as well as measures to prevent future breaches.

By diligently applying these practices, researchers can uphold the trust placed in them by research participants and ensure that ethical standards concerning confidentiality and privacy are maintained throughout the research process. This not only protects participants but also enhances the credibility and integrity of the research.

Confidentiality and Privacy

Confidentiality and privacy are paramount in research, safeguarding the personal information of participants and maintaining the integrity of the data collected. These principles ensure that sensitive information is handled with the utmost care and respect throughout the research process. Here's how confidentiality and privacy can be effectively upheld:

- **Secure Data Handling**: Implement robust data protection measures to ensure that all participant information is securely stored and accessed. This includes using encrypted databases, secure networks, and password protections to prevent unauthorized access to sensitive data.
- **Anonymity and Pseudonymity**: Whenever feasible, researchers should anonymize or pseudonymize participant data to prevent any personal information from being directly linked to specific individuals. Anonymity removes all identifying details entirely, while pseudonymity replaces them with artificial identifiers.
- **Clear Information on Privacy Practices**: During the informed consent process, clearly communicate to participants how their information will be used, who will have access to it, the steps taken to protect their privacy, and the duration of data retention. Transparency in these matters helps build trust and assures participants of their privacy.
- **Limit Data Collection**: Collect only the data that is necessary for achieving the research objectives. Superfluous data collection not only poses additional privacy risks but can also burden participants without adding value to the research.
- **Compliance with Legal Standards**: Adhere to applicable laws and regulations concerning data protection and privacy, such as the General

Data Protection Regulation (GDPR) in Europe or the Health Insurance Portability and Accountability Act (HIPAA) in the United States. These regulations set the standard for privacy practices and provide a framework for handling personal information.

- **Procedures for Data Breach**: Establish protocols for dealing with data breaches, including immediate response strategies to mitigate harm, notifying affected individuals, and taking steps to prevent future incidents. Being prepared for potential breaches is a critical component of privacy protection.
- **Ethical Disposal of Data**: Once the data is no longer needed, or once the research project concludes, ensure that all personal data is ethically disposed of in a manner that prevents recovery or misuse. This includes securely deleting electronic files and shredding physical documents.

By meticulously implementing these strategies, researchers can protect the confidentiality and privacy of their subjects, thereby upholding ethical standards and fostering a respectful and secure research environment.

Avoiding Harm to Participants

Avoiding harm to participants is a cornerstone of ethical research. Researchers have a duty to minimize the risk of harm and maximize benefits for participants, ensuring that the welfare of those involved in the study is prioritized at all stages. Here's how this ethical principle can be effectively implemented:

- **Risk Assessment**: Before beginning any study, conduct a thorough assessment of potential risks and benefits. This includes identifying physical, psychological, emotional, social, and economic risks. The aim is to understand and mitigate any potential harm that could arise from participation in the research.
- **Informed Consent**: Ensure that all participants are fully informed about the risks involved before they agree to take part. This process should be carried out honestly and transparently, allowing participants to make an educated decision about their involvement.
- **Minimize Risks**: Design the study in a way that minimizes potential risks to participants. This might involve choosing non-invasive methods, providing supports for participants who might be affected by the study, or selecting a safer experimental approach.

- **Monitor and Support**: Throughout the research process, continuously monitor the well-being of participants and provide adequate support as needed. If adverse effects are observed, take immediate action to address them, which may include providing medical attention, counseling, or discontinuing the participant's involvement in the study.
- **Debriefing**: After participation, provide a debriefing session to inform participants about the study's findings and its purposes. This is also an opportunity to identify any lingering effects from their participation and to offer further support if necessary.
- **Vulnerable Populations**: Take extra precautions when dealing with vulnerable populations (such as children, the elderly, or individuals with cognitive impairments). This includes obtaining consent from guardians when necessary and ensuring that additional protections are in place to safeguard their well-being.
- **Ethical Review and Oversight**: Submit the research protocol for review by an ethics committee or institutional review board (IRB). This review ensures that the research meets ethical standards and that appropriate measures are in place to protect participants from harm.

By adhering to these guidelines, researchers can uphold their ethical obligations to protect participants from harm. This not only ensures the integrity of the research but also builds trust between researchers and the community, fostering a positive environment for future studies.

2.3.2 Guidelines and Best Practices

Ethical Guidelines by Professional Organizations

Professional organizations across various disciplines establish ethical guidelines to steer the conduct of research and ensure that it adheres to universally accepted ethical standards. These guidelines serve as a framework for researchers, helping them navigate the complex ethical considerations involved in conducting research. Here's an overview of the role and impact of these guidelines:

- **Standardizing Ethical Practices**: Ethical guidelines provided by professional organizations create a standard of conduct that researchers are expected to follow. This helps in maintaining consistency in ethical practices across different studies and disciplines.
- **Addressing Specific Ethical Issues**: Many professional organizations tailor their guidelines to address the unique challenges and ethical

dilemmas specific to their field. For instance, the American Psychological Association (APA) provides detailed guidelines on issues like confidentiality, informed consent, and the ethical treatment of subjects.

- **Providing a Basis for Accountability**: These guidelines form the basis for evaluating the ethical conduct of researchers. They provide a benchmark against which research activities can be assessed, ensuring that researchers are accountable for their ethical responsibilities.
- **Educational Resource**: For new researchers and students, these guidelines serve as an essential educational tool, helping them understand the ethical considerations of their profession and the importance of ethical compliance in their work.
- **Support for Ethical Decision-Making**: In complex situations where ethical dilemmas arise, these guidelines offer guidance and support, helping researchers make decisions that align with the best practices of their profession.
- **Promotion of Public Trust**: By adhering to established ethical guidelines, researchers help build and maintain public trust in research activities. This is crucial for the ongoing support and funding of research endeavors.
- **Dynamic and Evolving**: As new ethical challenges emerge with advancements in technology and methodology, professional organizations regularly update their guidelines to reflect these changes, ensuring that they remain relevant and effective.

Researchers are encouraged to familiarize themselves with the ethical guidelines of their respective professional organizations and incorporate these principles into their research practices. This not only ensures the ethical integrity of their work but also enhances the quality and reliability of the research outcomes.

Institutional Review Boards (IRBs)

Institutional Review Boards (IRBs) are critical components in the research ethics landscape, tasked with overseeing the protection of human subjects in research. These boards review research proposals to ensure that they comply with ethical standards and that the rights and welfare of participants are safeguarded. Here's an in-depth look at the role and functions of IRBs:

- **Review and Approval**: IRBs conduct thorough reviews of research proposals to assess the risk to participants against the potential benefits of the research. They ensure that the plans for participant protection are adequate and that informed consent processes are clear and robust.
- **Monitoring Research**: Beyond initial approvals, IRBs are also involved in the ongoing monitoring of approved studies. This can include the review of any proposed modifications to the research protocol and conducting periodic reviews to ensure ongoing compliance with ethical standards.
- **Ensuring Informed Consent**: IRBs scrutinize the process by which researchers plan to obtain informed consent to ensure it is free of coercion and that participants are fully informed about the nature of the research, including any potential risks.
- **Protecting Vulnerable Populations**: Special attention is given to research proposals involving vulnerable groups such as children, prisoners, pregnant women, or individuals with mental disabilities. IRBs ensure that additional safeguards are in place to protect these populations.
- **Educational Role**: IRBs often provide educational resources and guidance to researchers on ethical issues and the application of ethical standards in research. This role is crucial in fostering a culture of ethics in institutions.
- **Regulatory Compliance**: IRBs help ensure that research activities comply with both national and international laws and regulations related to research with human subjects. This includes regulations from bodies like the U.S. Department of Health and Human Services and the Food and Drug Administration, among others.
- **Addressing Complaints and Concerns**: IRBs also serve as a resource for participants to voice any concerns or complaints about the research process, ensuring that these issues are addressed promptly and effectively.

By fulfilling these roles, IRBs play a pivotal role in maintaining ethical standards in research involving human subjects. They not only protect participants but also help to uphold the integrity of the research process and the validity of the research outcomes.

Best Practices for Ethical Research Conduct

Ethical research conduct is foundational to the integrity of the scientific process. It involves adhering to established ethical principles to ensure the rights, dignity, and safety of all participants are respected. Here are some best practices for maintaining high ethical standards in research:

- **Transparency in Methodology**: Be clear and open about your research methods and procedures. This includes providing detailed descriptions in study protocols and publications to allow for scrutiny and reproducibility by other researchers.
- **Maintain Integrity and Honesty**: Avoid practices such as data fabrication, falsification, or manipulation. Report findings truthfully, including results that may not support your hypotheses or that are unexpected.
- **Ensure Confidentiality and Privacy**: Safeguard the confidentiality and privacy of research participants. Implement data protection measures, use data anonymization techniques where appropriate, and handle sensitive information with care.
- **Obtain Informed Consent**: Always obtain informed consent from participants. Ensure they understand the research, what is expected of them, the risks involved, and their rights to withdraw from the study at any time without penalty.
- **Protect Vulnerable Populations**: Implement special measures when involving individuals who may be less able to protect their own interests, such as children, prisoners, pregnant women, or individuals with cognitive impairments. Ensure their participation is justified and they are given additional protections.
- **Fair Subject Selection**: Ensure that the selection of research subjects is fair and equitable. Avoid selecting subjects solely based on ease of availability, compromised position, or manipulability.
- **Avoid Conflicts of Interest**: Disclose any potential conflicts of interest that may influence the research outcomes. Manage these conflicts to prevent them from compromising the research.
- **Ethical Problem Solving**: Be prepared to face ethical dilemmas and have strategies in place to address them. Consult with colleagues, adhere to guidelines from professional organizations, and engage with Institutional Review Boards (IRB) or ethics committees when in doubt.
- **Continuous Ethical Education**: Keep up-to-date with the latest developments in research ethics. Participate in ongoing training and education to improve your understanding and implementation of ethical practices.

- **Respect for All Participants**: Show respect for all individuals participating in or affected by the research. This includes respecting their culture, lifestyle, and privacy.

By adhering to these best practices, researchers can ensure that their studies are conducted ethically and responsibly, thereby contributing to the trustworthiness and social value of their research findings.

CHAPTER THREE

TECHNICAL WRITING AND REPORTING

3.1 Basics of Technical Writing

3.1.1 Key Principles and Styles

Clarity and Precision

Clarity and precision are fundamental principles in technical writing, ensuring that information is communicated effectively and accurately. These principles are essential for creating documents that are both understandable and reliable, particularly in fields that rely heavily on detailed data and instructions. Here's how clarity and precision manifest in technical writing:

- **Clarity**: This involves using straightforward language and a logical structure to ensure that the reader can easily follow and understand the content. Clarity means avoiding ambiguous terms and complex sentence constructions that could confuse the reader. Instead, use simple, direct language and clearly defined terms. Organize information in a way that logically flows from one section to the next, making use of headings, subheadings, and bullet points to break up text and highlight key points.
- **Precision**: This refers to the accuracy of the information presented and the specificity with which it is described. In technical writing, it is crucial to be exact with details such as specifications, measurements,

and descriptions. Precision ensures that there is no room for misinterpretation or error, which is particularly important in technical fields where a small mistake could have significant consequences. Use specific data and quantifiable information where possible, and be exact in your descriptions.

- **Consistency**: Consistency in terminology, formatting, and style helps maintain clarity and precision throughout a document. Use the same terms to describe the same concepts throughout your text to avoid confusion. Consistently apply formatting choices such as capitalization, fonts, and layout styles.
- **Conciseness**: While detail is important, unnecessary verbosity should be avoided. Be concise in your writing by eliminating redundant words and focusing on essential information. This helps in maintaining the reader's attention and ensures that the writing is efficient and to the point.
- **Audience Awareness**: Understanding the audience is crucial in technical writing. Tailor your language, style, and depth of information to the knowledge and expectations of your audience. This might mean simplifying complex topics for lay readers or providing detailed technical descriptions for expert audiences.

By integrating these principles, technical writing can effectively convey complex information in a manner that is accessible and useful to the intended audience. This not only enhances the usability of the documents but also supports accurate implementation and application of the information provided.

Objectivity and Formality

Objectivity and **formality** are essential attributes of technical writing that contribute to its credibility and professionalism. Here's how these principles are applied and why they are crucial:

- **Objectivity**: This involves presenting information in an unbiased and impartial manner. In technical writing, the focus should be on factual data and evidence-based conclusions, rather than personal opinions or speculative statements. Objectivity ensures that the content is trustworthy and can be relied upon for accurate, factual information. To maintain objectivity, use neutral language and avoid emotionally charged or subjective terminology. Additionally, always support claims with data or well-documented evidence, and clearly distinguish between established facts and hypotheses.

- **Formality**: Technical writing typically adheres to a formal style to reinforce the seriousness and professionalism of the content. This includes using a professional tone, avoiding colloquialisms or slang, and employing precise technical vocabulary appropriate for the subject matter. Formality also extends to the structure of the document; it should be well-organized with a clear hierarchy of headings and subheadings, and it should follow any specific formatting guidelines relevant to the field or institution.
- **Consistent Voice**: A formal and objective tone is often achieved through the use of a consistent voice, typically the passive voice in technical writing. This helps to remove the focus from the author and places it on the information being conveyed, further supporting the objective nature of the document. For instance, instead of writing "I measured the sample," use "The sample was measured."
- **Precision in Language**: Formality also requires precision in language. This means choosing words that accurately convey the intended meaning without ambiguity. Technical terms should be defined when they are first introduced, and acronyms should be spelled out initially to ensure clarity and enhance understanding for all readers.
- **Professional Formatting**: The formal nature of technical documents is also reflected in their presentation. This includes consistent use of fonts, margins, and spacing, as well as adhering to professional standards for tables, graphs, and figures. These elements should be neatly arranged and clearly labeled to contribute to the overall formal appearance of the document.

Incorporating objectivity and formality in technical writing not only enhances the clarity and precision of the document but also ensures that the information is presented in a professional manner that respects the norms and expectations of the technical and scientific communities.

Audience Awareness

Audience awareness is a pivotal aspect of technical writing, shaping both the content and presentation of information to meet the specific needs and understanding levels of the intended readers. Here's how this principle is applied and why it's crucial:

- **Identifying the Audience**: The first step in applying audience awareness is identifying who the readers are. Technical documents can have a range of audiences, from experts in the field to laypersons, or from decision-makers to practitioners. Understanding who the audience is allows the writer to tailor the complexity, depth, and type of information accordingly.
- **Adjusting Technical Level**: Depending on the audience's familiarity with the subject, the technical level of the document should be adjusted. For instance, writing for experts allows for the use of jargon and complex concepts without extensive explanations. Conversely, if the audience is not specialized, technical terms need to be defined, and concepts should be broken down into more digestible parts.
- **Clarifying Purpose**: Different audiences may require information for different purposes. Some may seek an overview, while others might need detailed procedural guidance or technical specifications. Understanding the purpose behind the audience's need for the document will guide the writer in structuring and prioritizing content effectively.
- **Engaging and Accessible Language**: Even within technical writing, the language should be as accessible as possible while still being appropriate for the audience. This involves avoiding unnecessary complexity and ensuring that the document is readable and engaging. For broader audiences, this might mean simplifying information and using more universal examples that resonate with a diverse group of readers.
- **Visual Aids**: Depending on the audience, visual aids such as charts, diagrams, and tables can enhance understanding. These should be used judiciously to help clarify complex information, especially when addressing less technical audiences who might benefit from visual explanations.
- **Feedback Mechanisms**: Incorporating mechanisms for feedback, such as contact information, Q&A sections, or user forums, can help writers receive direct responses from their audience. This feedback can provide insights into whether the document meets the audience's needs and how it might be improved.
- **Cultural Sensitivity**: Being aware of cultural differences is essential, especially in global or diverse settings. This includes using culturally appropriate examples, avoiding potential cultural biases, and considering

translation needs if the document will be used across different language groups.

By maintaining a strong awareness of the audience, technical writers can create documents that are not only informative but also appropriately tailored to the needs and expectations of their readers. This enhances the effectiveness of the communication and ensures that the document achieves its intended purpose.

3.1.2 Structuring a Technical Document

Logical Organization

Logical organization is essential in structuring a technical document. It ensures that information is presented in a coherent and accessible manner, facilitating understanding and ease of use for the reader. Here's how to effectively organize a technical document:

- **Define the Purpose**: Start by clearly defining the purpose of the document. Understanding what you need to convey will guide how you organize the content. Whether the document is meant to instruct, inform, or persuade will influence its structure.
- **Identify Key Points**: List out the main points or sections that need to be covered. This includes identifying all necessary topics, subtopics, and the relationship between them. Ensure that each section logically flows into the next.
- **Use Standard Structures**: Depending on the type of technical document, certain structures may be more appropriate. For instance:
    - **Reports** typically follow a structure of Introduction, Methods, Results, and Discussion (IMRaD).
    - **Manuals** or **guides** might be organized according to the chronological steps of a process or grouped by function or component.
    - **Proposals** might be organized into sections that outline the problem, proposed solution, budget, and qualifications.
- **Hierarchical Formatting**: Utilize headings and subheadings to create a clear hierarchy and make the document easier to navigate. This not only breaks the information into manageable chunks but also helps readers

quickly find the information they need.

- **Logical Flow**: Ensure there is a logical flow to the information presented. This may mean organizing content from the most to the least important (deductive), or building from basic to more complex information (inductive). The flow should match the way the intended audience is expected to process the information.
- **Consistent Layout**: Use a consistent layout throughout the document. This includes consistent use of fonts, heading styles, and spacing. Such consistency helps in reinforcing the logical flow and makes the document more professional and easier to read.
- **Use of Lists and Bullet Points**: For procedures, lists, or key points, use bullet points or numbered lists to make the information more digestible and to highlight important steps or considerations.
- **Conclusion and Summaries**: Include a conclusion or summary at the end of sections, particularly in longer documents. This helps in reinforcing what has been covered and aids in the retention of the information.
- **Appendices and References**: If the document includes supplemental information that is too detailed for the main body, use appendices. Likewise, include a references section if referencing external sources, following appropriate citation styles.

By organizing a technical document logically, you not only enhance its clarity and usability but also ensure that it effectively communicates the intended message to the target audience. This structured approach is fundamental in achieving the goals of technical communication.

Use of Headings and Subheadings

The use of headings and subheadings is a critical aspect of structuring technical documents. They organize content into clearly defined sections, making it easier for readers to navigate the document and find specific information. Here's a detailed look at how to effectively use headings and subheadings:

- **Hierarchy of Information**: Establish a clear hierarchy using different levels of headings. Typically, headings are formatted in descending order of importance. For instance, use larger or bolder fonts for main headings and progressively smaller or less bold fonts for subheadings. This visual distinction helps readers understand the structure of the document and the relative importance of each section.

- **Consistency in Formatting**: Maintain consistency in the style and format of headings and subheadings throughout the document. This includes consistent use of font size, typeface, and style (e.g., bold or italic). Consistent formatting aids in the visual organization of the content and enhances the overall readability.
- **Descriptive Titles**: Make headings and subheadings descriptive and concise. They should clearly indicate what the following section is about, allowing readers to quickly ascertain the content and decide whether it is relevant to their needs. Avoid vague titles that might confuse the reader or obscure the content of the section.
- **Spacing and Placement**: Proper spacing around headings and subheadings improves readability. Typically, more space is left before a heading than after, helping to visually separate it from the preceding content. This spacing acts as a visual cue, signaling a new section or topic.
- **Numbering System**: In longer documents, a numbering system can help in tracking the progression and organization of content. For example, main sections might be numbered (1, 2, 3, etc.), with sub-sections using a decimal system (1.1, 1.2, 1.3, etc.). This not only aids in navigation but also helps in referencing specific parts of the document in discussions or presentations.
- **Avoid Over-Sectioning**: While it's important to break the text into manageable sections, avoid excessive use of headings and subheadings. Over-sectioning can fragment the content too much, making it choppy and disrupting the flow of information.
- **Integration with Lists and Bullet Points**: Subheadings can be effectively combined with lists and bullet points to break down complex information into clear, actionable items or key points. This is especially useful in manuals, guidelines, or any document where step-by-step instructions are necessary.
- **Interactive Table of Contents**: For digital documents, integrate an interactive table of contents that links directly to various headings. This feature enhances the usability of the document, allowing readers to easily navigate to different sections with a click.

Effectively using headings and subheadings enhances the organization, navigability, and professionalism of technical documents. By guiding the reader through the content in a structured way, you can ensure that the information is accessible and easy to understand.

Consistent Formatting and Style Guides

Consistent formatting and adherence to style guides are vital in technical writing to ensure clarity, professionalism, and ease of communication. These elements help in maintaining a uniform appearance and structural coherence throughout the document, which is especially important in collaborative environments or when the documents are intended for a wide audience. Here's how to implement consistent formatting and utilize style guides effectively:

- **Choosing a Style Guide**: Select a style guide that is appropriate for your field and type of document. Common style guides include the American Psychological Association (APA) for social sciences, the Chicago Manual of Style for general publishing, and IEEE for engineering and technical fields. These guides provide detailed instructions on formatting, citation, and presentation standards.
- **Document Templates**: Use templates that align with the chosen style guide. Templates can pre-set elements like margins, fonts, headings, and other layout features, ensuring consistency throughout the document. This is particularly useful for organizations that produce multiple documents, as it helps maintain a uniform brand and professional appearance.
- **Font and Typography**: Choose fonts that are easy to read and appropriate for professional documents, such as Times New Roman, Arial, or Calibri. Maintain consistent use of font sizes and styles for body text, headings, and special sections like captions or quotations.
- **Heading Hierarchy**: Define a clear hierarchy for headings and subheadings, as discussed previously, and stick to it throughout the document. This includes consistent use of font size, weight (bold, italics), and numbering systems.
- **Paragraph and Line Spacing**: Consistent paragraph and line spacing improve readability. Typically, technical documents use single or 1.5-line spacing with a clear space between paragraphs. Avoid excessive

spacing, which can disrupt the flow of text.

- **Consistent Margins**: Standardize margins to ensure that text is neatly aligned and the document looks tidy. Common margins are 1 inch (2.54 cm) on all sides, but this may vary based on the specific formatting guidelines of your organization or the style guide in use.
- **Citation and Referencing**: Follow the citation style specified in your style guide consistently. This includes how references are cited within the text and how they are listed at the end of the document. Consistency in citations not only supports the credibility of your document but also helps avoid issues of plagiarism.
- **Use of Visual Elements**: Maintain consistency in the use of visual elements such as tables, charts, and figures. This includes consistent labeling, captioning, and formatting styles. Visual consistency aids in the reader's ability to quickly interpret and compare data presented in different sections of the document.
- **Quality Control Measures**: Implement quality control measures such as peer reviews, proofreading sessions, and editing protocols to ensure that the document adheres to the intended formatting and style guidelines. This is crucial in catching inconsistencies or deviations from the established standards.

By ensuring consistent formatting and adhering to style guides, technical documents can achieve a level of professionalism and reliability that supports effective communication and reinforces the credibility of the content.

3.2 Writing Research Reports

3.2.1 Components of a Research Report

Title Page

The title page is the first component of a research report and serves as the face of your document. It provides the necessary preliminary information to identify the nature and scope of the research, and it sets the tone for the content that follows. Here's how to effectively craft a title page:

- **Title of the Report**: The title should be clear, concise, and descriptive. It should accurately reflect the content of the report and ideally be specific enough to give the reader a solid understanding of the topic of research without needing to look further. Avoid ambiguous terms and overly broad statements.
- **Author's Name**: Include the full name of the author or authors. If the report is a collaborative effort, list the names in the order of their contributions, or alphabetically if contributions are equal. This is also the place to indicate affiliations if relevant, such as academic institutions or organizations.
- **Date of Publication**: The date when the report is completed or published should be prominently displayed. This helps to contextualize the research within a specific time frame, which is particularly important for scientific studies where data may evolve over time.
- **Affiliations and Logos**: If the research is affiliated with any institutions, universities, or companies, their names and logos should be included on the title page. This not only gives credit to the supporting entities but also adds a level of professionalism and authority to the report.
- **Course or Department (if applicable)**: In academic contexts, include the course name, code, or department for which the report was prepared. This information can be crucial for instructors or academic committees in identifying the relevance and categorization of the report.
- **Instructor or Supervisor's Name**: If the report is an assignment or part of a project, include the name of the instructor or project supervisor. This shows whom the report is prepared under or reviewed by, which can be important in academic or professional settings.
- **Contact Information**: Depending on the purpose of the report, it might be appropriate to include contact information for further correspondence. This can be an email address, a telephone number, or even a mailing address.

The title page should be formatted according to the general style guidelines applicable to the entire document, ensuring it is not only informative but also aesthetically pleasing and professional. It should be free of clutter, well-organized, and visually balanced, making a good first impression on the reader.

Abstract

The abstract is a crucial component of a research report, providing a concise summary of the entire study. It gives readers a quick overview of the main aspects of the report, including the purpose, methodology, results, and conclusions. Here's how to effectively write and structure an abstract:

- **Conciseness**: Typically, an abstract should be between 150 and 250 words, depending on the guidelines provided by the journal or institution. It needs to be succinct while still providing a clear and comprehensive overview of the research.
- **Purpose of the Study**: Start by clearly stating the purpose or objectives of the research. This helps readers understand the central focus of the study and its rationale. Mention the problem being addressed or the hypothesis that the study aims to test.
- **Methodology**: Briefly describe the methods used to conduct the research. This might include the type of research design, data collection techniques, and the tools or instruments employed. The aim here is to provide enough detail for the reader to understand how the research was conducted without going into the depth that the main body of the report will cover.
- **Results**: Summarize the key findings or results of the study. Highlight the most significant data points and outcomes of the research. Be specific about the results, using quantifiable information when possible to give a clear picture of the findings.
- **Conclusions**: Outline the conclusions drawn from the research. This should directly relate to the research objectives stated earlier and reflect the outcomes derived from the data. Mention any significant implications or potential applications of the findings.
- **Keywords**: Often, abstracts include a list of keywords at the end. These keywords should be specific to the research and are used for indexing purposes and to help others find the report through search engines or databases.

When writing an abstract, maintain a neutral and professional tone. Avoid using first-person pronouns and keep the language straightforward and objective. The abstract should stand alone, meaning it must make sense to the reader who might not read the rest of the document. This part of the report is often what readers use to decide whether to read the full document, so it's important to ensure that it is clear, compelling, and accurately reflects the content of the research report.

Introduction

The introduction of a research report sets the stage for the entire document, outlining the background, context, and purpose of the research. It should capture the interest of the reader and provide all necessary information to understand why the research was conducted. Here's how to effectively construct an introduction:

- **Background Information**: Begin by providing context for the research. This might include a brief overview of the field, a summary of relevant existing research, and any gaps in knowledge that your study aims to fill. This section should build a foundation for understanding the problem at hand and its significance.
- **Research Problem**: Clearly state the research problem. Describe what you are investigating and why it is important. This is where you justify the necessity of your study and its relevance to the field or broader societal issues.
- **Objectives and Hypotheses**: Specify the objectives or specific questions that your research aims to address. If your study is hypothesis-driven, clearly state the hypotheses you are testing. This section should be precise, as it directs the focus of the entire research.
- **Rationale**: Explain the rationale behind the study. Discuss why this particular method, location, or population was chosen and what the expected contributions of your research are. This could involve a discussion of the theoretical implications of the research or its practical applications.
- **Scope of the Study**: Define the scope of your research, including any limitations in terms of geography, time, population, or data. Setting the scope helps readers understand the bounds within which your findings are applicable.
- **Structure of the Report**: Conclude the introduction by outlining the structure of the rest of the report. Briefly describe what each subsequent section will cover. This helps orient the reader and provides a roadmap for what to expect in the document.

The introduction should be engaging yet informative, providing all the necessary background to understand and appreciate the research undertaken. It's important to write clearly and concisely, avoiding overly complex language to ensure that the introduction is accessible to a broad audience, including those who may not be specialists in the field.

Methodology

The methodology section of a research report is critical as it outlines the procedures and techniques used in the study, providing enough detail for the research to be replicable. This section should clearly describe how the research was conducted, including the design, data collection, and analysis methods. Here's how to effectively detail the methodology in a research report:

- **Research Design**: Start by describing the overall design of the study. Specify whether it was experimental, correlational, qualitative, quantitative, or a mixed-methods approach. Explain the rationale behind choosing this particular design and how it supports the objectives of your study.
- **Participants or Subjects**: Detail the participants or subjects involved in the research. Include information on how they were selected, any inclusion or exclusion criteria, and the demographic characteristics relevant to the study. For non-human subjects, describe the relevant features (e.g., species, strain).
- **Materials and Instruments**: List the materials, tools, and instruments used in the study. This could include laboratory equipment, tests, surveys, or computer software. Provide details about any specific models, versions, or brands used, especially if such details could impact the study's replicability.
- **Procedure**: Clearly outline the steps taken during the research. Describe each phase of the study in the order it occurred, including any preparations, interventions, and methods of data collection. This part should be detailed enough that another researcher could replicate the study based on your description.
- **Data Collection Methods**: Explain how data was collected. If surveys or questionnaires were used, consider attaching or describing them. If observational methods were used, describe how observations were

recorded.

- **Data Analysis**: Describe the methods used for data analysis. Specify the statistical tests used, the software employed, and any techniques for ensuring data integrity and accuracy. If the study involved qualitative data, describe the coding, sorting, and interpretation methods.
- **Ethical Considerations**: Address any ethical issues related to the study. Mention any approvals obtained from ethics committees or institutional review boards. Describe how informed consent was obtained from participants, and how their confidentiality and anonymity were protected.
- **Limitations**: Acknowledge any potential limitations in the methodology that could impact the results or their generalizability. Discuss how these limitations were addressed or why they may be acceptable given the context of the study.

By providing a comprehensive and transparent account of the methodology, you allow readers to critically evaluate the reliability and validity of your research findings. This section is fundamental not only for reproducibility but also for adding credibility to your research efforts.

Results

The results section of a research report is where you present the data collected during your study without bias or interpretation. This section should clearly convey what was found through the research methodologies employed, allowing readers to understand the outcomes and judge their significance. Here's how to structure and present the results effectively:

- **Presentation of Data**: Begin by presenting the data in a logical sequence that aligns with the research questions or hypotheses outlined in the methodology section. Use tables, graphs, and charts to display data clearly and efficiently. Visual aids should be well-labeled, easy to read, and relevant to the discussion.
- **Descriptive Statistics**: Provide descriptive statistics such as means, standard deviations, ranges, and percentages to give a clear picture of the data. This is particularly important for quantitative research where the magnitude and variability of observations are central to understanding the results.

- **Significant Findings**: Highlight significant findings from the analysis. For experimental studies, report the outcomes of statistical tests, including p-values, confidence intervals, and effect sizes. Clearly indicate whether your hypotheses were supported or refuted by the data.
- **Subgroup Analyses**: If relevant, present the results of subgroup analyses to show how outcomes vary among different groups within the study population. This can provide insights into the consistency of your findings across different segments and might indicate areas for further exploration.
- **Non-Significant Results**: It's important to report non-significant results as well. These outcomes can provide useful information about the research topic and help in understanding what does not influence or affect the variables of interest.
- **Textual Explanation**: Accompany each figure or table with a textual explanation that summarizes the key points. Ensure that the narrative aids in understanding what the visuals represent and emphasizes the relevant findings.
- **Avoid Interpretation**: In the results section, focus solely on presenting the data. Save any interpretation of what these results mean for the discussion section. This clear separation helps to maintain objectivity and clarity in reporting the outcomes of the research.

By carefully structuring the results section and presenting the data comprehensively and clearly, you provide the foundation for the discussion and conclusions that follow. Ensure that this section is factual and straightforward, with a focus on reporting what was found rather than discussing or explaining the findings.

Discussion

The discussion section of a research report interprets the results, explaining their implications and relating them to the existing knowledge in the field. This section should explore the significance of the findings, compare them with previous studies, and suggest possible explanations for the observed outcomes. Here's how to effectively construct the discussion section:

- **Interpretation of Results**: Begin by interpreting the main findings of your research. Discuss what the results mean in the context of the study's objectives and hypotheses. Explain how these findings contribute to the existing body of knowledge and what new insights they provide.

- **Comparisons with Previous Research**: Compare your results with those from previous studies. Highlight similarities and discrepancies, and discuss possible reasons for any differences. This comparison not only situates your study within the larger field but also helps in validating or challenging existing theories and results.
- **Theoretical Implications**: Discuss the theoretical implications of your findings. Consider how they support, extend, or challenge existing theories. This discussion should deepen the reader's understanding of the topic and suggest how your results refine or reshape theoretical perspectives.
- **Practical Implications**: If applicable, discuss the practical implications of your results. Consider how they can be applied in real-world settings, their relevance to industry practices, or policy-making. This aspect of the discussion helps to demonstrate the tangible value of your research.
- **Limitations of the Study**: Acknowledge the limitations of your research. Discuss how these limitations might affect the interpretation of the results and the generalizability of the findings. Being transparent about the constraints of your study enhances its credibility and helps guide future research.
- **Suggestions for Future Research**: Based on your findings and the limitations noted, suggest areas for future research. These suggestions should offer concrete ideas for how subsequent studies could overcome the limitations, explore unresolved questions, or further investigate the implications of your findings.
- **Concluding Remarks**: End the discussion with a strong conclusion that synthesizes the key aspects of your findings and their significance. This conclusion should effectively tie the discussion back to the research questions and overall objectives of the study.

By thoughtfully addressing these elements, the discussion section provides a comprehensive analysis of the research findings, situates them within the broader field, and offers insights into their broader relevance and implications. This section is crucial for demonstrating the value and impact of your research to the reader.

Conclusion

The conclusion section of a research report is essential for summarizing the study's findings, reaffirming its significance, and leaving a lasting impression on the reader. This section should succinctly encapsulate what was achieved through the research, the broader implications, and the potential next steps. Here's how to craft an effective conclusion:

- **Summary of Key Findings**: Begin by summarizing the main findings of the research. Recap the critical data and outcomes in a way that reinforces the significance of these results. This summary should reflect the objectives outlined in the introduction and provide a clear answer to the research questions.
- **Implications of the Research**: Discuss the broader implications of your findings. Explain how your research contributes to the existing body of knowledge and what it adds to the field. Highlight any surprising elements or particularly significant insights that emerged from the study.
- **Limitations and Future Directions**: Briefly reiterate the main limitations of your study. This acknowledgment not only demonstrates scholarly honesty but also contextualizes the findings. Following this, suggest potential future research directions. Indicate how further studies could build upon your work, address the limitations noted, or explore new areas that your findings have uncovered.
- **Practical Applications**: If applicable, mention the practical applications of your research. Discuss how the findings can be implemented or suggest ways in which they could influence policy, practice, or future research methodologies.
- **Concluding Thoughts**: End with a strong, impactful statement that underscores the value of the research and its contributions to the field. This could be a reflection on the evolution of the field, the importance of the topic in current contexts, or a call to action based on your findings.

The conclusion should not introduce new data or arguments but rather focus on bringing closure to the report by synthesizing the information presented. It should reinforce the importance of the research and leave the reader with a clear understanding of what was achieved and why it matters.

References

The references section of a research report is critical for providing the bibliographic details of the materials cited throughout the document. This section helps uphold the integrity of your research by acknowledging the sources of your information and allowing readers to verify and further explore those sources. Here's how to effectively manage and structure the references section:

- **Consistency in Formatting**: Choose a specific citation style (APA, MLA, Chicago, etc.) and consistently apply it throughout the reference list. Each citation style has specific rules for how to format different types of sources, including books, journal articles, websites, and more. Consistency helps maintain professionalism and makes it easier for readers to follow the references.
- **Alphabetical Order**: Typically, entries in the reference list are organized alphabetically by the last name of the first author. This standard organization allows readers to easily locate a source.
- **Completeness**: Each entry should provide enough information for readers to locate the source themselves. This typically includes the author(s), publication year, title of the work, publication or source title, volume and issue number (for articles), publisher (for books), and pages used.
- **Accuracy**: Ensure that every reference is accurate. This means double-checking that names are spelled correctly, titles are accurate, and all required information is included. Errors in the references can undermine the credibility of the entire research.
- **Cross-referencing**: Make sure that every source mentioned in your text is also listed in the references section and vice versa. This not only aids in validating your work but also ensures that you are giving proper credit to the original sources.
- **Digital Object Identifiers (DOIs) and URLs**: For electronic sources, include DOIs or URLs when available. DOIs provide a persistent link to content online and are preferable when available. If a DOI is not available, provide the direct URL where the source was accessed.

By carefully managing the references section, you demonstrate the rigor and thoroughness of your research process. It is a testament to the scholarly effort and integrity involved in your study, providing a foundation for trust in your work and facilitating further scholarly exploration by interested readers.

Tips for Clear and Concise Writing

Clear and concise writing is essential in research reports to ensure that the information is accessible and easily understood by a broad audience. Here's how to achieve clarity and conciseness in your writing:

- **Avoiding Jargon and Complex Sentences**:

    - **Jargon**: Minimize the use of specialized terminology or acronyms that may not be familiar to all readers, especially those outside your specific field. If you must use jargon, provide a definition upon its first use.
    - **Complex Sentences**: Avoid overly complex sentence structures that can confuse readers. Instead, break down complicated ideas into simpler sentences. Aim for clarity and simplicity to enhance understanding.

- **Using Active Voice Where Appropriate**:

    - **Active Voice**: Utilize active voice to make sentences clearer and more direct. For example, instead of writing "The experiment was conducted by the researcher," write "The researcher conducted the experiment." Active voice helps in making the writing more engaging and easier to follow.
    - **Passive Voice**: While active voice is generally preferred for clarity, passive voice can be useful in scientific writing to focus on the action rather than the actor, especially in methodological descriptions or where the "doer" is irrelevant. Use it judiciously to emphasize the important elements of your sentences.

- ### *Additional Tips:*

- *Be Concise: Use only as many words as necessary to convey your message. Avoid redundant phrases and filler words that do not add value to the content.*

- **Use Plain Language**: Whenever possible, use straightforward language that is easy to read and understand. This makes your report more accessible to readers who may not have a deep background in the subject.
- **Paragraph Structure**: Organize your paragraphs logically. Start with a topic sentence that introduces the main idea, followed by supporting sentences that elaborate on that idea, and a concluding sentence that ties back to the research's broader implications.
- **Transitional Phrases**: Use transitional words and phrases to connect sentences and paragraphs smoothly, which helps guide the reader through your arguments and results coherently.

By focusing on these elements, you can significantly enhance the clarity and readability of your research report, making it more effective and accessible to a diverse audience.

Ensuring Coherence and Cohesion

Coherence and cohesion are fundamental to writing an effective research report, as they ensure that the document is logically organized and ideas flow smoothly from one to another. Here are strategies to ensure your writing is both coherent and cohesive:

- **Logical Organization**: Structure your report in a logical sequence. Each section should naturally follow from the one before it, with clear connections that build upon each other. This helps readers understand how each part contributes to the overall purpose of the research.
- **Topic Sentences**: Use clear topic sentences at the beginning of each paragraph to introduce the main idea. This helps the reader understand what each paragraph will discuss and how it relates to the larger argument or findings.
- **Linking Words and Phrases**: Employ transitional words and phrases to connect sentences and paragraphs. Common examples include

"however," "moreover," "therefore," and "as a result." These transitions help smooth the flow of your narrative, indicating relationships between different ideas (e.g., contrast, cause, addition).

- **Consistency in Terms and Frameworks**: Maintain consistency in the terminology and frameworks used throughout the report. Switching terms or frameworks can confuse readers and disrupt the narrative flow. If you introduce a concept with a specific term, stick to it throughout the document.
- **Paragraph Linking**: Link paragraphs by ensuring that each paragraph flows into the next. You can achieve this by echoing a key term or idea from the previous paragraph at the start of the new one, or by posing a question in one paragraph that is answered in the next.
- **Reiteration and Synthesis**: At the end of sections or major points, summarize or reiterate key findings or ideas to reinforce them and show how they fit into the overall argument or study objective. This repetition helps reinforce the coherence of the report.
- **Visual Aids**: Use figures, tables, and charts effectively. Visual aids should be integrated smoothly into the text, with clear references and explanations of what they show. They should enhance the textual content, providing a clear visual representation of your data and arguments.

By focusing on these aspects, you can enhance the clarity, flow, and effectiveness of your research report, making it easier for readers to follow your arguments and understand your findings. Cohesion and coherence not only improve readability but also help to convey your ideas more powerfully and persuasively.

Revising and Editing for Clarity and Accuracy

Revising and editing are crucial steps in the writing process, especially for research reports, where clarity and accuracy are paramount. These processes involve refining your content to enhance readability and ensure factual correctness. Here's how to effectively revise and edit your report:

- **Review for Clarity**: Go through your document with the goal of improving clarity. Look for any complex sentences that can be simplified or broken into shorter, more digestible ones. Ensure that every sentence clearly conveys its intended message without ambiguity.

- **Check for Accuracy**: Accuracy is critical in research reporting. Verify all the facts, figures, names, dates, and other details. Pay close attention to your data presentation and ensure that all tables, charts, and graphs are correctly labeled and accurately reflect the data discussed in the text.
- **Eliminate Jargon**: Unless absolutely necessary for your target audience, eliminate jargon or highly technical terms that might confuse readers. If you must use specialized terminology, provide clear definitions upon their first occurrence.
- **Improve Sentence Structure**: Opt for the active voice in most cases as it makes sentences clearer and more direct. However, use the passive voice appropriately to emphasize the action rather than the actor, particularly in scientific writing where the focus should be on the process or results.
- **Consistency Checks**: Ensure consistency in terminology, formatting, and style throughout the document. Consistency helps prevent confusion and enhances the professional quality of your report.
- **Grammar and Spelling**: Correct any grammatical errors and spelling mistakes. These can detract from the credibility of your report and distract the reader from the content.
- **Feedback from Peers**: Obtain feedback from peers or mentors. Fresh eyes can catch errors you might have overlooked and provide insights into how your report can be further improved.
- **Read Aloud**: Reading your text aloud can help you notice issues in flow, awkward phrasing, or overly complex sentences that might not be as obvious when reading silently.
- **Multiple Revision Rounds**: Don't expect to catch everything in one go. Conduct multiple rounds of revisions, focusing on different aspects each time—first on structural issues, then word choice, and finally, on proofreading for typos and minor errors.
- **Use Editing Tools**: Consider using software tools that can help catch common errors and suggest stylistic improvements. Tools like Grammarly, Microsoft Editor, or others specific to academic writing can be beneficial.

By diligently applying these revision and editing techniques, you can significantly enhance the clarity, coherence, and accuracy of your research report, making it more effective and professional.

Importance of a Research Proposal

A research proposal is a critical document that outlines the intent, scope, methodology, and significance of your intended research. It serves multiple essential purposes in the academic and professional realms. Here's why a research proposal is fundamentally important:

- **Justifying the Need for the Research**: The primary aim of a research proposal is to demonstrate the necessity of the proposed study. This involves articulating a clear and compelling argument that addresses a specific gap in the existing body of knowledge or tackles a practical problem that requires resolution. The proposal must convincingly outline why the research is important, who will benefit from it, and why it should be carried out now. This justification is crucial for gaining support from academic supervisors, funding bodies, or other stakeholders.
- **Defining the Research Questions and Objectives**: A well-crafted proposal clearly defines the research questions and objectives. This clarity helps in focusing the research efforts and ensures that the study remains on track. By establishing specific objectives, the proposal sets the boundaries of the study, dictating what will and will not be considered within the scope of the research.
- **Outlining the Methodology**: The proposal provides a detailed plan of how the research will be conducted. This includes the research design, the methods for data collection and analysis, and the techniques for validating the results. A thorough and feasible methodology is vital to convince reviewers of the reliability and validity of the proposed research.
- **Reviewing the Literature**: Including a literature review in the proposal helps to frame the research within the existing academic discourse. It shows the historical progression of the field, identifies where the proposed research fits within that progression, and highlights how it aims to contribute new knowledge or insights.
- **Planning the Research Timeline**: The proposal outlines a timeline for completing the research, breaking down the process into manageable stages with realistic deadlines. This helps in organizing the research more efficiently and demonstrates to reviewers that the project has been thoroughly planned and is achievable within the proposed timeframe.

- **Budget Considerations**: For proposals seeking funding, presenting a detailed budget is essential. This includes costs for resources, materials, travel, and time. A well-justified budget reassures funders that the money will be spent efficiently and that the research team has carefully considered the financial aspects of the project.
- **Ethical Considerations**: The proposal should address any ethical issues related to the research, especially if it involves human or animal subjects. This includes how consent will be obtained, how confidentiality will be maintained, and how the subjects will be treated during and after the study.

A research proposal is not just a formality but a crucial tool for planning and executing research. It helps to ensure that the research is thoughtfully considered and structured, increasing its chances of success and its contribution to the field.

Securing Funding and Approval

Securing funding and approval for a research project is a critical component of the research proposal process. It often determines whether a project will have the necessary resources to proceed. Here's how a research proposal can be effectively utilized to secure funding and gain approval:

- **Clear Articulation of the Research Value**: Funders and approval bodies need to understand the value and significance of the proposed research. The proposal should clearly articulate how the research will advance knowledge, address significant problems, or have practical applications. Demonstrating the potential impact of the research can significantly increase its chances of receiving funding and approval.
- **Comprehensive Budget Justification**: A detailed and well-justified budget is crucial for securing funding. The proposal should include a thorough breakdown of all expected costs, including personnel, equipment, travel, and other expenses. Each cost should be clearly linked to specific aspects of the research, showing funders exactly what their money will support. This transparency builds trust and shows that the project has been meticulously planned.
- **Strong Methodological Framework**: A robust methodology increases a proposal's credibility. It reassures funders and approval committees that

the research is feasible and that the results will be reliable and valid. Detailing the methods for data collection, analysis, and interpretation helps convince stakeholders of the project's scientific merit.

- **Demonstration of Research Team's Expertise**: Including information about the qualifications and experience of the research team can bolster a proposal's strength. Demonstrating that the team has the necessary skills and background to execute the proposed research effectively reassures funders and committees of the project's likelihood of success.
- **Addressing Ethical Considerations**: Addressing ethical issues upfront in the proposal is crucial, especially for research involving human or animal subjects. Providing a clear ethical framework and detailing how ethical challenges will be handled not only fulfills a necessary requirement for most funding and regulatory bodies but also enhances the credibility of the research proposal.
- **Alignment with Funding Objectives**: Tailoring the proposal to align with the specific interests and objectives of the funding body can greatly enhance its chances of success. Understanding what funders are particularly interested in supporting—whether it's a type of research, a specific field, or broader impact initiatives—and demonstrating how your project aligns with these interests can make your proposal more compelling.
- **Effective Presentation and Submission**: Ensuring that the proposal is well-written, clear, and professionally presented is crucial. It should be free of jargon, concise, and tailored to the audience's level of expertise. Moreover, adhering to all specific submission guidelines and deadlines is essential. This professionalism helps make a positive impression on the review panel.

By addressing these areas effectively, a research proposal can significantly enhance its chances of securing the necessary funding and approvals, paving the way for the successful execution of the research project.

Planning and Guiding the Research Process

A research proposal is instrumental in planning and guiding the research process from its inception to completion. This strategic document serves as a roadmap, detailing every aspect of the project and ensuring that each phase is thoughtfully planned and aligned with the overall objectives. Here's how a research proposal aids in planning and guiding the research process:

- **Defining the Research Framework**: The proposal sets out the research questions, hypotheses, and objectives clearly. This framework acts as the foundation for the entire project, guiding what data needs to be collected, what methods will be used, and how the findings will be evaluated. This clarity prevents scope creep and ensures that the research stays focused on its primary goals.
- **Detailed Methodology**: A well-crafted proposal outlines the methodology in detail, specifying the research design, data collection methods, and analysis techniques. This comprehensive planning helps anticipate potential challenges and solutions, ensuring the research can be conducted smoothly and efficiently. It also assures stakeholders that the project is well-conceived and feasible.
- **Timeline for Execution**: The proposal includes a timeline that outlines key milestones and deadlines. This schedule is crucial for managing time effectively throughout the project. It helps in tracking progress, ensuring that the research does not fall behind and that resources are allocated efficiently over the duration of the project.
- **Resource Allocation**: By detailing what resources are needed—whether financial, human, or material—the proposal helps in the allocation and management of these resources. It ensures that the necessary tools, personnel, and funding are available as needed, which is essential for the smooth execution of the project.
- **Risk Management**: The proposal should also identify potential risks and challenges associated with the research, along with strategies for mitigating these risks. This proactive approach to risk management is critical for navigating uncertainties and ensuring the project's success.
- **Ethical Considerations**: Planning for ethical considerations is another crucial aspect covered in the proposal. It outlines how the research will comply with ethical standards, including gaining informed consent, ensuring confidentiality, and minimizing harm to participants. This not only protects the subjects involved but also enhances the legitimacy and integrity of the research.
- **Evaluation and Adaptation Strategies**: Finally, the proposal should include mechanisms for ongoing evaluation and possible adaptation of the research strategy. This allows for flexibility in responding to

unexpected findings or challenges, ensuring that the research can adapt to new information or conditions without losing its direction or focus.

In essence, the research proposal is not just a document for securing funding and approval; it is a strategic tool that guides every step of the research process, ensuring that the project is well-planned, feasible, ethically sound, and aligned with its stated objectives. By meticulously detailing each aspect of the research, the proposal acts as both a guide and a checkpoint, ensuring that the project progresses as intended.

Format and Key Elements of a Research Proposal

A well-structured research proposal follows a specific format that facilitates a clear presentation of the research idea, its significance, and the plan for its execution. Understanding the format and key elements involved is essential for crafting a compelling proposal. Here are the details regarding some of the critical components of a research proposal format:

- **Title:**
    - The title of the proposal should be concise yet descriptive. It should clearly convey the essence of the research project and, if possible, hint at the research question or area of study. A good title is straightforward and avoids ambiguous terms, allowing readers to understand the topic at a glance.
- **Abstract:**
    - The abstract is a brief summary of the research proposal, typically ranging between 150-300 words. It should cover the main objectives of the research, the methodology to be used, and the expected outcomes. The abstract should be succinct and informative, designed to give the reader a clear overview of what the proposal contains and the significance of the research being proposed.

These elements serve as the preliminary introduction to the proposal, setting the stage for a detailed discussion of the research plan. They are crucial for making a strong first impression, as they are often the first sections read by reviewers or funding bodies.

- **Background and Literature Review:**
  - **Background:**
    - The background section provides a detailed context for the research question or problem being addressed. It sets the stage by outlining the current state of knowledge in the field and situating the research within that context. This section should demonstrate the relevance of the topic and build a strong case for why this particular research is necessary. It often includes a discussion of the historical development of the topic, key findings from previous research, and the existing gaps that the proposed study aims to fill.
  - **Literature Review:**
    - The literature review systematically evaluates and synthesizes the existing research related to the research topic. This section not only shows the researcher's comprehensive understanding of the field but also helps in identifying and justifying the research gap that the proposal aims to address. A well-conducted literature review outlines major theories, concepts, and studies that have shaped the field, highlighting both their strengths and limitations. It should be critical and selective, focusing on the most relevant and current literature to support the rationale for the new study.

These components are fundamental in setting up the foundation of the research proposal. They provide the necessary background and justification for the research, demonstrating the researcher's knowledge and the significance of the proposed study.

-

Research Objectives and Hypotheses:

  - **Research Objectives:**

  - Research objectives clearly state what the researcher intends to achieve through the study. These should be specific, measurable, attainable, relevant, and time-bound (SMART). Objectives guide the research process, dictating the direction and scope of the study. They help stakeholders understand the purpose and the intended outcomes of the research. For instance, an objective might be to "determine the effect of X on Y among Z population within a 12-month period." Each objective should align with the overall aim of the research, contributing directly to answering the research question.

- **Hypotheses**:

  - Hypotheses are testable statements that predict a relationship between two or more variables. They are formulated based on the literature review and the theoretical framework of the study. Hypotheses provide a focused direction for research activities, suggesting possible outcomes that the study seeks to confirm or refute. A well-formulated hypothesis should be clear and concise, providing a basis for scientific investigation. For example, a hypothesis might state, "There is a significant positive relationship between X (independent variable) and Y (dependent variable) among Z (population)."

These elements are essential for structuring the research and providing a clear framework for what the study aims to achieve and how it will contribute to existing knowledge. They also facilitate the design of the methodology section, as the objectives and hypotheses determine the type of data to be collected, the nature of the analysis, and the overall approach of the study.

- **Methodology**:

  - The methodology section is one of the most critical components of a research proposal, detailing how the research will be conducted. It should provide enough detail for the study to be replicable, addressing several key elements:

- **Research Design:**
    - Describe the overall strategy that you will use to integrate the different components of the study in a coherent and logical way, thereby ensuring you effectively address the research problem. This could involve experimental design, correlational studies, case studies, ethnography, etc., depending on the nature of the question and the objectives of the research.
- **Sampling Method:**
    - Specify how participants or items will be selected to be part of the study (e.g., random sampling, convenience sampling, stratified sampling). Include details about the population, sample size, and the rationale for these choices to ensure representativeness and reliability of the results.
- **Data Collection Methods:**
    - Clearly outline the techniques for gathering data (e.g., surveys, interviews, observation, archival research). Provide details about any instruments you will use, such as questionnaires or specialized equipment. If existing instruments are used, mention their previous use and reliability.
- **Data Analysis Procedures:**
    - Describe the statistical or qualitative techniques you will use to analyze the data collected. Explain how these methods are suited to address the research objectives and test the hypotheses. Include any software or tools that will be utilized.
- **Validity and Reliability:**
    - Discuss how you will ensure the validity and reliability (or credibility and dependability in qualitative research) of your findings. This might include pilot testing, triangulation, and other verification techniques.

- **Ethical Considerations**:
    - Address any ethical issues related to the research, such as how informed consent will be obtained, how confidentiality will be maintained, and how potential harm to participants will be minimized. Detail any ethical approvals required for the study.
- **Potential Limitations**:
    - Acknowledge any potential limitations of your research approach and how you plan to mitigate them. This transparency helps build trust in the rigor of your research process.

This section is vital as it not only demonstrates your understanding of conducting scientific research but also reassures readers (including potential funders or academic supervisors) that the study is well-planned and feasible, and that the researcher is prepared to handle the practical aspects of the research process.

- **Budget and Timeline**:
    - These components are essential in demonstrating the feasibility and planning of the research project. They provide a detailed forecast of the resource allocation and timeline required to successfully complete the research.
        - **Budget**:
            - The budget should detail all the financial requirements necessary to carry out the research. This includes direct costs like salaries for research assistants, costs for materials and supplies, travel expenses for fieldwork, and any other resources that are essential to the project. It should also consider indirect costs, such as administrative support and overheads. Each item on the budget should be justified in terms of its necessity for the project's success. A well-prepared budget reflects the researcher's understanding of the project's

scope and a realistic appraisal of what it will take to achieve the research objectives.

- **Timeline**:

    - The timeline outlines the major milestones and deadlines of the research project. It should be presented in either a tabular or a Gantt chart format, showing the start and end dates of each major activity, such as literature review, data collection, data analysis, and report writing. The timeline helps to manage the project effectively, ensuring that the research is conducted within a feasible timeframe and resources are allocated efficiently. It also reassures funders and supervisory committees that the project has been carefully planned and is likely to be completed on schedule.

These elements of the research proposal are crucial for demonstrating to reviewers, whether they are academic advisors, institutional review boards, or potential funders, that the researcher has a clear and practical plan for carrying out the research. They show that the researcher has thought through the logistics and resources required, which increases the likelihood of the project's successful completion.

- **Preparing an Effective Presentation**:

    - When it comes time to present your research proposal to a review committee, preparation is key. This involves not only understanding your research thoroughly but also being able to communicate it effectively. Here are some crucial aspects to consider when preparing for a presentation to a review committee:

    - **Clarity and Conciseness**:

        - Your presentation should clearly articulate the purpose, significance, and methodology of your research in a concise manner. Avoid unnecessary jargon and overly complex explanations. The goal is to make your research accessible to all members of the committee, some of whom may not be specialists in your specific field.

- **Visual Aids:**
    - Use visual aids, such as PowerPoint slides, charts, and graphs, to enhance your presentation. These should support your verbal communication, not replace it. Ensure that all visuals are clear, professionally designed, and free of clutter. Each slide should focus on one main idea and visually complement what you are saying.
- **Practice:**
    - Rehearse your presentation multiple times to ensure smooth delivery. Practice helps you refine your timing, allows you to adjust your content for clarity and impact, and builds your confidence. If possible, practice in front of peers or mentors who can provide constructive feedback.
- **Anticipate Questions:**
    - Be prepared to answer questions from the committee. Anticipate potential queries and criticisms regarding your research methodology, budget, timeline, and expected outcomes. Having thoughtful responses ready will demonstrate your thorough understanding of the project and your preparedness to address any concerns.
- **Engagement and Enthusiasm:**
    - Show your passion for the research topic. Your enthusiasm can be contagious and can help persuade the committee of the importance and viability of your research. However, maintain professionalism at all times.
- **Summary and Closure:**

- Conclude your presentation with a strong summary of your research proposal's key points. Reinforce the significance of the research and its potential impact. Thank the committee for their time and attention, and invite any further questions.

Preparing an effective presentation involves not just a clear exposition of your research proposal but also readiness to engage with the review committee interactively and responsively. This preparation demonstrates your commitment to the project and your capability to execute it as planned.

- **Anticipating and Addressing Potential Questions**:
  - Successfully defending a research proposal involves not just presenting your work but also being prepared to address questions and concerns from the review committee. This preparation is crucial for demonstrating the robustness of your proposal and your capability as a researcher. Here's how you can effectively anticipate and address potential questions:
    - **Understand the Committee's Perspective**:
      - Try to understand the concerns and interests of the committee members. Each member may have different priorities, such as the feasibility of the methodology, the ethical considerations, or the practical impact of your research. Tailoring your responses to their perspectives can help address their specific concerns effectively.
    - **Common Areas of Inquiry**:
      - Prepare for questions that commonly arise in research defenses. These include inquiries about the choice of methodology, the justification for the research topic, how you plan to handle unexpected results or difficulties, and the significance of your research to the field. Also, be ready to discuss your research's theoretical and practical implications.

- **Methodological Justification:**
    - Be prepared to defend your methodological choices. Understand the strengths and limitations of your chosen methods and be ready to discuss why they are the most appropriate for addressing your research questions. Having alternative methodologies in mind can also be helpful in case the committee challenges your initial choice.
- **Budget and Timeline Scrutiny:**
    - Expect detailed questions about your proposed budget and timeline. You should be able to justify each item in your budget and the time allocated to each phase of your research. Be realistic and prepared to explain how you will manage if unexpected costs arise or if activities take longer than planned.
- **Handling Critiques:**
    - It's important to remain open and responsive to critiques. View them as an opportunity to strengthen your proposal rather than as an attack. If you encounter a question or critique that you haven't considered, acknowledge its validity and express your willingness to look into it further. This shows openness to feedback and a commitment to rigorous research.
- **Evidence of Preliminary Work:**
    - Be ready to show any preliminary data or pilot studies that support your research proposal. This can be particularly persuasive in demonstrating the feasibility of your research and your capability to carry it out successfully.
- **Ethical Considerations:**
    - Prepare to discuss how you will address ethical issues related to your research. Be clear about how you will obtain informed consent, ensure confidentiality, and handle sensitive data.

Preparing answers to potential questions involves a deep understanding of every aspect of your proposal and a readiness to engage thoughtfully and comprehensively with the review committee. This preparation not only helps in smoothing the review process but also enhances the credibility and feasibility of your research proposal.

CHAPTER FOUR

INTRODUCTION TO INTELLECTUAL PROPERTY RIGHTS

4.1 Nature of Intellectual Property

4.1.1 Overview of Patents

- **Definition:**
  - A patent is a legal right granted by a government to an inventor, giving the inventor exclusive rights to use, make, sell, and distribute their invention for a limited period, typically 20 years from the filing date of the patent application. This legal protection is designed to encourage innovation by allowing inventors the opportunity to reap the commercial benefits of their inventions without fear of unauthorized use or imitation by others.
- **Purpose:**
  - The primary purpose of a patent is to promote innovation and technical progress by providing inventors with a temporary monopoly on their creations. This exclusivity not only helps inventors to recover the financial outlay involved in research and development but also incentivizes further innovation. In return for this exclusive right, the inventor must disclose detailed information about the invention to the public. This disclosure contributes to the pool of public knowledge and may inspire further innovation and

development in the field, thereby fostering an environment of continuous technological advancement. Patents thus serve a dual function: protecting inventors' interests while enhancing the overall technological and economic development of society.

- **Types of Patents:**
  - Patents can be categorized into three main types, each serving a different purpose and covering specific kinds of inventions. Understanding these distinctions is crucial for inventors and businesses to protect their innovations appropriately.
    - **Utility Patents:**
      - Utility patents are the most common type of patent. They are granted for the invention of a new and useful process, machine, manufacture, or composition of matter, or a new and useful improvement thereof. This includes things like new technologies, chemical formulas, machines, and other manufactured goods. The key criteria for obtaining a utility patent are that the invention must be novel, non-obvious, and useful.
    - **Design Patents:**
      - Design patents protect the ornamental design of a functional item. This type of patent is concerned with the appearance of the product and not its function. For example, the unique shape or surface ornamentation of items can be protected under a design patent, provided the design is new and not obvious in light of what has already been known. Design patents are crucial for industries where the aesthetic of a product plays a significant role in consumer preference, such as in the fashion or furniture industries.
    - **Plant Patents:**

  - Plant patents are granted to anyone who invents or discovers and asexually reproduces any distinct and new variety of plant. This includes cultivated sports, mutants, hybrids, and newly found seedlings, other than a tuber-propagated plant or a plant found in an uncultivated state. The plant must be clearly distinguishable from existing plants and must not have been sold or released more than one year prior to the patent application.

These types of patents provide inventors with exclusive rights to their creations, encouraging innovation and investment in new products and technologies. Each type of patent is specific to the nature of the invention it protects, offering a tailored form of intellectual property protection that is suited to the unique aspects of the invention's functionality, design, or biological makeup.

4.1.2 Overview of Designs

- **Industrial Designs and Their Protection:**
  - **Definition of Industrial Designs:**
    - Industrial designs encompass the aesthetic or ornamental aspect of an item. An industrial design may consist of three-dimensional features, such as the shape or surface of an item, or two-dimensional features, such as patterns, lines, or color. These designs are applied to a wide range of industrial products and handicrafts: from technical and medical instruments to watches, jewelry, and other luxury items; from household products to electrical appliances; from architectural structures to textile designs.
  - **Purpose of Protection:**
    - The protection of industrial designs aims to ensure the visual appeal of products and to prevent unauthorized copying or imitation of the designs. This form of intellectual property protection helps creators ensure that their design investments are profitable, providing an incentive to create and innovate visually

appealing and marketable products.

- **Criteria for Protection:**

    - To qualify for design protection, the design must be new or original and have an individual character. A design is considered new if no identical design has been made available to the public. It has individual character if the overall impression it produces on an informed user differs from the overall impression produced on such a user by any design which has been made available to the public. The design must also be separable from the product and must not be dictated solely by the product's technical function.

- **Legal Mechanisms:**

    - Protection for industrial designs can be obtained through registration at a national or regional intellectual property office, which grants the designer exclusive rights to use the design. These rights typically allow the owner to prevent others from making, selling, or importing items incorporating or copying the design, for a period of up to 25 years, depending on the jurisdiction. The duration of protection is often divided into renewable periods.

- **International Protection:**

    - Designers can also secure protection in multiple countries through international treaties such as the Hague Agreement concerning the international registration of industrial designs, administered by the World Intellectual Property Organization (WIPO). This agreement allows for a streamlined application process through which designers can apply for protection in over 70 participating countries with a single application.

The protection of industrial designs not only benefits the creator by providing a competitive edge but also enhances the richness and diversity of products available in the market, contributing to economic development. It plays a crucial role in sectors where consumer appeal and aesthetic innovation are key to market success.

4.1.3 Overview of Trade Secrets

- **Definition and Importance:**
  - **Definition:**
    - A trade secret is any information that is not generally known or reasonably ascertainable by others, which a business can use to obtain an economic advantage over competitors or customers. This information can include formulas, practices, processes, designs, instruments, patterns, or compilations of information. For example, the recipe for Coca-Cola is one of the most famous trade secrets.
  - **Importance:**
    - Trade secrets are crucial for businesses as they provide a competitive edge by keeping important information confidential. Unlike patents, trade secrets are protected without registration, which means they can potentially be protected indefinitely as long as the secrecy is maintained. This makes them particularly valuable for businesses whose competitive advantage depends on confidential methods or formulas. The protection of trade secrets encourages businesses to invest in new methods, techniques, and technologies.
- **Methods of Protection:**
  - **Legal Frameworks:**
    - While trade secrets do not require registration for protection, they are legally protected under various national laws and international agreements, such as the Agreement on Trade-Related Aspects of Intellectual Property Rights (TRIPS). In the United States, for example, the Uniform Trade Secrets Act and the Defend Trade Secrets Act provide a framework for the protection against misappropriation of trade secrets.

- **Practical Measures:**
    - To maintain the confidentiality of trade secrets, businesses must take practical security measures. These measures include:
        - **Non-disclosure Agreements (NDAs):** Employees, contractors, and business partners who have access to trade secrets are often required to sign NDAs, legally obligating them to keep the information confidential.
        - **Physical Security:** Limiting physical access to facilities where sensitive information is kept, using locks, security badges, and surveillance systems.
        - **Digital Security:** Using strong cybersecurity measures such as encryption, secure servers, and access control systems to protect digital data.
        - **Employee Training:** Educating employees about the importance of trade secrets and their role in protecting those secrets.
- **Internal Policies and Procedures:**
    - Companies should develop and enforce policies that limit access to confidential information to essential personnel only. Regular audits and monitoring can help ensure that these policies are followed and that the information remains secure.

Protecting trade secrets requires a combination of legal tools and practical measures. Effective protection not only secures a company's valuable information but also supports long-term innovation and business success.

4.1.4 Overview of Copyrights

- **Scope and Coverage:**
    - **Definition:**
        - Copyright is a form of protection provided by the laws of a country to the creators of original works of authorship, including

literary, dramatic, musical, artistic, and certain other intellectual works, both published and unpublished. This protection is granted automatically upon the creation of a work and does not generally require registration.

- **Coverage**:
    - Copyright covers a wide range of creative expressions but does not protect facts, ideas, systems, or methods of operation. It typically covers:
        - **Literary Works**: Novels, poems, articles, essays, and even software code.
        - **Musical Works**: Songs, instrumental pieces, and their accompanying lyrics.
        - **Dramatic Works**: Plays, screenplays, and scripts.
        - **Artistic Works**: Paintings, drawings, sculptures, and photographs.
        - **Architectural Works**: Architectural designs and plans.
        - **Audiovisual Works**: Movies, television shows, and online videos.
        - **Sound Recordings**: Audio recordings of music or other sounds.
    - Copyright is meant to encourage the creation of art and culture by ensuring that creators can profit from their works without fear of misappropriation.

- **Rights of Authors and Creators**:
    - **Exclusive Rights**:
        - Copyright grants authors and creators certain exclusive rights, which typically include:
            - **Reproduction**: The right to make copies of the copyrighted work.
            - **Distribution**: The right to sell or otherwise distribute copies to the public.

- **Public Performance**: The right to perform the work publicly, as in the case of plays and concerts.
- **Public Display**: The right to display the work publicly, as in artworks in galleries or readings of literary works.
- **Adaptation**: The right to create adaptations of the work, known as derivative works (e.g., turning a novel into a movie script).

- **Moral Rights**:

  - In addition to economic rights, many jurisdictions recognize moral rights of authors, which may include:

    - **Right of Attribution**: The right to claim authorship of the work and to prevent others from claiming authorship falsely.
    - **Right of Integrity**: The right to object to any distortion, mutilation, or other modification of their work that would be prejudicial to the creator's honor or reputation.

- **Duration**:

  - Copyright protection typically lasts for the life of the author plus an additional 70 years after their death (depending on the jurisdiction). For corporate authorship, works are generally protected for 95 years from publication or 120 years from creation, whichever is shorter.

Copyrights are crucial for protecting the rights and financial interests of creators, enabling them to control how their works are used and to receive compensation for their efforts. This protection is foundational to the flourishing of creativity and the development of a diverse cultural landscape.

4.2 Importance of IPR in Research

4.2.1 Encouraging Innovation

- **Incentives for Researchers and Inventors**:

  - Intellectual Property Rights (IPR) provide a critical framework for rewarding creativity and innovation. By securing exclusive rights to their discoveries and creations, inventors and researchers can potentially reap financial benefits from their work. This monetary incentive is a powerful motivator for individuals and companies to invest time, effort, and resources into generating new ideas and technologies. The prospect of obtaining a patent, for instance, can justify the substantial research and development costs associated with bringing new products to market. Similarly, copyrights protect authors and artists, ensuring they can earn royalties from their works, thereby supporting their livelihood and continued creative output.

- **Role of IPR in Fostering Creativity**:

  - Beyond financial incentives, IPR plays a pivotal role in promoting a culture of continuous innovation and creative thinking. Intellectual property protections provide a safe space for experimentation and development, knowing that new ideas can be secured and protected from unauthorized use or duplication. This security encourages a more open exchange of ideas and collaboration, particularly in research and development-intensive sectors like pharmaceuticals, technology, and academia.
  - Moreover, IPR contributes to a competitive market environment where companies and individuals strive to out-innovate each other. This competition drives the advancement of technology and arts, leading to broader societal benefits including new products, services, and artistic expressions that enhance quality of life and cultural enrichment.
  - IPR also ensures that knowledge and innovation are disseminated through society via publications, patents, and public performances, among others. Patents, for instance, require the inventor to fully disclose the invention to the public, thus adding to the collective pool of knowledge and potentially spurring further innovation by others in the field.

The framework established by IPR thus not only incentivizes individual creativity and investment but also fosters a broader culture of innovation that drives scientific, technological, and cultural advancement. This dynamic is especially crucial in research environments where the development and sharing of new knowledge are fundamental to progress.

4.2.2 Protecting Inventions

- **Legal Frameworks for Protection**:

  - Intellectual Property Rights (IPR) are protected through a variety of legal frameworks designed to safeguard the creations of inventors and creators across different fields. These frameworks include:

    - **Patent Law**: Patents protect inventions by granting inventors exclusive rights to make, use, sell, and distribute their invention for a limited period, typically 20 years. The patent system is critical for inventions in industries such as pharmaceuticals, engineering, and technology.
    - **Copyright Law**: Copyrights protect the rights of authors and artists by giving them exclusive rights to reproduce, distribute, perform, display, and make derivative works from their original content for a specified period, which generally extends for the life of the creator plus 70 years after their death.
    - **Trademark Law**: Trademarks protect words, phrases, symbols, or designs identifying the source of goods or services and distinguishing them from others. Trademarks are crucial for maintaining brand identity and consumer trust.
    - **Design Rights**: These protect the visual design of objects that are not purely utilitarian. Design rights cover the appearance, shape, or configuration of an item, provided it is new and has individual character.
    - **Trade Secrets**: Trade secret protection is crucial for formulas, practices, processes, designs, instruments, commercial methods, and compilations of information that provide a business with a competitive edge. The protection of trade secrets does not expire as long as the information remains confidential.

- **Benefits of Securing Intellectual Property**:

  - Securing intellectual property rights offers numerous benefits, including:

- **Monetary Gain**: Intellectual property can be a significant source of revenue through licensing agreements, selling IP rights, or the commercialization of IP-protected products and services.
- **Market Position**: Strong IP rights can help a company establish a dominant position in the market. It can act as a barrier to entry for competitors and can be used strategically to maintain or extend market share.
- **Investment Attraction**: Companies with well-protected IP portfolios are often more attractive to investors, as these rights can increase the potential for market success and provide a clear competitive edge.
- **Global Expansion**: IP rights, especially those recognized in multiple jurisdictions, can facilitate the global expansion of business by providing the necessary legal framework to protect inventions and brands worldwide.
- **R&D Incentives**: With the protection of outcomes, companies and individuals are more likely to invest in research and development, knowing that their inventions and new technologies can be protected legally from competitors.

Protecting inventions through intellectual property laws not only secures the legal rights of creators and inventors but also fosters a healthy competitive environment that encourages innovation and promotes economic growth. These protections are essential for motivating the creation of new products, technologies, and artistic works, contributing significantly to technological advances and cultural enrichment.

4.3 Global Perspective on IPR

4.3.1 International Cooperation and Agreements

- **Key International Treaties and Organizations**:

  - Intellectual Property Rights (IPR) have a robust international framework governed by several treaties and organizations, ensuring cooperation across borders and jurisdictions:

    - **World Intellectual Property Organization (WIPO)**: WIPO is a specialized agency of the United Nations dedicated to developing a balanced and accessible international intellectual property (IP) system. It administers numerous treaties concerning the protection of IP and offers mediation services for IP disputes.

- **Agreement on Trade-Related Aspects of Intellectual Property Rights (TRIPS)**: Administered by the World Trade Organization (WTO), TRIPS sets minimum standards for many forms of intellectual property regulation as applied to nationals of other WTO Members. It was negotiated in the late 1980s and early 1990s and is a comprehensive multilateral agreement on intellectual property.
- **Paris Convention for the Protection of Industrial Property**: Dating back to 1883, this treaty was one of the first intellectual property treaties. It establishes a union for the protection of industrial property. The convention applies to industrial property in the widest sense, including patents, trademarks, industrial designs, utility models, service marks, trade names, and geographical indications.
- **Berne Convention for the Protection of Literary and Artistic Works**: This convention, established in 1886, deals primarily with the protection of works and the rights of their authors. It is one of the most important agreements on copyright protection, providing creators such as authors, musicians, poets, painters etc., with the means to control how their works are used, by whom, and on what terms.

- **Harmonization of IPR Laws Across Countries**:

  - The harmonization of intellectual property laws across countries aims to ensure that IP laws are consistent and operate similarly worldwide, which is crucial for global commerce and the international exchange of goods and services. This process is facilitated by international treaties like TRIPS and conventions managed by WIPO, which help to standardize regulations across countries, making it easier for multinational companies and creators to protect their intellectual property while operating in multiple jurisdictions.
  - Harmonization efforts have led to the adoption of similar standards for the granting of patents, the registration of trademarks and designs, and the enforcement of copyrights. These efforts reduce

complexity and increase predictability for IP rights holders when they seek to protect their IP in various countries.

- However, despite significant progress, complete harmonization is challenging due to the differences in domestic legal systems, cultural differences, and different levels of economic development. As such, while the broad frameworks may be aligned, the specific details and implementations can vary significantly from one country to another.

International cooperation and the harmonization of laws are critical for protecting intellectual property in the global market. These efforts help create a safer and more predictable environment for investors, creators, and businesses worldwide, promoting innovation and creativity across borders.

4.3.2 Comparative Study of IPR Systems

- **Differences in Patent Laws Globally**:
  - Patent laws vary significantly from one country to another, reflecting differences in legal traditions, economic development, and public policy priorities. These variations can affect the ease with which patents are obtained, the type of inventions that can be patented, and the duration and enforcement of patent rights. For instance:
    - **United States**: The U.S. operates under a "first-to-file" system, which grants patent rights based on who first files a patent application rather than who first invents. Patents are granted for 20 years from the filing date but require payment of maintenance fees to keep the patent in force.
    - **European Union**: The European Patent Office (EPO) allows inventors to seek patent protection in up to 38 countries through a single application process. Unlike the U.S., the EPO does not allow for patents on business methods and has stricter requirements for software-related inventions.
    - **Japan**: Known for its efficiency in processing patent applications, Japan also has a "first-to-file" system and offers a "patent opposition system," which allows third parties to submit evidence against the grant of a patent shortly after it has been issued.
- **Case Studies of International IPR Disputes**:

- International IPR disputes often highlight the complexities of navigating different legal systems and the global impact of IPR enforcement. Some notable case studies include:

  - **Apple vs. Samsung**: This series of lawsuits involved claims and counterclaims related to the infringement of various intellectual property rights, including patents and trademarks. The disputes spanned multiple countries, each with its legal proceedings and judgments, reflecting differing national laws on IP protection.
  - **Eli Lilly vs. Canada**: Pharmaceutical company Eli Lilly filed a suit against Canada under the North American Free Trade Agreement (NAFTA), claiming that Canadian courts' invalidation of patents for two of its drugs was in violation of its rights. This case raised questions about the balance between national health policies and international patent rights.
  - **Roche vs. Cipla**: This dispute involved the Indian pharmaceutical company Cipla producing a generic version of Roche's patented cancer drug, which was still under patent protection. The case was notable for addressing issues related to compulsory licensing and access to life-saving medicines in developing countries.

These examples demonstrate how variations in national patent laws can lead to complex international legal battles that can be costly and time-consuming. They underscore the importance of careful strategic planning for IP management on a global scale and highlight the need for ongoing efforts to harmonize international IP laws to facilitate smoother international operations and dispute resolution.

4.4 Procedure for Grants of Patents

4.4.1 Steps for Patent Application

- **Preparing the Patent Application**:

  - The preparation of a patent application is a crucial step that requires meticulous attention to detail to ensure that the invention is clearly and comprehensively described. This includes:

    - **Detailed Description**: The application must include a full disclosure of the invention, explaining how it works and how it is to be used. This should be done in such a way that someone skilled in the relevant field can replicate the invention.

- **Claims**: The most critical part of the patent application. Claims define the scope of the protection sought and must be clear and specific to establish exactly what the invention covers.
- **Drawings and Diagrams**: If the invention can be illustrated, drawings must be included to aid in the understanding of the invention. These must be detailed enough to complement the written description and claims.
- **Abstract**: A summary of the disclosure in the patent application, including what the invention is about and its crucial technical aspects.

- **Filing with the Patent Office:**

  - Once the patent application is prepared, it must be filed with the appropriate patent office where protection is sought. This step involves several important considerations:

    - **Choosing the Right Office**: If protection is only sought in one country, the application will be filed with the national patent office. However, if protection is desired in multiple countries, one might consider filing through international agreements like the Patent Cooperation Treaty (PCT) which simplifies the process of filing in its member countries.
    - **Application Fees:** Filing a patent application requires the payment of fees, which can vary depending on the type of application, the number of claims, and whether the filing is national or international.
    - **Examination Process**: After filing, the patent office will conduct an examination process to determine if the invention meets all legal requirements for patentability, such as novelty, non-obviousness, and usefulness. This process can take several years and may require responding to objections raised by patent examiners.
    - **Publication**: Typically, 18 months after filing, the patent application is published, allowing the public to see the invention details. This publication starts the process of protecting the

invention while the examination continues.

Successfully navigating the patent application process requires not only a thorough understanding of one's invention but also the intricacies of patent law and procedures. This can often necessitate the assistance of patent attorneys or agents who specialize in intellectual property law to ensure that all procedural requirements are met and to maximize the chances of obtaining patent protection.

4.4.2 Examination and Approval Process

- **Patent Examination Procedures**:
  - After a patent application is filed, it enters the examination phase, which is a critical part of the patent granting process. This involves several key steps:
    - **Initial Assessment**: Initially, the patent office checks the application for compliance with filing requirements and administrative details, such as the correct submission of forms and fees.
    - **Search for Prior Art**: The examiner conducts a comprehensive search of existing patents, scientific literature, and other public disclosures (collectively known as "prior art") to assess whether the invention is novel and non-obvious.
    - **Substantive Examination**: The core of the examination process, where the examiner scrutinizes the claims of the patent application to determine if they meet legal standards of patentability. This includes evaluating the invention's novelty, inventive step (non-obviousness), and industrial applicability.
    - **Communication**: Throughout the examination process, the patent office may issue communications or "office actions" to the applicant, detailing any concerns about the application, such as unclear claims or similarities to prior art.
- **Addressing Objections and Revisions**:
  - Responding to objections raised during the examination process is a pivotal aspect of securing a patent. Key considerations include:

- **Responding to Office Actions**: Applicants must carefully address any objections or rejections issued by the patent office. This typically involves amending the claims, arguing against the objections, or providing additional information to clarify the invention's novelty and utility.
- **Amendment of Claims**: Often, claims need to be amended to clarify their scope, distinguish the invention from prior art, or tighten their focus to enhance their enforceability. These amendments must not stray from the original disclosure to avoid adding new matter, which is generally not permissible.
- **Negotiation and Re-examination**: Sometimes, a back-and-forth negotiation occurs between the patent examiner and the applicant or their attorney. This can involve multiple rounds of responses and further amendments until the issues are resolved or the examiner's objections are overcome.
- **Final Decision**: Once all objections are addressed, and the examiner is satisfied that the patent application meets all patentability criteria, the patent is granted. If the examiner's objections cannot be overcome, the application may be refused, although most jurisdictions offer an appeal process.

The examination and approval process for patents is thorough and can be complex, requiring a deep understanding of both the invention and patent law. Success often depends on the applicant's ability to effectively communicate the uniqueness and utility of their invention, as well as their willingness to carefully navigate the legal and procedural hurdles of the patent system.

4.4.3 Patenting under the Patent Cooperation Treaty (PCT)

- **Overview of the PCT Process**:

  - The Patent Cooperation Treaty (PCT) is an international treaty administered by the World Intellectual Property Organization (WIPO). It simplifies the process of filing patents in multiple countries by allowing inventors to file a single international patent application that has the effect of a national patent application in all contracting states of the PCT. Here are the key steps in the PCT process:

- **Filing**: The applicant files an international patent application, typically in one language, and pays fees that cover both the international search and preliminary examination.
- **International Search**: An International Searching Authority (ISA) identifies the published documents and prior art which may affect the patentability of the invention. The ISA then issues an International Search Report (ISR) and a written opinion regarding the patentability of the invention.
- **Supplementary International Search** (optional): An additional search by a second ISA aimed at finding prior art possibly missed in the initial search.
- **International Publication**: Around 18 months after the priority date (the earliest filing date in one of the member countries), the application is published by WIPO.
- **International Preliminary Examination** (optional): This step involves a more detailed review of the patentability of the application. The applicant can request amendments to the claims to address any issues raised.
- **National Phase**: After the PCT process, the applicant must enter the national phase, in which the international application is converted into separate national applications in the countries where protection is sought. This typically occurs 30 months from the priority date.

- **Benefits and Challenges of International Patenting**:

  - **Benefits**:

    - **Simplified Process**: The PCT system consolidates the filing process and defers the cost and effort of multiple national filings until the international reviews are completed.
    - **Strategic Planning**: Applicants have more time (up to 30 months from the earliest filing date) to decide in which countries to pursue patent protection based on the business importance, market size, and ISR findings.
    - **Cost Efficiency**: Initial costs are lower because the applicant avoids multiple national filing fees and translations at the early stages of the patent lifecycle.

- **Challenges**:
  - **Complexity and Cost in Later Stages**: During the national phase, the costs can escalate significantly as each country's specific requirements come into play, including translations and local agent fees.
  - **Variability in National Laws**: The PCT process does not standardize substantive patent law across all jurisdictions, meaning the outcomes of patent examinations can vary significantly from country to country.
  - **Extended Timeline**: The process from filing to final patent grant can be lengthy, particularly if international preliminary examination and national phase entries are pursued, potentially delaying enforcement.

Using the PCT system can provide strategic advantages in managing international patent filings, but it requires careful planning and consideration of the costs and complexities involved in the subsequent national phase entries.

CHAPTER FIVE

THE PATENT SYSTEM

5.1 Understanding Patents

5.1.1 Definition and Scope

- **What Constitutes a Patent**:
    - A patent is a form of intellectual property that grants the patent holder exclusive rights to make, use, sell, and distribute an invention for a limited period, typically 20 years from the filing date of the patent application. The purpose of a patent is to provide a reward for inventiveness and technical contribution to the public domain by offering a temporary monopoly in exchange for the public disclosure of the invention. Here's what specifically constitutes a patent:
        - **Inventive Step**: The invention must show some new characteristic which is not known in the body of existing knowledge (prior art) in its technical field. This step must represent a sufficient advance over what would be obvious to someone with knowledge and experience in the area.
        - **Novelty**: The invention must be fundamentally new. No public disclosure, use, sale, or publication of the invention should have occurred prior to the patent application. It must differ significantly in some way from previous knowledge or products.
        - **Utility**: The invention must be useful. This means it must be operable and provide a practical benefit. Generally, speculative inventions without a demonstrable utility do not qualify for patent protection.

- **Legally Patentable Subject Matter**: The invention must fall within the categories of patentable subject matter, which generally include processes, machines, manufactures, and compositions of matter. Some things, such as abstract ideas, natural phenomena, and purely artistic creations, are not patentable.

These components—novelty, inventive step, utility, and qualifying subject matter—are crucial for an invention's eligibility for patent protection. The scope of the patent is defined primarily by its claims, which are detailed descriptions of the technical boundaries of the invention. These claims outline what the patent does and does not cover, essentially delineating the legal protection conferred by the patent.

- **Types of Patents**:

  - Patents can be categorized into different types based on the nature of the invention they protect. Each type serves a specific purpose and caters to a particular category of invention:

    - **Utility Patents**: These are the most common type of patents issued and they protect new and useful processes, machines, articles of manufacture, or compositions of matter, or any new and useful improvement thereof. Utility patents are what most people refer to when they talk about patents and provide protection for the functional aspects of an invention. They typically last for 20 years from the date the application is filed.
    - **Design Patents**: Design patents protect the ornamental design of a functional item. This could include new, original, and ornamental designs for an article of manufacture. It's important to note that a design patent protects only the appearance of the article and not its structural or functional features. Design patents in the United States last for 15 years from the date of patent grant.
    - **Plant Patents**: These patents are granted to anyone who invents or discovers and asexually reproduces any distinct and new variety of plant, including cultivated sports, mutants, hybrids, and newly found seedlings, other than a tuber-propagated plant or a plant found in an uncultivated state. Plant patents protect the inventor's right to exclude others from asexually reproducing, selling, or

using the plant so reproduced. Plant patents last for 20 years from the date the patent application is filed.

Each type of patent requires a different approach and understanding of what is protected under the law. Utility patents focus on function, design patents on appearance, and plant patents on genetic uniqueness. Understanding these distinctions is crucial for effectively protecting and leveraging intellectual property in various fields.

- **Criteria for Patentability**:
  - For an invention to be eligible for patent protection, it must meet several key criteria set by patent laws, which ensure that only truly deserving inventions receive this valuable form of intellectual property protection. The primary criteria include:
    - **Novelty**: An invention must be novel, meaning it must not have been previously known or used by others in public before the patent application is filed. Anything that has been publicly disclosed, used, sold, or published before the filing date, anywhere in the world, can potentially prevent a patent from being granted if it includes the same or very similar technology or process as the invention.
    - **Non-obviousness (Inventive Step)**: The invention must involve an inventive step that is not obvious to someone with knowledge and skills in the technical field of the invention. This criterion is meant to ensure that the patent system rewards only those inventions that contribute something significant and not merely trivial modifications or improvements that any skilled individual could make.
    - **Utility**: The invention must be useful, which means it must have a practical application and must operate to perform its intended purpose. The utility requirement is relatively broad, but it prevents the patenting of inventions that do not function properly or have no real-world benefit.

These criteria collectively ensure that the patent system rewards inventors for genuine, substantive contributions to their fields while preventing the overcrowding of the patent landscape with trivial modifications or broadly known technologies. Meeting these criteria can often be challenging and typically requires careful preparation and presentation of the patent application to demonstrate how the invention stands out from prior art and meets all the legal requirements for patentability.

5.1.2 Process of Patenting and Development

- **Concept to Patent: Stages of Development**:
  - The journey from an initial idea to securing a patent involves several crucial stages. Each stage serves to refine the concept, assess its viability, and ensure that it meets the stringent requirements of patent law.
    - **Idea Conception**: This is the genesis of the process, where an idea or innovation is conceived. It involves recognizing a problem and developing a novel solution. At this stage, it's essential to document every step meticulously to establish a clear timeline of development.
    - **Preliminary Research and Documentation**: Before proceeding, it's critical to document the invention in detail and conduct preliminary research. This includes searching patent databases and other resources to check if the invention or something similar has already been patented or disclosed.
    - **Prototype Development**: Developing a working model or prototype helps to test the practical application of the concept and identify any operational flaws. This step is crucial for inventions that are complex and require proof of concept before a patent application is filed.
    - **Patentability Analysis**: At this point, the inventor or an appointed patent attorney conducts a thorough analysis to determine if the invention meets the criteria of novelty, non-obviousness, and utility. This analysis often includes a more extensive patent search and consultation with experts to assess the invention's eligibility for patent protection.
    - **Drafting and Filing the Patent Application**: Once it's confirmed that the invention is likely patentable, the next step involves

drafting the patent application, which includes detailed descriptions, drawings, and claims of the invention. The application is then filed with the appropriate patent office, either nationally or internationally.

- **Patent Examination**: After filing, the patent office reviews the application to ensure it meets all the necessary legal criteria. This may involve correspondence with the applicant to clarify aspects of the invention or modify parts of the application. The examination process can take several years, depending on the complexity of the invention and the backlog at the patent office.
- **Grant of Patent**: If the patent office is satisfied that the invention fulfills all requirements, a patent is granted, providing the inventor exclusive rights to the invention for a specified period. This right enables the inventor to exclude others from making, using, or selling the invention without permission.
- **Commercialization and Maintenance**: After the patent is granted, the inventor can move towards commercializing the invention, either through manufacturing and selling it directly or licensing the rights to another party. Maintaining a patent often requires periodic fees and management of legal rights, especially if the patent is registered in multiple countries.

Each of these stages is critical in transforming an abstract idea into a fully patented, marketable invention. The process requires a blend of creative, technical, and legal expertise to navigate successfully.

- **Research and Documentation Required**:

  - To successfully navigate the patenting process, comprehensive research and meticulous documentation are critical. These components help establish the invention's originality and patentability, and they provide a robust foundation for the patent application. Here's what typically needs to be done:

    - **Initial Invention Documentation**: The first step involves documenting the initial concept of the invention as soon as it is conceived. This documentation should include detailed descriptions, sketches, and any other records that outline the idea and its development. Keeping a dated inventor's notebook or journal where all observations, experiments, and revisions are logged can be beneficial.

- **Prior Art Search**: Conducting a thorough search of existing patents and other public disclosures (collectively known as prior art) is essential. The purpose of this search is to determine whether the invention is novel and non-obvious. This involves searching through patent databases, scientific journals, and other publications to find related technologies. Online patent databases like those of the United States Patent and Trademark Office (USPTO), European Patent Office (EPO), and World Intellectual Property Organization (WIPO) can be valuable resources.
- **Detailed Description of the Invention**: The inventor must prepare a comprehensive description of the invention that covers every technical detail and possible variation of the invention. This should include the purpose of the invention, how it works, and the specific components or steps involved in its operation. The description should be clear enough that someone skilled in the relevant field could replicate the invention without additional inventive work.
- **Drawings and Diagrams**: For most patents, especially those involving complex machinery or devices, detailed drawings and diagrams are required. These visuals should clearly illustrate the invention from various angles and include labels for all important components.
- **Comparative Analysis with Prior Art**: This involves analyzing how the invention differs from and improves upon existing solutions. This analysis can help in writing the claims of the patent application, which define the scope of protection granted by the patent.
- **Claims Drafting**: Claims are the most critical part of a patent application as they define the legal protection conferred by the patent. Drafting precise claims requires understanding the technical nuances of the invention as well as the legal standards for patentability. This often requires the expertise of a patent attorney or agent.
- **Legal and Regulatory Documents**: Depending on the nature of the invention, additional legal and regulatory documentation

might be necessary. This could include safety analyses, environmental impact assessments, or approvals for clinical trials if the invention is a pharmaceutical product.

Proper documentation and thorough research are not just about supporting the patent application; they also provide a legal safeguard against potential infringement and challenges to the patent's validity in the future. By ensuring that every aspect of the invention and its development is well-documented and supported by robust research, inventors can strengthen their cases for patent grants and defend their intellectual property effectively in competitive markets.

- **Provisional vs. Non-Provisional Applications:**
  - When filing for a patent, inventors have the option to submit either a provisional or a non-provisional patent application. Each type serves different purposes and offers distinct advantages depending on the inventor's needs and the stage of development of the invention.
    - **Provisional Patent Application:**
      - **Purpose:** A provisional application is a preliminary step that allows the inventor to establish an early filing date for the invention while providing additional time (up to one year) to refine the invention, explore market potential, or seek funding. It is not examined for patentability by the patent office and will not directly result in a patent.
      - **Content Requirements:** Provisional applications generally require less formal documentation and do not require formal patent claims. However, they must contain a thorough and detailed description of the invention and any drawings necessary to understand it. The content must be sufficient to support a subsequent non-provisional application.
      - **Advantages:** The main advantage of filing a provisional application is the ability to secure an early filing date. It is also typically less expensive to prepare and file compared to a non-provisional application. Inventors can use the term "Patent Pending" during the period the provisional application is

active.

- **Duration**: A provisional patent application only lasts for 12 months. Before this period expires, the inventor must file a corresponding non-provisional application to benefit from the earlier provisional filing date.

- **Non-Provisional Patent Application**:

  - **Purpose**: This is the complete application that is reviewed by the patent office for meeting the patentability criteria, including novelty, non-obviousness, and utility. Filing a non-provisional application is necessary to obtain a patent.
  - **Content Requirements**: A non-provisional application must include a full patent specification, claims that define the scope of the invention, an oath or declaration by the inventor, and any required drawings. It must be comprehensive enough to enable someone skilled in the relevant field to make and use the invention.
  - **Advantages**: Once granted, a non-provisional patent application results in the issuance of a patent that provides legal protection, allowing the holder to exclude others from making, using, selling, or importing the patented invention.
  - **Duration**: The duration of protection for a utility patent is typically 20 years from the filing date of the non-provisional application, subject to periodic fees to maintain the patent's validity.

5.2 Patent Application Process

- **5.2.1 Steps for Applying for a Patent**:

  - The process of applying for a patent is detailed and requires careful planning and execution. Here are the essential steps involved in applying for a patent:

    - **Initial Research and Patent Search**:

- **Purpose**: Before preparing a patent application, it is crucial to conduct initial research to determine if the invention is patentable. This involves assessing novelty, non-obviousness, and utility—key criteria for patentability.
- **Process**: The inventor or a patent professional conducts a comprehensive patent search to identify existing patents and public disclosures that might affect the patentability of the invention. This search typically involves databases like those of the USPTO, EPO, WIPO, and others, looking at patents, patent applications, and other technical documents.
- **Outcome**: The results of this search will guide the inventor in understanding the landscape of existing inventions and help refine the invention or its patent application to emphasize novel aspects. A thorough patent search can also help in drafting the patent claims, which define the scope of protection sought.

- **Drafting the Patent Application**:

  - **Purpose**: The primary goal of drafting the patent application is to provide a full and clear description of the invention, including how it works and how it is distinct from prior art. The application must be detailed enough to enable someone skilled in the related field to replicate the invention.
  - **Process**: This involves preparing several key components of the application:

    - **Description**: A detailed explanation of the invention, its operation, and its potential variations.
    - **Drawings**: Visual depictions of the invention, if applicable, showing all features and how they interrelate.
    - **Claims**: These are the most critical part of the application, legally defining the scope of protection. The claims must be clear and specific, delineating the boundaries of what the inventor considers their proprietary invention.
    - **Abstract**: A brief summary of the invention and its purpose.

- **Outcome**: A well-drafted application increases the likelihood of the patent being granted and can provide robust legal protection against infringement.

- **Filing the Patent Application**:

  - **Purpose**: Filing officially submits the patent application to the patent office, starting the formal process of obtaining a patent.
  - **Process**: The application can be filed with national patent offices or through international treaties, such as the Patent Cooperation Treaty (PCT), depending on the scope of protection desired. Filing fees are usually required at this stage.
  - **Outcome**: Once filed, the application will receive a filing date, which is crucial as it establishes the priority of the invention over others in the same field filed after that date.

- **Examination by the Patent Office**:

  - **Purpose**: The examination process is designed to ensure that the application meets all legal requirements and that the invention is indeed patentable.
  - **Process**: A patent examiner reviews the application to assess the invention against criteria including novelty, non-obviousness, and utility. The examiner may issue queries or objections, leading to correspondence with the applicant, who will have the opportunity to amend the application or argue against the objections.
  - **Outcome**: If the examiner is satisfied, the patent will be granted. If not, the application may be rejected, and the applicant may have options to appeal the decision or make further amendments.

- **Granting of Patent**:

  - **Purpose**: The final step in the patent application process is the granting of the patent, which legally protects the inventor's rights to the invention.

- **Process**: Once all objections and requirements are satisfied, and fees paid, the patent office issues a patent grant. This document provides the inventor with exclusive rights to the invention for a specific period.
- **Outcome**: With a patent granted, the inventor can enforce their rights to stop others from making, using, selling, or importing the invention without permission in the countries where the patent is valid.

Each step in the patent application process requires careful attention to detail and often the assistance of professionals specializing in patent law. This ensures the best chance of securing comprehensive protection for your invention.

5.2.1 Steps for Applying for a Patent

- **Drafting the Patent Application**:

  - **Purpose**: Drafting the patent application is a critical step where the inventor details every aspect of their invention to formally communicate its uniqueness and utility to the patent office. This documentation must be comprehensive, clear, and precise to meet the stringent requirements for patent approval.
  - **Components of a Patent Application**:

    - **Description**: The description, also known as the specification, must encompass a detailed narrative of the invention, including its background, a summary of related technologies, and a full disclosure of the invention. It should explain how the invention works, its advantages, and possible variations, ensuring that someone skilled in the relevant technical field can reproduce the invention.
    - **Claims**: These are arguably the most crucial part of the application, as they define the legal boundaries of the invention's protection. Claims must be clear, specific, and supported by the description. They should be written in a precise format to distinctly point out what the invention is and what it is not, delineating the scope of protection sought.

- **Drawings**: Almost all patent applications require drawings if the invention can be illustrated graphically. These must clearly show every feature of the invention as claimed. Drawings need to be professionally done, adhering to the patent office's specific requirements, illustrating all aspects and components of the invention from multiple views.
- **Abstract**: This is a concise summary of the content of the application, providing a snapshot of the technical information and the essence of the invention. The abstract should be brief but detailed enough to convey the core idea and utility of the invention.

- **Drafting Process**:

  - **Collaboration with Professionals**: Many inventors opt to work with patent attorneys or agents experienced in drafting patent applications. These professionals can help ensure that the application meets all legal standards, significantly enhancing the likelihood of patent grant.
  - **Technical and Legal Review**: The draft should undergo rigorous technical and legal reviews to ensure that the description is accurate and the claims are correctly formulated. This review helps in identifying potential weaknesses in the patent application that could be exploited by competitors.
  - **Refinement**: The application may need several iterations to refine the claims and ensure that the description fully supports them. This iterative process is crucial to align the legal scope of protection with the technical aspects of the invention.

- **Outcome**: A well-drafted patent application not only facilitates the examination process but also maximizes the scope of legal protection for the invention. It acts as a critical document in defending the patent during infringement cases and can significantly enhance the commercial value of the invention.

Effective drafting requires an understanding of both the invention's technical complexity and the legal framework governing patents. This ensures that the final patent provides robust and enforceable rights to the inventor.

5.2.1 Steps for Applying for a Patent

- **Filing the Application with the Patent Office:**
  - **Purpose:** The act of filing the patent application with the appropriate patent office is the formal step that officially starts the patent process. This is when the inventor submits their well-prepared patent application to seek exclusive rights for their invention.
  - **Process:**
    - **Selection of Patent Office:** Depending on the geographical coverage desired for the patent protection, inventors may choose to file nationally (in one country), regionally (covering multiple countries, like the European Patent Office), or internationally (using systems such as the Patent Cooperation Treaty, PCT).
    - **Preparation of Required Documents:** Before filing, all necessary documentation, including the completed patent application form, detailed descriptions, claims, drawings, abstract, and any additional documents required by the specific patent office, must be prepared.
    - **Payment of Fees:** Filing a patent application usually involves various fees, such as basic filing fees, examination fees, and additional fees if the number of claims or drawings exceeds a certain limit. These fees vary by patent office and the type of application filed.
    - **Submission:** The application can be submitted through traditional paper forms or, increasingly, via online submission portals provided by many patent offices. Online submissions are typically faster and more reliable, providing immediate confirmation of receipt.
    - **Obtaining a Filing Date:** Once the application is submitted and the initial fees are paid, the patent office assigns a filing date. This date is crucial as it establishes the priority of the invention relative to other filings, which is especially important in "first to file" jurisdictions.
  - **Outcome:**

- **Acknowledgment of Receipt**: After filing, the patent office acknowledges receipt of the application and provides a filing receipt that includes the application number and filing date. This receipt is an important document that should be safely stored as it is proof of the patent application filing.
- **Preliminary Examination**: Some patent offices conduct a preliminary examination to ensure that the application meets basic filing requirements. This may involve checking the completeness of the application, including the presence of all required parts like claims and drawings.
- **Waiting for Examination**: Once the application is deemed complete, it enters a queue for substantive examination, where the details of the invention will be assessed against patentability criteria. This phase can take several years, depending on the patent office and the complexity of the invention.

Filing the application is a critical step that requires precision and attention to detail, as errors or omissions can delay the process or affect the patent's scope of protection. It is often advisable to seek the assistance of patent professionals to ensure that all procedural requirements are met efficiently and accurately. This ensures that the patent application is correctly positioned for the subsequent examination phase and maximizes the chances of obtaining a robust patent.

5.2 Patent Application Process

- **5.2.2 Examination and Approval Process:**

  - **Purpose**: The examination process is a crucial phase where the patent office rigorously assesses the patent application to determine if it meets all the legal criteria for patentability, including novelty, inventive step (non-obviousness), and industrial applicability (utility).
  - **Patent Examination Procedures:**

    - **Initial Formalities Check**: After filing, the patent office first conducts a formality examination to ensure that the application complies with all required formal aspects, such as proper formatting, inclusion of all necessary parts, and payment of fees.

- **Search for Prior Art**: The next step is a comprehensive search for prior art. This involves identifying existing patents, published patent applications, and other public documents (like scientific papers) that might be relevant to assessing the novelty and inventive step of the claimed invention. The results are compiled in a search report, which is typically sent to the applicant.
- **Substantive Examination**: This is the core of the examination process. A patent examiner reviews the application in detail, considering the prior art identified in the search report. The examiner evaluates whether the invention as claimed in the application meets the criteria for patentability:

  - **Novelty**: The invention must be new, meaning it has not been publicly disclosed in the same form before the filing date.
  - **Inventive Step (Non-obviousness)**: The invention must not be obvious to someone with knowledge and experience in the subject area.
  - **Industrial Applicability (Utility)**: The invention must be useful and have a practical application.

- **Communication with the Applicant**: During the examination, the examiner may issue queries or objections, known as office actions, to which the applicant must respond. These might relate to the clarity of the claims, the invention's patentability, or issues with prior art. The applicant has the opportunity to amend the claims, argue against the objections, or provide additional information to support the application.
- **Final Decision**: After evaluating the application and considering the applicant's responses to any objections, the examiner makes a decision. If the application meets all the criteria, the patent is granted. If not, the application may be refused, but typically there are options to appeal or request further examination.

- **Outcome**:

  - **Grant of Patent**: A successful examination results in the issuance of a patent. The granted patent document is then published and the inventor is awarded exclusive rights to exploit the invention for a set period (usually 20 years from the filing date).

- **Publication of Grant:** The grant of the patent is published, notifying the public and other inventors in the field of the new patented invention. This publication marks the beginning of the period during which the patent holder has exclusive rights to the invention.

The examination and approval process is meticulous and can be lengthy, often taking several years. It is designed to ensure that only truly novel, non-obvious, and useful inventions receive patent protection. This rigorous scrutiny maintains the balance between innovator rights and public interest, preventing the patenting of unworthy inventions that do not meet the high standards set by law.

5.2.2 Examination and Approval Process

- **Responding to Office Actions and Objections:**
  - **Purpose:** Responding effectively to office actions, which are official communications from a patent examiner detailing any objections or issues with a patent application, is crucial in the patent approval process. These responses are an opportunity for the applicant to clarify misunderstandings, amend claims, and argue for the patentability of their invention.
  - **Understanding Office Actions:**
    - **Types of Objections:** Common objections might include issues with novelty, inventive step, or clarity of the claims. The examiner may also point out formal issues like improper formatting or missing documents.
    - **Detailed Review:** The first step in responding is to thoroughly review the office action to understand the examiner's concerns. It's important to analyze each objection to determine its basis and the specific areas of the application it affects.
  - **Crafting a Response:**
    - **Amending Claims:** Often, objections can be overcome by amending claims to make them more specific, narrow their scope,

or clarify the language used. This can help in distinguishing the invention from prior art and addressing concerns regarding the inventive step.

- **Providing Arguments and Evidence**: If the applicant believes that the examiner's objections are unfounded, they can provide a detailed argument supported by technical explanations and, if available, additional experimental results or evidence. This might include a detailed explanation of why the invention is novel or involves an inventive step.
- **Further Experiments or Data**: Sometimes, additional data or experiments may be necessary to demonstrate the invention's efficacy or to clarify its innovative nature. Submitting this additional data can be crucial in convincing the examiner of the invention's merits.
- **Consulting with a Patent Attorney**: Handling office actions can be complex, and legal expertise is often required. A patent attorney can help in interpreting the legal and technical aspects of the objections and in drafting a robust response that adheres to legal standards.

- **Submission of the Response**:

  - **Timely Response**: It is critical to respond within the deadlines set by the patent office, which can vary from one jurisdiction to another. Failure to respond on time can result in the abandonment of the patent application.
  - **Formal Requirements**: The response must comply with any formal requirements specified by the patent office, including the way amendments to claims are made or how additional documents are filed.

- **Outcome**:

  - **Further Communication**: The examination process is iterative. The examiner may issue subsequent office actions if the initial response does not fully resolve the issues or if new issues arise from the amendments.

- **Eventual Resolution**: The process continues until all objections are addressed satisfactorily, leading either to the rejection or the grant of the patent. In cases of rejection, there might be further options for appeal or continuation of the application.

Responding to office actions is a critical skill in the patent process, requiring both technical knowledge and legal acumen. Effective responses can greatly increase the chances of securing patent protection by addressing all the examiner's concerns in a comprehensive and legally sound manner.

5.2.2 Examination and Approval Process

- **Grant of the Patent and Publication**:

  - **Purpose**: The final stage of the patent application process is the grant of the patent, following a successful examination where all objections have been resolved. This step officially confers the exclusive rights of the invention to the applicant and makes the details of the invention publicly available.
  - **Granting the Patent**:

    - **Issuance**: Once the patent examiner is satisfied that the application meets all patentability criteria—novelty, inventive step, and utility—and all procedural requirements are met, the patent office issues a notice of allowance. The applicant may need to pay a final issuance fee before the patent is officially granted.
    - **Patent Document**: Upon payment of the issuance fee, the patent office prepares a formal patent document that contains the full details of the granted patent, including the inventor's name, the patent number, and the claims that define the scope of the patent protection. This document is legally binding and enforces the rights of the patent holder.

  - **Publication**:

    - **Disclosure to the Public**: Following the grant, the patent is published in an official patent journal or a public database, making the information accessible to the public. This publication includes all details of the patent, such as the description, claims, and drawings.

- **Purpose of Publication**: The publication serves multiple purposes:

  - **Transparency**: It ensures transparency in the patent system by disclosing the full scope and details of patented inventions.
  - **Prevents Infringement**: It notifies the public and potential competitors about the existence and scope of the patent rights, which helps in preventing inadvertent infringements.
  - **Encourages Innovation**: By making the technical details of the invention available, it allows other inventors to understand the new technology, which can spur further innovation and development in related fields.

- **Outcome**:

  - **Legal Protection**: The grant of a patent confers exclusive rights to the patent holder to exploit the invention commercially, prevent others from using, selling, manufacturing, or distributing the patented invention without permission, and take legal action against infringers.
  - **Starting Point for Enforcement**: The date of publication often marks the start of the term during which these rights can be legally enforced, usually 20 years from the filing date for most types of patents.

The grant and publication of a patent are crucial as they not only confer legal rights to the inventor but also add to the collective technical knowledge shared with the public. This process is essential for the advancement of technology and promotes further innovation by clearly delineating protected technologies and encouraging inventors to build on existing knowledge.

5.3 Patenting under the Patent Cooperation Treaty (PCT)

- **5.3.1 Overview of the PCT Process:**

  - **Purpose of the PCT:**

- **Simplifying the Patenting Process**: The primary purpose of the Patent Cooperation Treaty (PCT) is to simplify the process of filing patent applications on a global scale. Instead of having to submit separate applications in each country where protection is sought, the PCT allows inventors to file a single international patent application that has the same effect as national applications in all contracting states to the treaty.
- **Delaying Expenses**: The PCT process provides applicants with the option to delay the significant costs associated with pursuing patent protection in multiple countries. Applicants can delay making decisions about which countries to enter into the national phase for up to 30 or 31 months from the priority date, which allows more time to assess the potential commercial value of their invention.

- **Benefits of the PCT**:

  - **International Search Report (ISR) and Written Opinion**: One major advantage of the PCT process is the generation of an International Search Report and a Written Opinion on the patentability of the invention. This provides valuable feedback on the likelihood of obtaining patents in the national phase, helping inventors make informed decisions about whether and where to pursue patent protection.
  - **Global Reach**: The PCT covers over 150 countries, making it an effective tool for securing potential patent protection almost worldwide. This extensive coverage is crucial for inventors looking to market their inventions globally.
  - **Strategic Planning**: The additional time provided before entering the national phase allows applicants to refine their patent strategies based on the search report, market conditions, or development of their invention. This can include securing funding, conducting further research, or initiating partnerships.
  - **Cost-Effective**: Although the initial filing fee for a PCT application might be higher than that of a national application, it eliminates the need for multiple separate filings in the initial stages. This consolidated approach can lead to substantial cost savings, particularly for applicants seeking broad international protection.

The PCT process is a cornerstone of international patent law, designed to facilitate the protection of inventions across multiple countries through a streamlined and cost-effective approach. This process not only aids inventors in managing their patent portfolios more efficiently but also supports the global dissemination of technological information, fostering innovation worldwide.

5.3 Patenting under the Patent Cooperation Treaty (PCT)

- **Steps Involved in PCT Application:**
  - **Filing the International Application**: The first step in the PCT process is to file an international patent application, which can be done up to 12 months after filing a national or regional patent application (this initial filing is known as the priority application). The international application can be filed in one of the authorized languages, and it must designate all PCT member countries where the applicant may eventually seek patent protection.
  - **Receiving an International Search Report (ISR)**:
    - **Assignment of International Searching Authority (ISA)**: Upon filing, one of the designated ISAs (selected based on the applicant's choice or jurisdiction) conducts a search for prior art that could affect the patentability (novelty, inventive step, and industrial applicability) of the invention.
    - **Delivery of the ISR**: The ISA provides an International Search Report and a written opinion regarding the patentability of the invention, usually within 16 months from the priority date.
  - **International Publication**:
    - **Timing**: The application is published by the International Bureau of the World Intellectual Property Organization (WIPO) 18 months from the earliest priority date.
    - **Purpose**: Publication makes the application and the findings of the ISR available to the public, increasing transparency and potentially attracting commercial interest or partners.
  - **Supplementary International Search (Optional)**:

- **Additional Search**: An optional supplementary search may be requested to cover literature not included in the initial search, conducted by a different ISA to ensure broader patentability analysis.

- **International Preliminary Examination (Optional)**:

  - **Request**: After the ISR, the applicant can request an optional detailed preliminary examination of the application's patentability, conducted by one of the International Preliminary Examining Authorities (IPEA).
  - **Outcome**: The IPEA issues an International Preliminary Report on Patentability (IPRP), providing a strong indication of whether the application meets patentability criteria under the PCT.

- **Entering the National Phase**:

  - **Deadline**: Typically, the applicant must decide to enter the national phase in each designated country or region within 30 months (or in some cases 31 months) from the priority date.
  - **National Processing**: Each designated patent office begins national processing of the application, applying local laws to decide if a patent can be granted.

- **Grant of Patents**:

  - **Final Decision**: The final decision on the grant of a patent is made by each national or regional patent office. The process and requirements can vary significantly, involving additional examinations, fees, and legal hurdles.

The PCT application process is designed to streamline the management of international patent filings and provides a structured pathway for obtaining patent protection in multiple jurisdictions. It significantly aids inventors in navigating the complex landscape of international patent law.

5.3 Patenting under the Patent Cooperation Treaty (PCT)

- **Role of the International Searching Authority (ISA) and International Preliminary Examining Authority (IPEA):**

  - **International Searching Authority (ISA):**

    - **Purpose and Function:** The ISA is responsible for conducting a thorough search of the relevant prior art. This includes published patent applications and other technical literature that may affect the patentability (novelty, inventive step, and industrial applicability) of the invention claimed in the PCT application.
    - **International Search Report (ISR):** The ISA compiles the International Search Report, which lists all the relevant prior art documents that have been identified during the search. Alongside the ISR, the ISA also provides a written opinion on the potential patentability of the invention based on the identified prior art.
    - **Impact on Patent Application:** The report and opinion from the ISA are critical as they give the applicant a preliminary assessment of whether the invention is likely patentable, guiding decisions about proceeding to the national phase in various countries.

  - **International Preliminary Examining Authority (IPEA):**

    - **Purpose and Function:** For applicants seeking a more detailed analysis of the patentability of their invention, the IPEA conducts what is known as an International Preliminary Examination. This examination is optional and goes beyond the initial search to include an in-depth review of the application in light of the claims and the identified prior art.
    - **International Preliminary Report on Patentability (IPRP):** The IPEA issues this report, which includes an analysis of the patentability aspects of the application—particularly focusing on novelty, inventive step, and industrial applicability. The report provides a final opinion on these matters before the application enters the national phase.
    - **Strategic Importance:** The IPEA's report helps the applicant understand the strengths and weaknesses of the patent application more comprehensively. It offers a chance to make amendments or arguments before entering the national phase, potentially

reducing the likelihood of facing objections from national patent offices.

- **Collaborative Roles:**
  - **Guidance for Applicants:** Both ISA and IPEA play crucial roles in guiding the applicant through the international phase of the patent process under the PCT. Their assessments help the applicant make informed decisions about where and how to pursue patent protection effectively.
  - **Cost and Time Efficiency:** By providing early and detailed feedback on the patentability of inventions, these authorities help streamline the process, potentially saving applicants time and money by reducing the likelihood of costly disputes and rejections during the national phase.

The roles of ISA and IPEA are integral to the PCT system, providing essential services that help maintain the integrity and effectiveness of international patent protection. Their evaluations are pivotal in determining the strategy for entering national phases and significantly influence the overall success of patent applications globally.

5.3 Patenting under the Patent Cooperation Treaty (PCT)

- **5.3.2 Advantages and Challenges of PCT:**
  - **Simplification of the International Patent Process:**
    - **Streamlined Filing Procedure:** The PCT provides a unified procedure for filing patent applications to seek protection in multiple countries. Applicants can file one international application in a single language and pay one set of fees, which simplifies the initial steps of seeking international patent protection.
    - **Extended Decision Period:** By utilizing the PCT process, applicants gain up to 30 or 31 months from the priority date to decide in which member countries to pursue patent protection. This extended timeframe allows applicants to better assess the commercial viability of their invention in different markets and

make more informed decisions.

- **Centralized Examination**: The preliminary examination conducted by the ISA and IPEA helps streamline the patent process by identifying potential issues early. This centralized examination can reduce the likelihood of facing objections and rejections during the national phase, potentially saving time and resources.

- **Cost Efficiency**:

    - **Reduced Initial Costs**: Filing a single international application under the PCT can be more cost-effective compared to filing separate applications in multiple countries. The PCT process also delays the need for translations and national filing fees until the national phase, which can help manage upfront costs.
    - **Harmonized Procedures**: The PCT standardizes the procedures for filing, searching, and examining patent applications, which reduces the administrative burden on applicants and can lead to cost savings in managing the patent process across different jurisdictions.

- **Enhanced Patent Quality**:

    - **Comprehensive Search and Examination**: The International Search Report (ISR) and the International Preliminary Report on Patentability (IPRP) provide applicants with detailed assessments of the patentability of their invention. These reports help applicants refine their applications and address potential issues before entering the national phase, leading to stronger patent applications.
    - **Global Recognition**: The PCT system is recognized by patent offices worldwide, which can enhance the credibility and acceptance of the application in different jurisdictions. This global recognition can facilitate smoother processing and examination in national patent offices.

- **Challenges of PCT**:

- **Complexity and Administrative Requirements**: While the PCT simplifies many aspects of the international patent process, it still involves complex procedures and strict deadlines. Applicants must carefully manage their applications to ensure compliance with PCT requirements and timelines.
- **Initial Costs**: Although the PCT can reduce costs in the long term, the initial fees for filing an international application and conducting the international search and examination can still be substantial. Applicants need to be prepared for these upfront expenses.
- **National Phase Costs**: Entering the national phase in multiple countries can be costly, as it involves paying national filing fees, translation costs, and legal fees for each jurisdiction. Applicants must budget for these expenses and plan their international patent strategy accordingly.
- **Potential for Delays**: The centralized examination process under the PCT can introduce additional steps and timelines, which may delay the overall patenting process. Applicants seeking rapid protection in specific countries might need to consider alternative strategies alongside the PCT process.

The PCT offers significant advantages in terms of simplifying the international patent process, reducing initial costs, and enhancing the quality of patent applications. However, it also presents challenges related to complexity, administrative requirements, and costs associated with the national phase. Understanding these advantages and challenges is crucial for applicants to effectively navigate the PCT system and maximize the benefits of international patent protection.

5.3 Patenting under the Patent Cooperation Treaty (PCT)

- **5.3.2 Advantages and Challenges of PCT:**

  - **Simplification of the International Patent Process:**

    - **Streamlined Filing Procedure**: The PCT provides a unified procedure for filing patent applications to seek protection in multiple countries. Applicants can file one international application in a single language and pay one set of fees, which simplifies the initial steps of seeking international patent protection.

- **Extended Decision Period**: By utilizing the PCT process, applicants gain up to 30 or 31 months from the priority date to decide in which member countries to pursue patent protection. This extended timeframe allows applicants to better assess the commercial viability of their invention in different markets and make more informed decisions.
- **Centralized Examination**: The preliminary examination conducted by the ISA and IPEA helps streamline the patent process by identifying potential issues early. This centralized examination can reduce the likelihood of facing objections and rejections during the national phase, potentially saving time and resources.

- **Cost Efficiency**:

  - **Reduced Initial Costs**: Filing a single international application under the PCT can be more cost-effective compared to filing separate applications in multiple countries. The PCT process also delays the need for translations and national filing fees until the national phase, which can help manage upfront costs.
  - **Harmonized Procedures**: The PCT standardizes the procedures for filing, searching, and examining patent applications, which reduces the administrative burden on applicants and can lead to cost savings in managing the patent process across different jurisdictions.

- **Enhanced Patent Quality**:

  - **Comprehensive Search and Examination**: The International Search Report (ISR) and the International Preliminary Report on Patentability (IPRP) provide applicants with detailed assessments of the patentability of their invention. These reports help applicants refine their applications and address potential issues before entering the national phase, leading to stronger patent applications.

- **Global Recognition**: The PCT system is recognized by patent offices worldwide, which can enhance the credibility and acceptance of the application in different jurisdictions. This global recognition can facilitate smoother processing and examination in national patent offices.

- **Challenges of PCT**:

  - **Complexity and Administrative Requirements**: While the PCT simplifies many aspects of the international patent process, it still involves complex procedures and strict deadlines. Applicants must carefully manage their applications to ensure compliance with PCT requirements and timelines.
  - **Initial Costs**: Although the PCT can reduce costs in the long term, the initial fees for filing an international application and conducting the international search and examination can still be substantial. Applicants need to be prepared for these upfront expenses.
  - **National Phase Costs**: Entering the national phase in multiple countries can be costly, as it involves paying national filing fees, translation costs, and legal fees for each jurisdiction. Applicants must budget for these expenses and plan their international patent strategy accordingly.
  - **Potential for Delays**: The centralized examination process under the PCT can introduce additional steps and timelines, which may delay the overall patenting process. Applicants seeking rapid protection in specific countries might need to consider alternative strategies alongside the PCT process.

- **Cost Considerations and Strategic Planning**:

  - **Budgeting for PCT and National Phases**: It is crucial for applicants to plan their budget carefully, taking into account both the initial PCT filing fees and the subsequent costs of entering the national phase in each desired country. Proper financial planning ensures that applicants can sustain the costs associated with the entire patenting process.

- **Strategic Country Selection**: Applicants should strategically choose the countries in which they seek patent protection based on market potential, manufacturing locations, and competitive landscape. Focusing on key markets can help optimize costs and ensure that resources are allocated efficiently.
- **Timing and Resource Allocation**: The extended decision period provided by the PCT allows applicants to align their patenting activities with their overall business strategy. By assessing the commercial success and strategic importance of their invention, applicants can make informed decisions about where and when to invest in national phase entries.
- **Utilizing Professional Expertise**: Engaging with patent attorneys and professionals who specialize in international patent law can help navigate the complexities of the PCT process. Expert guidance can optimize the patent application, ensure compliance with various national requirements, and maximize the chances of obtaining robust patent protection.

The PCT system offers significant advantages by simplifying the international patent process, reducing initial costs, and enhancing patent quality. However, it also presents challenges related to complexity, administrative requirements, and costs associated with the national phase. Strategic planning and cost considerations are essential for effectively navigating the PCT process and achieving successful international patent protection.

5.4 Patent Rights and Licensing

- **5.4.1 Scope and Limitations:**
  - **Rights Conferred by a Patent:**
    - **Exclusive Rights to the Invention**: A patent grants the holder the exclusive rights to make, use, sell, and distribute the patented invention for a limited period, typically 20 years from the filing date. These rights provide the patent holder with a legal monopoly over the invention, preventing others from exploiting it without permission.

- **Right to Exclude Others**: One of the primary benefits of holding a patent is the ability to exclude others from making, using, selling, or importing the patented invention without the patent holder's consent. This exclusionary right is a powerful tool for controlling the commercial exploitation of the invention and can be enforced through legal actions against infringers.
- **Licensing and Monetization**: Patent holders can monetize their patents through licensing agreements. By granting licenses to other parties, patent holders can generate revenue while allowing licensees to use the patented technology. Licensing can be exclusive, granting rights to a single licensee, or non-exclusive, allowing multiple parties to use the invention.
- **Transfer and Assignment**: Patents are considered intellectual property and can be transferred or assigned to other entities. The patent holder can sell or transfer the ownership rights of the patent to another individual or organization, allowing the new owner to exercise all the rights conferred by the patent.

- **Limitations of Patent Rights:**

- **Geographical Scope**: Patent rights are territorial, meaning they are only enforceable within the jurisdiction where the patent is granted. For international protection, inventors must seek patents in each country or region where they wish to enforce their rights. This can involve significant costs and administrative efforts.
- **Duration of Protection**: Patent protection is limited to a fixed period, typically 20 years from the filing date for utility patents. After this period, the patented invention enters the public domain, and anyone can use it without restriction. This time-limited nature of patents encourages innovation by eventually making new technologies available for public use.
- **Disclosure Requirements**: To obtain a patent, inventors must fully disclose the details of their invention in the patent application. This disclosure is intended to advance public knowledge and enable others to understand and build upon the invention. However, this requirement means that trade secrets cannot be protected through patents, and once the patent is granted, the disclosed information becomes publicly accessible.

- **Challenges and Invalidity**: Patents can be challenged and invalidated through legal proceedings. Competitors or other parties may seek to invalidate a patent by proving that it does not meet the criteria of novelty, non-obviousness, or utility. Additionally, procedural errors or misrepresentations in the patent application process can lead to the revocation of the patent.
- **Ethical and Regulatory Constraints**: Certain inventions may be subject to ethical considerations and regulatory constraints that limit the enforceability of patent rights. For example, patents related to pharmaceuticals, biotechnology, or environmental technologies may face regulatory scrutiny, and ethical concerns can influence public acceptance and use of the patented inventions.

The scope of patent rights provides inventors with significant control over the commercialization and use of their inventions, offering opportunities for revenue generation and competitive advantage. However, these rights come with limitations, including territorial restrictions, finite duration, mandatory disclosure, vulnerability to challenges, and ethical and regulatory constraints. Understanding the scope and limitations of patent rights is crucial for inventors and organizations to effectively leverage their patents and navigate the complex landscape of intellectual property.

5.4 Patent Rights and Licensing

- **5.4.1 Scope and Limitations:**
  - **Rights Conferred by a Patent:**
    - **Exclusive Rights to the Invention**: A patent grants the holder the exclusive rights to make, use, sell, and distribute the patented invention for a limited period, typically 20 years from the filing date. These rights provide the patent holder with a legal monopoly over the invention, preventing others from exploiting it without permission.
    - **Right to Exclude Others**: One of the primary benefits of holding a patent is the ability to exclude others from making, using, selling, or importing the patented invention without the patent holder's consent. This exclusionary right is a powerful tool for controlling

the commercial exploitation of the invention and can be enforced through legal actions against infringers.

- **Licensing and Monetization**: Patent holders can monetize their patents through licensing agreements. By granting licenses to other parties, patent holders can generate revenue while allowing licensees to use the patented technology. Licensing can be exclusive, granting rights to a single licensee, or non-exclusive, allowing multiple parties to use the invention.
- **Transfer and Assignment**: Patents are considered intellectual property and can be transferred or assigned to other entities. The patent holder can sell or transfer the ownership rights of the patent to another individual or organization, allowing the new owner to exercise all the rights conferred by the patent.

- **Limitations of Patent Rights:**

  - **Geographical Scope**: Patent rights are territorial, meaning they are only enforceable within the jurisdiction where the patent is granted. For international protection, inventors must seek patents in each country or region where they wish to enforce their rights. This can involve significant costs and administrative efforts.
  - **Duration of Protection**: Patent protection is limited to a fixed period, typically 20 years from the filing date for utility patents. After this period, the patented invention enters the public domain, and anyone can use it without restriction. This time-limited nature of patents encourages innovation by eventually making new technologies available for public use.
  - **Disclosure Requirements**: To obtain a patent, inventors must fully disclose the details of their invention in the patent application. This disclosure is intended to advance public knowledge and enable others to understand and build upon the invention. However, this requirement means that trade secrets cannot be protected through patents, and once the patent is granted, the disclosed information becomes publicly accessible.
  - **Challenges and Invalidity**: Patents can be challenged and invalidated through legal proceedings. Competitors or other parties may seek to invalidate a patent by proving that it does not meet the criteria of novelty, non-obviousness, or utility.

Additionally, procedural errors or misrepresentations in the patent application process can lead to the revocation of the patent.

- **Ethical and Regulatory Constraints**: Certain inventions may be subject to ethical considerations and regulatory constraints that limit the enforceability of patent rights. For example, patents related to pharmaceuticals, biotechnology, or environmental technologies may face regulatory scrutiny, and ethical concerns can influence public acceptance and use of the patented inventions.

- **Duration and Territorial Limitations**:

  - **Time-Bound Protection**: The protection provided by a patent is not indefinite. Utility patents, which cover new and useful inventions or discoveries, generally last for 20 years from the filing date. Design patents, which protect new, original, and ornamental designs for articles of manufacture, have a term of 15 years from the date of grant. Plant patents, which are granted for new and distinct varieties of plants, also last for 20 years from the filing date. Once the patent term expires, the patented invention enters the public domain, and anyone can use, produce, or sell the invention without needing to obtain permission from the original patent holder.
  - **Geographical Limitations**: Patent rights are territorial in nature, meaning that they are only valid within the jurisdiction in which they are granted. This means that a patent granted by the United States Patent and Trademark Office (USPTO) is only enforceable within the United States. To protect an invention in other countries, the inventor must apply for and obtain patents in each of those countries. This can be done through individual national patent offices or through international systems like the Patent Cooperation Treaty (PCT), which facilitates the process of seeking patent protection in multiple countries. However, even with the PCT, the inventor must eventually pursue national phase entries in each desired country, which involves additional costs and legal considerations.

Understanding the scope, limitations, duration, and territorial constraints of patent rights is essential for inventors and organizations. It enables them to strategically manage their intellectual property, maximize the value of their innovations, and navigate the complexities of patent law effectively.

5.4 Patent Rights and Licensing

5.4.1 Scope and Limitations

- **Rights Conferred by a Patent**

  - **Exclusive Rights to the Invention**: A patent grants the holder exclusive rights to make, use, sell, and distribute the patented invention for a limited period, typically 20 years from the filing date. These rights provide the patent holder with a legal monopoly over the invention, preventing others from exploiting it without permission.
  - **Right to Exclude Others**: One of the primary benefits of holding a patent is the ability to exclude others from making, using, selling, or importing the patented invention without the patent holder's consent. This exclusionary right is a powerful tool for controlling the commercial exploitation of the invention and can be enforced through legal actions against infringers.
  - **Licensing and Monetization**: Patent holders can monetize their patents through licensing agreements. By granting licenses to other parties, patent holders can generate revenue while allowing licensees to use the patented technology. Licensing can be exclusive, granting rights to a single licensee, or non-exclusive, allowing multiple parties to use the invention.
  - **Transfer and Assignment**: Patents are considered intellectual property and can be transferred or assigned to other entities. The patent holder can sell or transfer the ownership rights of the patent to another individual or organization, allowing the new owner to exercise all the rights conferred by the patent.

- **Limitations of Patent Rights**

  - **Geographical Scope**: Patent rights are territorial, meaning they are only enforceable within the jurisdiction where the patent is granted. For international protection, inventors must seek patents in each country or region where they wish to enforce their rights. This can involve significant costs and administrative efforts.

- **Duration of Protection**: Patent protection is limited to a fixed period, typically 20 years from the filing date for utility patents. After this period, the patented invention enters the public domain, and anyone can use it without restriction. This time-limited nature of patents encourages innovation by eventually making new technologies available for public use.
- **Disclosure Requirements**: To obtain a patent, inventors must fully disclose the details of their invention in the patent application. This disclosure is intended to advance public knowledge and enable others to understand and build upon the invention. However, this requirement means that trade secrets cannot be protected through patents, and once the patent is granted, the disclosed information becomes publicly accessible.
- **Challenges and Invalidity**: Patents can be challenged and invalidated through legal proceedings. Competitors or other parties may seek to invalidate a patent by proving that it does not meet the criteria of novelty, non-obviousness, or utility. Additionally, procedural errors or misrepresentations in the patent application process can lead to the revocation of the patent.
- **Ethical and Regulatory Constraints**: Certain inventions may be subject to ethical considerations and regulatory constraints that limit the enforceability of patent rights. For example, patents related to pharmaceuticals, biotechnology, or environmental technologies may face regulatory scrutiny, and ethical concerns can influence public acceptance and use of the patented inventions.

- **Duration and Territorial Limitations**

  - **Time-Bound Protection**: The protection provided by a patent is not indefinite. Utility patents, which cover new and useful inventions or discoveries, generally last for 20 years from the filing date. Design patents, which protect new, original, and ornamental designs for articles of manufacture, have a term of 15 years from the date of grant. Plant patents, which are granted for new and distinct varieties of plants, also last for 20 years from the filing date. Once the patent term expires, the patented invention enters the public domain, and anyone can use, produce, or sell the invention without needing to obtain permission from the original patent holder.

- **Geographical Limitations**: Patent rights are territorial in nature, meaning that they are only valid within the jurisdiction in which they are granted. This means that a patent granted by the United States Patent and Trademark Office (USPTO) is only enforceable within the United States. To protect an invention in other countries, the inventor must apply for and obtain patents in each of those countries. This can be done through individual national patent offices or through international systems like the Patent Cooperation Treaty (PCT), which facilitates the process of seeking patent protection in multiple countries. However, even with the PCT, the inventor must eventually pursue national phase entries in each desired country, which involves additional costs and legal considerations.

Understanding the scope, limitations, duration, and territorial constraints of patent rights is essential for inventors and organizations. It enables them to strategically manage their intellectual property, maximize the value of their innovations, and navigate the complexities of patent law effectively.

5.4.2 Infringement and Enforcement of Patent Rights

- **Infringement of Patent Rights**

  - **Types of Infringement**: Patent infringement occurs when an unauthorized party makes, uses, sells, or imports a patented invention without the patent holder's permission. There are several types of infringement, including direct infringement, which involves unauthorized use of the patented invention, and indirect infringement, which includes contributory infringement (supplying components of a patented invention) and induced infringement (encouraging others to infringe a patent).
  - **Identification of Infringement**: Patent holders must actively monitor the market and industry to identify potential infringement. This can involve regular surveillance of competitors' products, attending industry trade shows, and conducting patent searches to identify products that may infringe on their patents. Once potential infringement is identified, patent holders can conduct a detailed

analysis to determine whether the unauthorized product or process falls within the scope of the patent claims.

- **Enforcement of Patent Rights**

  - **Legal Remedies for Infringement**: Patent holders have several legal remedies available to enforce their rights against infringers. These remedies can be pursued through civil litigation in court. The primary legal remedies for patent infringement include:

    - **Injunctions**: Patent holders can seek injunctive relief, which is a court order preventing the infringer from continuing their unauthorized activities. Injunctions can be preliminary (issued before the final judgment) or permanent (issued after the final judgment).
    - **Damages**: Patent holders can seek monetary compensation for the infringement. Damages can include lost profits, reasonable royalties, and, in some cases, enhanced damages for willful infringement. The court may also award interest and attorney fees.
    - **Seizure and Destruction**: In some cases, the court may order the seizure and destruction of infringing products to prevent further infringement.

  - **Alternative Dispute Resolution (ADR)**: To avoid lengthy and costly litigation, patent holders and alleged infringers can opt for alternative dispute resolution methods, such as mediation or arbitration. These methods offer a more informal and flexible approach to resolving patent disputes and can lead to mutually agreeable settlements.
  - **International Enforcement**: Enforcing patent rights internationally can be challenging due to differences in patent laws and legal systems across countries. Patent holders seeking to enforce their rights in multiple jurisdictions must navigate the specific procedures and requirements of each country. International treaties and agreements, such as the Patent Cooperation Treaty (PCT) and the World Trade Organization's Agreement on Trade-Related Aspects of Intellectual Property Rights (TRIPS), provide frameworks for international cooperation and enforcement of patent rights.

- **Role of Customs Authorities**: Patent holders can also seek the assistance of customs authorities to prevent the importation of infringing products. Many countries have procedures in place for patent holders to register their patents with customs authorities, enabling the authorities to identify and seize infringing goods at the border.

Effectively enforcing patent rights requires a strategic approach that combines legal action, monitoring, and, when appropriate, alternative dispute resolution. By understanding the types of infringement and the available enforcement mechanisms, patent holders can protect their intellectual property and maintain their competitive advantage in the market.

5.4 Patent Rights and Licensing

5.4.2 Licensing and Transfer of Technology

- **Types of Licensing Agreements**:

  - **Exclusive Licensing**:

    - **Definition**: An exclusive license grants the licensee sole rights to use, make, sell, and distribute the patented invention. The patent holder agrees not to grant similar rights to any other party, including retaining those rights for themselves.
    - **Advantages**: This type of license can be highly attractive to the licensee as it provides a competitive advantage and the ability to fully exploit the market potential of the invention. It also typically results in higher royalty payments or upfront fees for the patent holder.
    - **Considerations**: Exclusive licenses often come with higher expectations and responsibilities for the licensee, including performance obligations and milestones. It also means the patent holder must carefully select the licensee, as they are entrusting their invention to a single entity.

  - **Non-Exclusive Licensing**:

  - **Definition**: A non-exclusive license allows multiple licensees to use, make, sell, and distribute the patented invention. The patent holder retains the right to use the invention and can grant licenses to other parties.
  - **Advantages**: This type of license enables the patent holder to maximize the commercial potential of their invention by granting rights to multiple entities. It also spreads the risk and can create multiple revenue streams from different licensees.
  - **Considerations**: The licensee does not receive the competitive advantage provided by an exclusive license, which might result in lower royalty rates. The patent holder must manage multiple licensees and ensure compliance with the terms of each licensing agreement.

- **Compulsory Licensing**:

  - **Definition**: Compulsory licenses are granted by a government authority, allowing a third party to use, make, sell, and distribute a patented invention without the consent of the patent holder. This usually occurs in situations where the patent holder is not making the invention available to the public or in cases of national emergency.
  - **Advantages**: Compulsory licensing can help address public health needs, ensure access to essential medicines, and prevent anti-competitive practices by patent holders. It can also promote technological advancement by allowing broader access to patented technologies.
  - **Considerations**: For the patent holder, compulsory licensing can mean a loss of control over their invention and potentially lower revenues. However, they are typically compensated with a reasonable royalty set by the government. Compulsory licenses are generally subject to specific legal criteria and processes, which vary by jurisdiction.

5.4.2 Licensing and Transfer of Technology

- **Structure and Terms of Licensing Agreements**:

- **Financial Terms**: This includes details about upfront fees, royalties, milestone payments, and any minimum payment obligations. The financial terms must balance the interests of both the patent holder and the licensee to ensure mutual benefit and incentivize performance.
- **Scope of Rights**: The agreement should clearly define the scope of the licensed rights, including the geographical territory, the duration of the license, and any field-of-use restrictions. These terms determine how and where the licensee can exploit the patented invention.
- **Performance Obligations**: The licensee may be required to meet certain performance obligations, such as achieving sales targets, investing in marketing, or further developing the technology. These obligations ensure that the licensee actively works to commercialize the invention.
- **Quality Control and Compliance**: To maintain the integrity and value of the patented invention, the license agreement should include provisions for quality control and compliance. This ensures that the licensee maintains certain standards in the use and manufacturing of the invention.
- **Confidentiality and IP Protection**: Licensing agreements often include confidentiality clauses to protect proprietary information and trade secrets. They also address how IP rights will be enforced, including procedures for handling infringement by third parties.
- **Termination and Dispute Resolution**: The agreement should outline the conditions under which the license can be terminated by either party and provide mechanisms for resolving disputes, such as arbitration or mediation.

- **Transfer of Technology**:

  - **Technology Transfer Agreements**: Beyond licensing, technology transfer agreements facilitate the movement of technological knowledge and innovations from one organization to another. These agreements are common in academia-industry collaborations, joint ventures, and international partnerships.
  - **Benefits**: Technology transfer can accelerate innovation, drive economic growth, and enhance competitiveness by allowing

organizations to leverage external technological advancements. It can also foster collaboration and knowledge sharing across different sectors and regions.

- **Challenges**: Effective technology transfer requires careful negotiation of terms to protect the interests of both parties. Issues such as IP ownership, confidentiality, and the scope of the transferred technology must be clearly defined. Cultural differences, regulatory environments, and differences in technological capabilities can also pose challenges in international technology transfer agreements.

Licensing and technology transfer are powerful tools for maximizing the value of patents and driving innovation. By carefully structuring licensing agreements and managing technology transfer processes, patent holders can create new opportunities for revenue generation and collaboration while advancing the development and dissemination of new technologies.

CHAPTER SIX

INTELLECTUAL PROPERTY DATABASES AND RESOURSES

6.1 Patent Information and Databases

6.1.1 Key Databases for Patent Information

6.1.1.1 USPTO (United States Patent and Trademark Office)

- Overview:
  - The United States Patent and Trademark Office (USPTO) is the federal agency responsible for granting U.S. patents and registering trademarks. The USPTO provides extensive resources and databases that are essential for patent search, filing, and management.
- USPTO Patent Database:
  - **Content and Coverage**: The USPTO patent database contains detailed information about patents granted and patent applications published in the United States. It includes bibliographic data, full-text documents, images of patent drawings, and legal status information. This database is a comprehensive resource for researching prior art, understanding patent landscapes, and tracking the status of patent applications.

- **Search Tools**: The USPTO offers various search tools to help users find relevant patent information:

    - **PatFT (Patent Full-Text and Image Database)**: This tool allows users to search full-text patents from 1976 to the present and full-page images from 1790 to the present. Users can search by keywords, patent numbers, classifications, and other criteria.
    - **AppFT (Patent Application Full-Text and Image Database)**: This tool provides access to published patent applications from March 2001 to the present. Similar to PatFT, it supports searches by various criteria, enabling users to track the progress of patent applications and understand emerging trends in technology.

- **Global Dossier**: This feature allows users to access dossier information for related applications filed in multiple jurisdictions. It provides a consolidated view of examination reports, office actions, and other key documents from participating patent offices, facilitating a global perspective on patent prosecution.
- **Public PAIR (Patent Application Information Retrieval)**: Public PAIR provides access to the status and history of patent applications. Users can view documents, track the examination process, and monitor the progress of their applications. It includes information on rejections, amendments, and correspondence with the USPTO.

- **Benefits of Using the USPTO Patent Database**:

    - **Comprehensive Coverage**: The USPTO database offers extensive coverage of U.S. patents and published applications, making it an essential resource for anyone conducting patent research or due diligence.
    - **Accessibility**: The database is freely accessible to the public, providing open access to a wealth of patent information. This democratizes access to patent data and supports innovation by making information readily available to inventors, researchers, and businesses.
    - **Search Flexibility**: The USPTO provides powerful search tools that allow users to tailor their searches to specific needs. Whether searching by keywords, patent numbers, classifications, or other

criteria, users can efficiently locate relevant patent documents.

- **Legal and Procedural Insights**: By accessing the legal status and history of patent applications through Public PAIR, users can gain insights into the procedural aspects of patent prosecution, including examiner decisions and applicant responses.

- **Challenges and Considerations**:

  - **Complexity**: Navigating the USPTO database and interpreting patent documents can be complex, particularly for users who are not familiar with patent terminology and procedures. Training or assistance from patent professionals may be necessary.
  - **Timeliness**: While the USPTO database is comprehensive, there can be delays in the publication of certain documents and updates. Users should be aware of these potential delays when conducting time-sensitive research.

The USPTO patent database is a critical resource for accessing comprehensive information on U.S. patents and published applications. Its powerful search tools, extensive coverage, and accessibility make it indispensable for inventors, researchers, and businesses engaged in patent-related activities.

6.1.1.2 EPO (European Patent Office)

- **Overview**:

  - The European Patent Office (EPO) is a key institution in the field of intellectual property, responsible for examining and granting European patents. The EPO offers robust databases and search tools that provide access to a vast repository of patent information across Europe and beyond.

- **EPO Patent Database**:

  - **Content and Coverage**: The EPO patent database contains information on European patents and patent applications, as well as patents from other jurisdictions. It includes bibliographic data, full-text documents, images of patent drawings, and legal status information. The EPO database is essential for researching European patent landscapes, prior art, and monitoring patent activity.

- **Search Tools**:

    - **Espacenet**: Espacenet is the EPO's free online patent search tool, offering access to over 120 million patent documents from around the world. It allows users to search for patents using keywords, patent numbers, classifications, and other criteria. Espacenet supports both simple and advanced search options, making it suitable for users with varying levels of expertise.
    - **Global Dossier**: Similar to the USPTO's Global Dossier, this tool provides integrated access to dossier information from multiple patent offices. It offers a comprehensive view of the examination process, including office actions and correspondence for related patent applications filed in different jurisdictions.
    - **European Patent Register**: This register provides detailed information on the legal status of European patent applications and granted patents. Users can track the progress of applications, view procedural documents, and monitor oppositions and appeals. It includes information on fees, legal events, and changes in ownership.
    - **Patent Translate**: This tool offers automatic translation of patent documents into 32 languages, facilitating access to non-English patent literature and enabling users to understand patents from different countries.

- **Benefits of Using the EPO Patent Database**:

    - **Extensive Coverage**: The EPO database covers a wide range of patents from European and other international patent offices, making it a comprehensive resource for patent research and analysis.
    - **Advanced Search Capabilities**: Espacenet and other EPO tools provide powerful search functionalities, allowing users to conduct precise and targeted searches. The ability to search by various criteria and access full-text documents enhances the depth and accuracy of research.
    - **Global Perspective**: With integrated tools like Global Dossier and Patent Translate, the EPO database offers a global perspective on

patent prosecution and multilingual access to patent documents. This is particularly valuable for international patent strategy and competitive analysis.

- **Legal and Procedural Insights**: The European Patent Register provides detailed legal status information, enabling users to track the lifecycle of European patents, understand procedural nuances, and stay informed about legal events and oppositions.

- **Challenges and Considerations:**

  - **Complexity of Use**: The EPO's databases and tools can be complex to navigate, especially for users unfamiliar with patent documentation and search techniques. Training or guidance from patent professionals may be necessary to maximize the utility of these resources.
  - **Language Barriers**: Although Patent Translate helps mitigate language barriers, automatic translations may not always capture the full technical nuances of patent documents. Users should exercise caution and, if necessary, seek professional translations for critical documents.

The EPO patent database is a vital resource for accessing extensive patent information across Europe and internationally. Its advanced search tools, comprehensive coverage, and global perspective make it indispensable for inventors, researchers, and businesses involved in patent-related activities. By leveraging the EPO's resources, users can enhance their understanding of the patent landscape, identify opportunities for innovation, and make informed decisions about their intellectual property strategies.

6.1.1.3 WIPO (World Intellectual Property Organization)

- Overview:

  - The World Intellectual Property Organization (WIPO) is a specialized agency of the United Nations dedicated to promoting and protecting intellectual property (IP) rights globally. WIPO administers international treaties and provides a wide range of services, including comprehensive databases for patent information.

- **WIPO Patent Database:**

  - **Content and Coverage:** WIPO's databases encompass international patent applications filed under the Patent Cooperation Treaty (PCT) as well as national patent data from various countries. These databases include bibliographic data, full-text documents, patent families, legal status information, and international preliminary reports on patentability.
  - **Search Tools:**

    - **PATENTSCOPE:** PATENTSCOPE is WIPO's global patent search system, providing access to over 90 million patent documents, including PCT applications and national patent data from multiple jurisdictions. It offers powerful search capabilities, including keyword searches, Boolean operators, and advanced search options.
    - **Global Dossier:** This tool provides integrated access to dossier information from multiple patent offices, enabling users to view examination reports, office actions, and other key documents for related patent applications filed in different countries.
    - **CLIR (Cross-Lingual Information Retrieval):** This feature allows users to search for patent information across different languages, leveraging machine translation to bridge language barriers. It enhances the ability to conduct comprehensive prior art searches and access patent documents from non-English-speaking regions.

- **Benefits of Using the WIPO Patent Database:**

  - **Comprehensive Global Coverage:** WIPO's PATENTSCOPE database offers extensive coverage of international patent applications and national patents from various countries. It is a valuable resource for conducting global patent searches and understanding international patent landscapes.
  - **Advanced Search Functionalities:** PATENTSCOPE provides robust search capabilities, allowing users to perform detailed and targeted searches using keywords, classifications, patent numbers, and more. The advanced search options enable precise retrieval of relevant patent documents.

  - **Multilingual Access**: With tools like CLIR and machine translation, WIPO's databases facilitate access to patent information in multiple languages, making it easier to understand and analyze patents from different regions. This is particularly beneficial for international IP strategy and research.
  - **Legal and Procedural Insights**: WIPO's Global Dossier and other tools offer insights into the legal status and examination history of patent applications across different jurisdictions. This information helps users track the progress of applications, understand examiner decisions, and monitor legal events.

- **Challenges and Considerations**:

  - **Complexity and Learning Curve**: Navigating WIPO's databases and utilizing advanced search functionalities can be complex, especially for users who are not familiar with patent terminology and search techniques. Training or assistance from patent professionals may be required to effectively use these resources.
  - **Timeliness and Completeness**: While WIPO's databases are comprehensive, there may be delays in the inclusion of certain national patent data. Users should be aware of potential gaps and verify information with national patent offices when necessary.

WIPO's patent databases, particularly PATENTSCOPE, are invaluable resources for accessing global patent information and conducting international patent research. The advanced search tools, extensive coverage, and multilingual capabilities provided by WIPO support inventors, researchers, and businesses in navigating the complex landscape of international intellectual property. By leveraging WIPO's resources, users can enhance their understanding of global patent trends, identify opportunities for innovation, and develop effective IP strategies.

6.1.1.4 Other National Patent Offices and Databases

- **Japan Patent Office (JPO)**:

  - **Overview**: The Japan Patent Office (JPO) is responsible for the examination and granting of patents in Japan. It provides access to comprehensive patent information through its databases and online tools.

- **J-PlatPat**: J-PlatPat is the JPO's free online patent search tool. It allows users to search for Japanese patents, utility models, designs, and trademarks. The database includes bibliographic data, full-text documents, and patent family information.
- **Benefits**:
    - **Extensive Coverage**: J-PlatPat provides detailed information on Japanese patents, making it a valuable resource for understanding the patent landscape in Japan.
    - **Multilingual Support**: J-PlatPat offers machine translation services, enabling users to access patent documents in English and other languages.
- **Challenges**:
    - **Complex Navigation**: Users unfamiliar with Japanese patent documentation may find it challenging to navigate the database and interpret the search results.

- **Indian Patent Office (IPO)**:
    - **Overview**: The Indian Patent Office (IPO) is responsible for granting patents in India. It provides access to patent information through its online databases and search tools.
    - **Indian Patent Search System (IPSS)**: IPSS is the IPO's online search tool that allows users to search for Indian patents and published applications. The database includes bibliographic data, full-text documents, and legal status information.
    - **Benefits**:
        - **Comprehensive Data**: IPSS provides detailed information on patents filed and granted in India, offering insights into the Indian patent landscape.
        - **User-Friendly Interface**: The search tool is designed to be user-friendly, making it accessible to a wide range of users.
    - **Challenges**:

- **Limited Language Support**: The primary language of the database is English, which may pose challenges for users who prefer other languages.

- **Other Notable National Patent Databases**:

  - **European Patent Office (EPO)**: As previously mentioned, the EPO provides access to a wide range of patent information through Espacenet and other tools. It covers patents from European countries and other international jurisdictions.
  - **Korean Intellectual Property Office (KIPO)**:

    - **Overview**: KIPO is responsible for the administration of patents in South Korea. It offers a comprehensive patent search tool known as KIPRIS (Korea Intellectual Property Rights Information Service).
    - **KIPRIS**: KIPRIS provides access to Korean patent information, including bibliographic data, full-text documents, and legal status information. The tool supports multilingual searches and offers detailed patent family information.
    - **Benefits**:

      - **Extensive Coverage**: KIPRIS covers a wide range of Korean patents and provides detailed information on the legal status of applications.
      - **Multilingual Support**: KIPRIS offers machine translation services, enabling users to access patent documents in multiple languages.

    - **Challenges**:

      - **Complex Navigation**: Users may find it challenging to navigate the database and interpret the search results due to differences in patent documentation formats and terminology.

- **China National Intellectual Property Administration (CNIPA)**:

- **Overview**: CNIPA is responsible for granting patents in China. It provides access to patent information through its online databases and search tools.
- **China Patent Search and Service System (CPSS)**: CPSS is CNIPA's online search tool that allows users to search for Chinese patents and published applications. The database includes bibliographic data, full-text documents, and legal status information.
- **Benefits**:

  - **Comprehensive Data**: CPSS provides detailed information on patents filed and granted in China, offering insights into the Chinese patent landscape.
  - **Multilingual Support**: CPSS offers machine translation services, enabling users to access patent documents in multiple languages.

- **Challenges**:

  - **Complex Navigation**: Users may find it challenging to navigate the database and interpret the search results due to differences in patent documentation formats and terminology.

Each of these national patent offices and their databases provide valuable resources for accessing patent information specific to their respective jurisdictions. By leveraging these tools, inventors, researchers, and businesses can gain insights into patent landscapes, identify potential areas for innovation, and develop effective IP strategies tailored to different regions.

6.1.2 How to Search and Use These Resources

6.1.2.1 Basic Search Techniques

- **Keyword Searches**:

  - **Purpose**: Keyword searches are fundamental to finding relevant patent documents based on specific terms related to the invention. This method involves using one or more words that describe the key features or functions of the invention.

- **Technique**:
    - **Identify Keywords**: Start by identifying a list of keywords and phrases that describe the core aspects of your invention. Consider synonyms and variations of these terms.
    - **Boolean Operators**: Use Boolean operators (AND, OR, NOT) to refine your search. For example, using "AND" between keywords ensures that all terms must appear in the results, while "OR" includes results with any of the keywords.
    - **Quotation Marks**: Use quotation marks to search for exact phrases. For instance, searching for "solar panel" will return documents containing that specific phrase.

- **Classification Searches**:
    - **Purpose**: Patent classification systems, such as the International Patent Classification (IPC) or the Cooperative Patent Classification (CPC), categorize patents based on technical features. Searching by classification can yield more precise results, especially for highly technical inventions.
    - **Technique**:
        - **Identify Relevant Classes**: Determine the relevant classification codes that correspond to your invention. You can find these codes by searching classification directories or reviewing the classifications of similar patents.
        - **Search by Classification**: Enter the classification codes into the search field of the patent database to retrieve documents categorized under those codes. This method helps in finding patents that might not be easily located through keyword searches alone.

- **Patent Number Searches**:
    - **Purpose**: If you already know the patent number of a specific document, you can perform a direct search to retrieve that particular patent.
    - **Technique**:

- **Enter Patent Number**: Simply enter the patent number into the search field. Ensure you include any necessary prefixes or country codes (e.g., US for United States patents, EP for European patents).
- **Verify Details**: After retrieving the document, verify its details to ensure it matches the patent you are looking for.

- **Assignee or Inventor Searches**:

  - **Purpose**: Searching by assignee (the entity that owns the patent) or inventor can help you find all patents filed by a particular company or individual.
  - **Technique**:

    - **Enter Name**: Input the name of the assignee or inventor in the search field. Be mindful of variations in spelling or format (e.g., "IBM" vs. "International Business Machines").
    - **Refine Results**: Use additional filters or search criteria to narrow down the results, especially if the assignee or inventor has a common name.

- **Citation Searches**:

  - **Purpose**: Citation searches involve looking for patents that cite or are cited by a particular patent. This method helps in identifying related technologies and tracking the evolution of an invention.
  - **Technique**:

    - **Identify Cited Patents**: Review the "References Cited" section of a patent to find other patents cited by it.
    - **Search Citing Patents**: Use the citation search function in the database to find patents that cite the patent you are investigating. This can reveal newer developments and related technologies.

- **Advanced Search Techniques**:

  - **Purpose**: Advanced search techniques allow for more complex queries, combining multiple search criteria to refine results further.

- **Technique**:
  - **Combine Criteria**: Use a combination of keywords, classifications, assignees, inventors, and date ranges to narrow down search results. Advanced search forms typically provide fields for each of these criteria.
  - **Use Filters**: Apply filters for publication dates, jurisdictions, legal status, and other relevant parameters to target your search more precisely.

By mastering these basic search techniques, users can effectively navigate patent databases and retrieve relevant documents. This proficiency is crucial for conducting thorough prior art searches, assessing the patentability of inventions, monitoring competitor activities, and making informed decisions about intellectual property strategies.

6.1.2.1 Basic Search Techniques

Boolean Operators

Boolean operators are essential tools in database searches, including those for patents, academic research, and even general web queries. They refine the search process by connecting keywords in ways that allow for more precise retrieval of information. Here's how each of the primary Boolean operators works:

- **AND**:
  - **Purpose**: The AND operator is used to ensure that all the search terms connected by it appear in the results. It narrows the search by combining terms, thus limiting the number of results to those that include all specified words.
  - **Example**: Searching for "solar AND panel" will return documents that contain both "solar" and "panel". This is useful when you want to find documents that specifically address solar panels, rather than documents that mention solar or panels separately.
- **OR**:

- **Purpose**: The OR operator is used to expand the search to include documents that contain any of the specified terms. It is helpful when looking for information that could be under various synonymous terms or related concepts.
- **Example**: Searching for "solar OR photovoltaic" will return documents that mention either "solar" or "photovoltaic". This approach is beneficial when you are not sure of the specific terminology used in the documents or when multiple terms are common in the field.

- NOT:

  - **Purpose**: The NOT operator excludes documents that contain the term that follows it. This is useful for filtering out unwanted information that contains a specific word or phrase.
  - **Example**: Searching for "solar NOT thermal" will return documents that mention solar but will exclude any documents that also include the word "thermal". This can be useful when you are interested in solar energy but not in the context of thermal energy systems.

- **NEAR** (sometimes represented as N):

  - **Purpose**: The NEAR operator is used to find documents where two or more terms appear close to each other within a certain number of words. It is useful for locating concepts that are likely to be discussed in relation to each other.
  - **Example**: Searching for "solar NEAR panel" might be set to return documents where "solar" and "panel" appear within 10 words of each other. This helps to find documents discussing the specific concept of solar panels rather than solar energy or panels in separate contexts.

- **Parentheses**:

  - **Purpose**: Parentheses are used to group terms and operators together. This allows the user to control the order of operations in the search, similar to their use in mathematics.
  - **Example**: Searching for "(solar OR photovoltaic) AND panel" will first combine the results for solar or photovoltaic and then narrow

those results to include only documents that also contain the word "panel".

Utilizing these Boolean operators effectively can greatly enhance the precision of search queries, leading to more relevant results. This is particularly important in fields like patent research, where the ability to pinpoint exact technologies or innovations can save substantial time and effort.

6.1.2.2 Advanced Search Techniques

Advanced search techniques build on basic search skills to provide more refined and specific results. These methods are especially useful in complex databases like those for patents, where precise querying can drastically improve the efficiency and relevance of your search results. Here's a breakdown of some effective advanced search techniques:

- **Field-Specific Searches**:
  - **Purpose**: Allows users to target specific fields within a database, such as the inventor's name, the patent title, the abstract, or the claims section.
  - **Technique**: Most patent databases provide field tags or dropdown menus that let you specify where to look for your keywords. For example, you might search for [inventor: "Jane Doe"] to find patents filed by a specific inventor or [title: solar] to find patents with the word "solar" in their titles.
  - **Benefit**: Enhances precision by focusing the search on areas of the document most likely to contain relevant information, reducing noise from irrelevant results.
- **Proximity Searches**:
  - **Purpose**: Finds documents where two or more keywords appear within a certain distance from each other, which can be crucial for finding patents where specific concepts are discussed in close correlation.

- **Technique**: Different databases may use different syntax for proximity searches. Common expressions include **NEAR**, **WITHIN X WORDS**, or using **N** (e.g., solar N5 panel, which finds documents where "solar" and "panel" are within five words of each other).
- **Benefit**: Allows for the discovery of more contextually relevant patents, where the proximity of terms can indicate a stronger relation between the concepts.

- **Combination Searches**:

  - **Purpose**: Combines multiple search criteria using Boolean operators to create complex queries that can filter results more effectively.
  - **Technique**: You can combine field-specific searches, keyword searches, and classification searches to create highly specific queries. For example, **[title: solar] AND [abstract: (efficiency OR performance)] AND [CPC: H02S]** would find solar-related patents in the title, mentioning efficiency or performance in the abstract, classified under the CPC code for solar energy generation.
  - **Benefit**: Yields highly targeted results, making it easier to sift through large volumes of data.

- **Date and Classification Filters**:

  - **Purpose**: Helps to narrow down search results by the date of publication or specific patent classification codes.
  - **Technique**: Most patent databases allow users to specify date ranges for their searches or to filter results by date after performing a search. Similarly, classification codes like the International Patent Classification (IPC) or Cooperative Patent Classification (CPC) can be specified to find patents within specific technological areas.
  - **Benefit**: Date filtering is particularly useful for tracking technological trends over time or ensuring that the search is restricted to the most recent developments. Classification searches are essential for identifying technologies within specific sectors.

- **Wildcards and Truncation**:

- **Purpose**: Allows for the search of variations of a root word to capture more comprehensive results.
- **Technique**: Wildcards are special characters that substitute for one or more characters in a search term. For example, using **solar*** might retrieve solar, solars, solarization, etc. Common wildcards include the asterisk (*) for multiple characters and the question mark (?) for a single character.
- **Benefit**: Wildcards expand the search to include various morphological variants of a word, increasing the thoroughness of the search results.

- **Saved Searches and Alerts**:

  - **Purpose**: Enables users to save their search queries and set up alerts for when new patents that match their criteria are added to the database.
  - **Technique**: Most modern patent databases allow users to create accounts where they can save their searches. Additionally, they can opt-in for email alerts or notifications.
  - **Benefit**: Saves time and ensures that researchers stay updated on the latest patents in their field of interest without having to perform repetitive searches.

These advanced search techniques are powerful tools for navigating patent databases efficiently. They help users to precisely define their search parameters, reduce the volume of irrelevant results, and track developments in specific technological fields effectively.

6.1.2.2 Advanced Search Techniques

Patent Classification Codes

Patent classification codes are a critical tool for organizing and accessing patent information. These codes help to categorize patents based on their technical content or specific characteristics, making it easier to conduct thorough searches and analyze trends within particular fields of technology. Here's an overview of the major classification systems used worldwide:

- **International Patent Classification (IPC)**:

- **Overview**: The IPC is managed by the World Intellectual Property Organization (WIPO) and is used internationally to classify patents. This hierarchical system divides technology into eight sections with approximately 70,000 subdivisions, ranging from general technology areas to very specific processes and products.
- **Usage**: Each patent document is assigned one or more classification codes based on its content. The codes consist of letters and numbers that correspond to various technical fields. For example, the code "H01L" refers to "Semiconductor devices; Electric solid state devices not otherwise provided for."
- **Benefit**: The IPC provides a universally recognized language for describing the nature of technology in patent documents, which facilitates the sharing and comparison of patent information across international borders.

- **Cooperative Patent Classification (CPC)**:

  - **Overview**: The CPC is a joint effort between the European Patent Office (EPO) and the United States Patent and Trademark Office (USPTO). It is a highly detailed and continuously updated patent classification system.
  - **Usage**: Similar to the IPC, the CPC uses a combination of letters and numbers to classify patents. It offers more granular classifications than the IPC, providing over 250,000 distinct symbols for categorizing innovations. For instance, "H01L 31/18" could specify a particular type of photovoltaic cell.
  - **Benefit**: The CPC provides a more detailed classification system, which can improve the precision of patent searches and the analysis of technological areas. It is particularly useful for identifying emerging technologies and trends in highly specialized fields.

- **United States Patent Classification (USPC)**:

  - **Overview**: Although largely phased out in favor of the CPC for new patents, the USPC system is still used for some administrative and search purposes within the USPTO.
  - **Usage**: The USPC system classifies patents based on their technological attributes using a series of numbers and sometimes

letters. It provides broad coverage of technology areas, similar to the IPC.

- **Benefit**: While it is being replaced by the CPC, the historical data contained in the USPC remains valuable for research and trend analysis in older patents.

- **Japanese Patent Classification (F-term)**:
  - **Overview**: The F-term system is used by the Japan Patent Office (JPO). It is designed to complement the IPC and offers detailed classifications based on themes that are specific to Japan's technology and industry sectors.
  - **Usage**: F-terms are a collection of terms selected from the viewpoints of "what to do" and "what to use" for the purpose of a specific invention, providing multiple perspectives on a single piece of technology.
  - **Benefit**: The F-term classification provides a unique insight into the functional aspects of Japanese inventions, making it a useful tool for searching and analyzing patents in Japan.

Using Patent Classification Codes in Searches

- **Enhanced Precision**: By using classification codes, researchers can quickly access a body of patents in a specific area of technology, bypassing the limitations of keyword searches that may miss relevant documents due to language or terminology differences.
- **Trend Analysis**: Classification codes make it easier to track technological trends and developments over time, especially when looking at large volumes of data.
- **Comparative Studies**: Researchers can compare innovations across different jurisdictions or time periods by examining the classifications assigned to similar technologies.

Understanding and effectively utilizing patent classification codes can significantly enhance the efficiency and effectiveness of patent searches and analysis. This knowledge is invaluable for inventors, businesses, and researchers looking to stay informed about advancements in specific technological areas.

6.1.2.2 Advanced Search Techniques

Citation Searching

Citation searching is a powerful method for exploring the intellectual relationships between patents and identifying the influence of specific patents on subsequent innovations. This technique involves tracking the citations to and from a patent document to uncover related research, trends, and the evolution of technology. Here's how citation searching can be effectively used in patent research:

- **Forward Citation Analysis**:
    - **Purpose**: Forward citation analysis looks at how many times a given patent has been cited by later patents. This can indicate the patent's influence or value within a specific field.
    - **Technique**: You can perform a forward citation search using most patent databases by accessing a patent document and reviewing its citations section to see subsequent patents that have referenced it.
    - **Benefit**: Forward citations help to identify how a particular innovation has shaped or contributed to later developments. Patents with a high number of forward citations are often considered to be highly influential and can be critical in assessing the impact of a technology.
- **Backward Citation Analysis**:
    - **Purpose**: This involves examining the citations within a patent document to see which earlier patents or publications it references. Backward citations provide insight into the foundational work upon which the patent is built.
    - **Technique**: In the citations section of a patent document, you can review all the referenced prior arts that the inventor used to build upon or differentiate their invention.
    - **Benefit**: By analyzing backward citations, researchers can trace the lineage of technological advancements and understand the base of

existing innovations. This can be particularly useful for new researchers entering a field, providing a historical context.

- **Co-citation Analysis:**
  - **Purpose:** Co-citation occurs when two patents are cited together by subsequent patents. This often indicates that the patents are related in terms of technology or application.
  - **Technique:** Identify patents that frequently appear together in the citations lists of later patents. This can often be done through specialized software or database features that allow for complex citation analysis.
  - **Benefit:** Co-citation analysis helps to identify clusters of patents that are technologically similar or complementary, which can be useful for identifying competitors or potential collaborators.

Using Citation Searching in Patent Research

- **Identifying Key Patents:** Citation analysis can help pinpoint key patents in a field that are considered foundational or particularly innovative, as evidenced by high citation counts.
- **Assessing Patent Strength:** A patent with a high number of forward citations may be seen as having greater technological impact and market value, which can be crucial information for businesses and inventors.
- **Exploring Patent Families:** By following the trail of citations, one can uncover related patents forming a "family," which can provide comprehensive insights into the development of a technology or product line.
- **Mapping Technology Evolution:** Citation patterns can reveal how technology has evolved over time and how different innovations are interconnected.

Citation searching adds a dynamic layer to patent analysis, offering a deeper understanding of the relationships and influences in the world of intellectual property. This technique not only aids in identifying the most impactful patents but also helps in understanding the broader context of technological advancements.

6.1.2.3 Analyzing Search Results

Analyzing search results effectively is crucial for extracting valuable insights from patent searches. This process involves sorting, evaluating, and interpreting the data obtained from your search to make informed decisions about your innovation, research, or competitive positioning. Here's how to effectively analyze patent search results:

- **Sorting and Filtering**:
    - **Purpose**: To manage large volumes of search results and focus on the most relevant patents.
    - **Technique**:
        - **Sort by Relevance or Date**: Most patent databases allow you to sort results by relevance to your search terms or by date of publication or application. Sorting by date is useful for understanding the most recent developments in a field.
        - **Filter by Criteria**: Use filters such as patent status (granted, application), jurisdiction (country or region), and patent classification codes to narrow down results to those most applicable to your needs.
    - **Benefit**: Sorting and filtering help reduce the volume of data to a manageable size and increase the relevance of the patents you review, saving time and increasing efficiency.
- **Reviewing Abstracts and Claims**:
    - **Purpose**: To quickly determine the relevance of each patent in the search results without delving into full documents.
    - **Technique**:
        - **Read Abstracts**: The abstract provides a summary of the patent and is a quick way to assess whether the patent is relevant to your search.

    - **Examine Claims**: The claims section defines the scope of the patent's protection and is crucial for understanding what exactly is patented.

  - **Benefit**: This step helps in short-listing patents that require a detailed review and eliminates those that do not meet your criteria.

- **Deep Dive into Selected Patents:**

  - **Purpose**: To gain a thorough understanding of patents that appear highly relevant based on your initial review.
  - **Technique:**

    - **Full Text Reading**: For selected patents, read the full text to understand the details of the invention, the background, and the specific claims made.
    - **Analyze Figures and Examples**: Review any diagrams, figures, or examples provided in the patent to better understand the technical aspects of the invention.

  - **Benefit**: Provides a deep understanding of the technological details and the potential impact or value of the patents.

- **Comparative Analysis:**

  - **Purpose**: To compare similar patents to identify differences, potential infringements, or gaps in the technology.
  - **Technique:**

    - **Side-by-Side Comparison**: Compare the claims and descriptions of similar patents to identify unique features or potential overlaps.
    - **Use of Analytical Tools**: Some databases offer tools that can visually compare aspects of different patents, such as citation analysis, legal status, or technological similarities.

  - **Benefit**: Helps in identifying competitive edges, potential partners, or risks related to patent infringement.

- **Utilizing Visualization Tools**:
  - **Purpose**: To visually analyze trends and patterns from the patent search results.
  - **Technique**:
    - **Trend Analysis**: Use tools that plot trends based on filing dates, patent classes, or jurisdictions to see how technology is evolving.
    - **Network Analysis**: Visualize connections between patents, such as citation networks or co-inventor networks, to understand relationships and clusters within the field.
  - **Benefit**: Visualization tools can reveal broader trends and patterns that might not be apparent from a simple review of individual documents.
- **Documenting Findings**:
  - **Purpose**: To keep a record of your search and analysis process, which is essential for further research, development, or legal purposes.
  - **Technique**:
    - **Create Summary Reports**: Document the key findings, including relevant patents, important technological trends, and potential areas of concern or opportunity.
    - **Maintain Search Logs**: Keep records of search queries, databases used, and the rationale behind selecting certain patents for a detailed review.
  - **Benefit**: Ensures that the search process is reproducible and that key information is accessible for future reference or for sharing with stakeholders.

Effective analysis of search results is fundamental in maximizing the utility of patent searches, whether for protecting intellectual property, enhancing research and development, or guiding business strategy.

6.1.2.3 Analyzing Search Results

Evaluating Relevance and Validity

Once you have a set of patent search results, it's critical to evaluate their relevance and validity to ensure that the information you are considering is applicable to your needs and legally accurate. Here's a structured approach to doing this effectively:

- **Relevance Assessment:**

    - **Purpose:** To determine how closely the patents match your research objectives or innovation needs.
    - **Technique:**

        - **Keyword Matching:** Check if the key terms used in your search appear in critical sections of the patent like the abstract, claims, and description.
        - **Scope of Invention:** Analyze the breadth and depth of the patent claims to assess if they cover the specific aspects of technology you are interested in.
        - **Technological Field:** Ensure the patent pertains to the same or a related field of technology as your area of interest.

    - **Benefit:** This helps in focusing on patents that are directly applicable to your project, thereby saving time and resources in reviewing irrelevant documents.

- **Validity Analysis:**

    - **Purpose:** To confirm that the patents are legally enforceable and have not been invalidated or superseded by later work.
    - **Technique:**

        - **Legal Status Check:** Use patent databases to check the current legal status of a patent, such as whether it is still in force, lapsed, or has been revoked.
        - **Expiry Date Verification:** Patents typically last for 20 years from the filing date; verifying this helps understand how long the patent

will continue to provide legal protection.
- **Citation Analysis**: Review citations both to and from the patent to assess its legal robustness and the extent to which it has been challenged or built upon.

- **Benefit**: Ensures that the patents you consider are not only relevant but also provide a reliable basis for further development or business planning without infringing on expired or invalid patents.

- **Cross-Referencing with Other Data**:

  - **Purpose**: To verify the information in the patent and gather more insights from different sources.
  - **Technique**:

    - **Scientific Literature and Market Reports**: Cross-reference information from patents with non-patent literature and market analysis reports to validate the significance and application of the patented technology in the real world.
    - **Database Cross-Checks**: Use multiple patent databases for cross-checking to ensure that no relevant patents have been missed and to confirm the accuracy of the data retrieved.

  - **Benefit**: Provides a holistic view of the technology landscape and helps validate the assumptions or claims made in patents.

- **Practical Application Considerations**:

  - **Purpose**: To evaluate how the technology covered by the patent can be practically implemented or commercialized.
  - **Technique**:

    - **Prototype and Testing Results**: Look for any information on prototyping, testing, or real-world applications of the patent to assess its practical utility.
    - **Commercialization Potential**: Evaluate whether there is market data or analysis available on the commercial success or potential of the patented technology.

- **Benefit:** Ensures that the patents you focus on have not only theoretical relevance and validity but also practical applicability and commercial viability.

Documenting Evaluations:

- **Purpose:** Keeping a detailed record of how each patent was evaluated for relevance and validity.
- **Technique:**
    - **Evaluation Sheets:** Create structured sheets or forms to record the results of relevance and validity checks for each reviewed patent.
    - **Notes on Decision-Making:** Document why certain patents were deemed relevant or valid and others were not, to provide context for future reference or decision-making.
- **Benefit:** Maintains transparency in the evaluation process and provides an audit trail that can be useful for future research or legal scrutiny.

By thoroughly assessing the relevance and validity of each patent, you can ensure that your focus remains on legally robust and directly applicable patents that contribute effectively to your research or commercial objectives.

6.1.2.3 Analyzing Search Results

Understanding Patent Documents (Claims, Descriptions, Drawings)

Navigating through patent documents effectively requires a comprehensive understanding of their key components—claims, descriptions, and drawings. Each of these elements plays a vital role in communicating the details of an invention and its legal protection scope. Here's how to understand and interpret these components:

- **Claims:**
    - **Purpose:** The claims of a patent define the legal boundaries of patent protection. They specify what the inventor claims as their exclusive right.

- **Technique**:

  - **Independent and Dependent Claims**: Start by reading the independent claims which stand alone in terms of the protection they seek. Dependent claims, which reference the independent claims, specify additional limitations or enhancements.
  - **Claim Structure and Terminology**: Pay attention to the structure and specific terms used in the claims. Terms like "comprising," "wherein," and "consisting of" have specific legal meanings that can affect the scope of the claim.

- **Benefit**: Understanding the claims helps in identifying the exact scope of what is protected by the patent and is crucial for avoiding infringement and assessing the potential for challenging existing patents.

- **Descriptions**:

  - **Purpose**: The description, also known as the specification, provides a detailed account of the invention and how to use or make it. It must be detailed enough for a person skilled in the art to replicate the invention.
  - **Technique**:

    - **Read Thoroughly**: Review the detailed description to understand the technical aspects and the functionality of the invention.
    - **Contextual Information**: Look for information on prior art and how the invention improves or differs from what's known, as this can provide insights into the novelty and utility of the patent.

  - **Benefit**: A thorough understanding of the description aids in comprehending the practical applications and technological advancements embodied in the patent.

- **Drawings**:

  - **Purpose**: Drawings are included in most patents to provide a visual representation of the invention. They are particularly important in understanding complex mechanical or structural aspects of a patent.

- **Technique**:

  - **Review All Figures**: Examine all drawings carefully as they often illustrate different embodiments or aspects of the invention.
  - **Refer to Description**: Cross-reference figures with the description to ensure a complete understanding of what is depicted and its relevance to the claims.

- **Benefit**: Drawings can often clarify elements of the invention that are not immediately apparent from the textual description alone and are invaluable for fully grasping the patented technology.

- **Practical Exercises**:

  - **Purpose**: To enhance your skill in interpreting patent documents.
  - **Technique**:

    - **Mock Analyses**: Conduct mock analyses where you dissect the claims, read through the descriptions, and interpret the drawings of a selected patent.
    - **Comparative Reviews**: Compare similar patents to see different approaches to describing and claiming similar technologies.

  - **Benefit**: Regular practice can significantly improve your ability to navigate patent documents quickly and efficiently.

Documenting Insights:

- **Purpose**: To keep a record of your analyses which can be referred to later or used in collaborative settings.
- **Technique**:

  - **Summaries and Notes**: Create summaries of your findings or detailed notes on key aspects of the patent documents you review.
  - **Reference Lists**: Maintain lists of patents with similar technologies or legal strategies for easy reference in future research or development projects.

- **Benefit**: Organized documentation ensures that valuable insights and data are preserved and accessible for future use, enhancing ongoing innovation and development efforts.

Understanding the intricate details of patent documents is critical for anyone working in fields where patents play a crucial role in guiding development and strategy. This knowledge not only aids in navigating the legal landscape but also enhances the ability to innovate within the bounds of existing technologies.

6.1.2.4 Practical Tips for Effective Searching

Using Patent Analytics Tools

In the world of intellectual property, efficient and effective patent searching is key. Utilizing patent analytics tools can significantly enhance the ability to search, analyze, and make informed decisions about patents. Here's how you can effectively employ these tools:

- **Selection of the Right Tools**:

    - **Purpose**: To choose analytics tools that best meet your research needs and budget.
    - **Technique**:

        - **Features Comparison**: Evaluate tools based on features like search capabilities, analytics functions, visualization options, and user support.
        - **Trial Versions**: Many services offer demos or trial periods; use these to test how well the tools match your needs before committing to purchase.

    - **Benefit**: Selecting the most suitable tool saves time and resources in the long run and enhances research accuracy.

- **Key Features to Look For**:

    - **Purpose**: To ensure that the tools you choose can perform comprehensive and insightful analysis.

- **Technique**:

    - **Advanced Search Capabilities**: Look for tools that allow complex query construction, such as Boolean logic, proximity searches, and wildcard usage.
    - **Data Visualization**: Tools that provide graphs, trends, and heat maps to visualize data can help in understanding large volumes of information quickly.
    - **Analytics Features**: Check for features that can analyze trends, track technology evolution, and benchmark against competitors.

- **Benefit**: Advanced features enable deeper insights and a more strategic approach to patent research.

- **Integrating Tools into Research Workflow**:

    - **Purpose**: To make the use of analytics tools a routine part of your patent search and analysis process.
    - **Technique**:

        - **Training and Onboarding**: Ensure that all users are trained on how to use the tools effectively, including understanding their features and limitations.
        - **Regular Use**: Integrate these tools into standard operating procedures to ensure they are used consistently across all relevant projects.

    - **Benefit**: Regular use maximizes the return on investment in these tools and ensures consistency in research quality.

- **Leveraging Analytics for Strategic Insights**:

    - **Purpose**: To use the analytical capabilities of these tools to gain competitive and strategic insights.
    - **Technique**:

        - **Patent Landscaping**: Use tools to perform patent landscaping to see the big picture of patent activity in your field, identify key

players, and spot emerging trends.
    - **Freedom to Operate (FTO) Analyses**: Use analytics to assess the risk of potential patent infringement before developing or launching new products.
    - **Portfolio Analysis**: Analyze your own or competitors' patent portfolios to identify strengths, weaknesses, and opportunities.

  - **Benefit**: Strategic insights help in making informed decisions about product development, risk management, and competitive positioning.

- **Continual Learning and Updates**:

  - **Purpose**: To keep up-to-date with the latest advancements and updates in patent analytics technology.
  - **Technique**:

    - **Professional Development**: Engage in ongoing training sessions, webinars, and industry conferences.
    - **Updates and Upgrades**: Regularly update the software to ensure you have the latest features and data.

  - **Benefit**: Staying current with technology and industry trends ensures that your patent searching remains effective and relevant.

Using patent analytics tools not only streamlines the search process but also provides a depth of analysis that can be critical for making strategic decisions in research and development. By carefully selecting, integrating, and leveraging these tools, you can enhance your ability to navigate the complex landscape of patents effectively.

6.1.2.4 Practical Tips for Effective Searching

Keeping Up-to-Date with New Filings and Publications

Staying informed about new patent filings and publications is crucial for anyone involved in research and development, intellectual property law, or corporate strategy. It ensures that you are aware of the latest innovations and potential competitive threats. Here's how you can keep up-to-date effectively:

- **Regular Alerts Setup**:
  - **Purpose**: To receive notifications about new patent filings and publications that are relevant to your field of interest.
  - **Technique**:
    - **Use of Alert Services**: Many patent databases and search platforms offer alert services where you can set up notifications based on specific search criteria such as keywords, inventors, companies, or classification codes.
    - **Email Alerts**: Configure these services to send you periodic email updates whenever new patents fitting your criteria are filed or published.
  - **Benefit**: Automated alerts save you time by delivering relevant patent information directly to your inbox, reducing the need for frequent manual searches.
- **Subscriptions to Patent Journals and Newsletters**:
  - **Purpose**: To gain insights from curated content that highlights recent patent filings and trends.
  - **Technique**:
    - **Professional Publications**: Subscribe to journals, magazines, and newsletters that focus on patent activity and intellectual property rights.
    - **Industry-Specific Updates**: Choose publications that cater to your specific industry to get targeted information that is more directly applicable to your needs.
  - **Benefit**: These publications often provide expert analysis and commentary, which can help you understand the implications of new patents and trends in a broader context.
- **Participating in Professional Networks and Forums**:

- **Purpose**: To exchange information and stay informed through discussions with peers in the intellectual property field.
- **Technique**:

  - **Online Forums and Social Media Groups**: Engage with professional communities on platforms like LinkedIn, specialized IP forums, and other social media where members frequently share and discuss new patent filings.
  - **Conferences and Webinars**: Attend industry conferences, seminars, and webinars that focus on recent developments in patenting.

- **Benefit**: Networking with other professionals can provide insights not only into new filings but also into emerging trends and legal interpretations that might affect patent strategy.

- **Utilizing Advanced Search and Analytics Platforms**:

  - **Purpose**: To harness powerful tools that offer comprehensive and up-to-date patent information and analytics.
  - **Technique**:

    - **Integration of Sophisticated Search Tools**: Implement advanced patent search platforms that provide real-time updates and detailed analytics.
    - **Data Visualization Tools**: Use tools that allow you to visualize data trends and patterns, making it easier to grasp the significance of new filings in the context of existing patents.

  - **Benefit**: Advanced tools provide a deeper and more quantitative analysis of patent activities, helping you make informed decisions based on the latest data.

- **Scheduled Review Sessions**:

  - **Purpose**: To allocate dedicated times for reviewing recent patent activities systematically.
  - **Technique**:

    - **Regular Review Meetings**: Set up regular meetings with your team to review recent patent filings and discuss their potential impact.
    - **Personal Review Time**: Schedule time in your calendar for personal review of recent patent updates to ensure you are always aware of the latest developments.

- **Benefit**: Regular, structured reviews ensure that new patent information is considered and assessed systematically, aiding in strategic planning and innovation.

Keeping abreast of new patent filings and publications is essential for maintaining a competitive edge and ensuring that your research and development efforts are not duplicating existing work or infringing on protected innovations. These practices not only keep you informed but also integrate seamlessly into strategic decision-making processes.

6.2 Geographical Indications

6.2.1 Definition and Significance

6.2.1.1 Definition of Geographical Indications (GIs)

A **Geographical Indication (GI)** is a sign used on products that have a specific geographical origin and possess qualities or a reputation that are due to that origin. The use of a GI acts as a certification that the product possesses certain qualities, is made according to traditional methods, or enjoys a certain reputation, all attributable to its geographical origin.

- **Legal Framework**:

  - **Purpose**: To protect the name of the product from misuse and unauthorized use which can mislead consumers or dilute the reputation of the GI.
  - **Technique**:

    - **Registration System**: Countries typically have a system for registering GIs, which provides legal protection to the use of the name in the marketplace.

- **Control by Local Authorities:** Local authorities or certified bodies often control the use of the GI, ensuring that products using this indication meet certain standards.

- **Benefit:** Registration helps maintain the product's exclusive characteristics and supports fair competition by preventing misleading practices that could deceive consumers.

- **Economic and Cultural Importance:**

  - **Purpose:** GIs hold significant economic and cultural value for local communities by promoting the uniqueness of regional products and contributing to rural development.
  - **Technique:**

    - **Marketing Tool:** GIs serve as a powerful marketing tool that enhances the brand value of products, allowing producers to potentially command higher prices.
    - **Cultural Preservation:** By linking products with their specific regions, GIs help preserve cultural heritage and traditional skills that are often centuries-old.

  - **Benefit:** The economic uplift supports local economies, and the preservation of cultural traditions enriches the cultural landscape.

- **Examples of GIs:**

  - **Purpose:** To illustrate the range of products that can be protected under GIs.
  - **Technique:**

    - **Agricultural Products:** Champagne from France, Darjeeling Tea from India.
    - **Handicrafts:** Murano Glass from Italy, Pashmina from Kashmir.

  - **Benefit:** These examples show how diverse products can gain international fame and legal protection through their geographical indications.

In summary, GIs are not just about geographical origin but also about the inherent qualities and reputation that come from that origin. This designation provides not only a form of intellectual property protection but also a tool for economic and cultural development, benefiting both producers and consumers by ensuring quality and authenticity.

6.2 Geographical Indications

6.2.1 Definition and Significance

6.2.1.2 Legal Framework and Protection Mechanisms

The legal framework surrounding Geographical Indications (GIs) provides a structured means for protecting these valuable identifiers at both national and international levels. Understanding how GIs are legally recognized and protected helps ensure their integrity and the economic and cultural benefits they confer to their respective regions.

- **National Legislation**:
  - **Purpose**: Different countries have established specific legal provisions for the protection of GIs, often tailored to the needs and characteristics of their own products and practices.
  - **Technique**:
    - **Registration Systems**: Most countries require GIs to be officially registered. The registration process typically involves proving the link between the product qualities or reputation and their geographical origin.
    - **Legal Enforcement**: Registered GIs are legally protected against unauthorized use and infringement, which includes misuse, imitation, or any other action that could mislead consumers about the true origin of the product.
  - **Benefit**: Strong national legal frameworks ensure that GIs maintain their market value and cultural significance, protecting both producers and consumers.
- **International Agreements**:

- **Purpose:** To provide cross-border protection for GIs, facilitating international trade and recognition.
- **Technique:**

  - **TRIPS Agreement:** The Agreement on Trade-Related Aspects of Intellectual Property Rights (TRIPS), administered by the World Trade Organization (WTO), is the key international agreement that includes provisions for GI protection. It requires all WTO members to provide legal means for protecting GIs.
  - **Bilateral and Multilateral Treaties:** Many countries enter into agreements to mutually recognize and protect each other's GIs, which often cover specific products like wines and spirits.

- **Benefit:** International agreements enhance the global reach of GI protection, helping producers enter new markets while safeguarding their products against imitation.

- **Control and Certification:**

  - **Purpose:** To ensure that products labeled with GIs meet certain standards and genuinely originate from the designated regions.
  - **Technique:**

    - **Quality Control Procedures:** Governing bodies or designated organizations often set and enforce strict production and quality criteria that products must meet to use a GI label.
    - **Certification Marks:** In some jurisdictions, GIs may also be protected through certification marks, which certify that a product possesses certain qualities or originates from a specific place.

  - **Benefit:** These mechanisms maintain the quality and authenticity of GI products, which in turn supports consumer trust and product reputation.

- **Enforcement and Legal Remedies:**

- **Purpose**: To actively enforce GI rights and provide legal recourse in case of infringement.
- **Technique**:
    - **Monitoring and Legal Action**: Authorities and organizations often monitor the market for unauthorized use of GIs and can take legal action against infringers, which may include lawsuits, fines, and injunctions.
    - **Public Awareness**: Educating consumers and producers about the value and meaning of GIs can also play a critical role in enforcement by reducing demand for counterfeit or misleading products.
- **Benefit**: Effective enforcement discourages infringement and ensures that the economic benefits of GIs are preserved for the legitimate stakeholders.

The protection of GIs through legal frameworks and mechanisms is not merely about safeguarding economic interests; it also involves preserving cultural heritage and ensuring sustainable practices in production. As such, GI protection serves multiple purposes, including legal, economic, cultural, and social objectives.

6.2 Geographical Indications

6.2.1 Definition and Significance

6.2.1.3 Economic and Cultural Importance of GIs

Geographical Indications (GIs) play a significant role in the economic and cultural landscapes of their regions. They are not only markers of origin but also symbols of quality and tradition that can drive economic growth and cultural preservation.

- **Economic Impact**:
    - **Purpose**: GIs can significantly boost the economy of a region by adding value to its products.
    - **Technique**:

- **Premium Pricing**: Products with GI status often command higher prices in the market due to their perceived quality and authenticity. This premium pricing allows producers to generate greater income.
- **Market Differentiation**: GIs serve as a tool for differentiating products in a crowded market. They provide a competitive edge that can attract both domestic and international consumers.

- **Benefit**: The economic benefits derived from GIs support rural development, improve the livelihoods of local producers, and can contribute to the economic resilience of regional economies.

- **Cultural Significance**:

  - **Purpose**: GIs help maintain cultural identity associated with specific regions and practices.
  - **Technique**:

    - **Preservation of Traditional Knowledge and Skills**: Many GI products are made using traditional methods that have been passed down through generations. By securing GI status, these practices are recognized and preserved.
    - **Promotion of Local History and Heritage**: GIs often tell a story about a place and its people, linking products with the history and heritage of the area.

  - **Benefit**: The cultural richness of a region is maintained and celebrated, fostering a sense of pride among community members and enhancing cultural tourism.

- **Social Benefits**:

  - **Purpose**: GIs contribute to social cohesion by fostering a sense of community and shared identity.
  - **Technique**:

    - **Community Engagement and Cooperation**: The process of obtaining and maintaining GI status often requires cooperation among producers, which can strengthen community ties.

    - **Sustainable Practices**: GIs encourage sustainable production practices that are environmentally friendly and socially responsible.

  - **Benefit**: Enhanced social cohesion and sustainability practices contribute to the overall well-being and resilience of communities.

- **Global Influence**:

  - **Purpose**: On a global scale, GIs can enhance the international reputation of regional products.
  - **Technique**:

    - **International Recognition**: As products gain international recognition through GIs, they can penetrate global markets, increasing exports.
    - **Cultural Exchange**: GIs facilitate cultural exchange by introducing consumers around the world to unique products and the cultures from which they originate.

  - **Benefit**: Increased international trade and cultural exchanges enrich both the producing and consuming regions, leading to a more interconnected world.

The economic and cultural importance of GIs thus extends beyond mere legal protection. They contribute to economic development, cultural preservation, social cohesion, and global interactions, making them invaluable assets for regions around the world.

6.2 Geographical Indications

6.2.2 Examples and Case Studies

6.2.2.1 Famous Geographical Indications

Champagne (France)

- **Overview**: Champagne is perhaps one of the most distinguished examples of a geographical indication. It refers to sparkling wine that is produced within the Champagne region of France, using specific production methods and grape varieties.

- **Legal Protection**:

  - **Protected Designation**: Champagne has been protected under French law since the early 20th century and is also covered under the European Union's Protected Designation of Origin (PDO) framework.
  - **International Agreements**: The name "Champagne" is protected worldwide due to various international treaties and agreements, including the Madrid system and bilateral treaties that France has with many countries.

- **Economic Impact**:

  - **Market Value**: The Champagne designation commands a premium price in global markets. The exclusivity associated with this GI not only boosts sales but also ensures that prices remain high due to controlled production and unmatched quality reputation.
  - **Brand Recognition**: Champagne is globally recognized as a symbol of luxury and celebration. This recognition supports a robust export market and significant economic benefits for the region.

- **Cultural Significance**:

  - **Heritage and Tradition**: The methods used to produce Champagne have been refined over centuries and are an integral part of the region's heritage. The strict regulations that govern its production ensure the continuation of these traditional methods.
  - **Tourism**: The Champagne region benefits from a significant number of tourists who visit vineyards, participate in wine tasting, and learn about the history of Champagne production.

- **Case Study Highlights**:

  - **Enforcement Challenges**: Despite strong legal protections, the Champagne name has faced challenges from misuse around the world, especially from producers in other countries labeling their sparkling wines as Champagne. Continuous legal efforts are required to enforce the GI.

- **Economic Sustainability**: The economic model of Champagne as a GI is highly sustainable due to the consistent global demand and the rigorous control of production, which preserves quality and prevents dilution of the brand.
- **Cultural Preservation**: The GI status helps in preserving not just the wine-making traditions but also the rural landscape and biodiversity of the Champagne region, aligning with both cultural preservation and environmental sustainability goals.

Conclusion: Champagne serves as a prime example of how geographical indications can protect regional products while adding significant economic and cultural value. The success of Champagne demonstrates the power of GIs in transforming a regional product into a globally recognized symbol of quality and heritage. This case underscores the importance of legal protection, strict production standards, and international cooperation in the successful management of GIs.

6.2 Geographical Indications

6.2.2 Examples and Case Studies

6.2.2.1 Famous Geographical Indications

Darjeeling Tea (India)

- **Overview**: Darjeeling tea, often referred to as the "Champagne of teas," is a GI that represents tea grown, cultivated, processed, and produced in the Darjeeling districts of West Bengal, India. Known for its distinctive aroma and delicate flavor, Darjeeling tea is one of the most famous and treasured teas worldwide.
- **Legal Protection**:

  - **Protected Status**: Darjeeling tea was among the first products in India to receive GI status in 2004. It is protected under the Geographical Indications of Goods (Registration and Protection) Act, 1999, which prevents any tea grown outside the designated regions from being sold as Darjeeling tea.

- **International Recognition**: The Darjeeling tea GI tag is also recognized in the European Union and other markets, ensuring international protection against misuse and counterfeiting.

- **Economic Impact**:
  - **Premium Pricing**: The GI status allows Darjeeling tea to command premium prices both in domestic and international markets. The unique characteristics attributed to its geographical origin justify these higher prices.
  - **Export Value**: Darjeeling tea is a significant export product for India, contributing considerably to the country's economy. The GI status boosts its export potential by assuring consumers of its authenticity and quality.

- **Cultural Significance**:
  - **Cultural Heritage**: The traditional methods of tea cultivation and production in Darjeeling are a key component of the local culture and heritage. The GI protection helps preserve these traditional practices and the local knowledge associated with tea production.
  - **Tourism**: Darjeeling, renowned for its picturesque tea gardens on rolling hills, attracts numerous tourists. Tea tourism is a growing sector, offering tea garden visits, tastings, and stays, enhancing the region's economic benefits from its GI status.

- **Case Study Highlights**:
  - **Community Impact**: The GI status of Darjeeling tea has a profound impact on the local communities involved in tea cultivation. It helps improve the livelihoods of tea garden workers by ensuring fair wages linked to the premium prices of the tea.
  - **Quality Control and Challenges**: Maintaining the high standards of quality that the GI tag demands poses challenges, especially with climate change impacting crop yields and quality. The Tea Board of India, responsible for the certification of Darjeeling tea, plays a crucial role in quality assurance.

- **Market Challenges**: The global tea market is competitive, and protecting the Darjeeling tea GI requires constant vigilance against infringement and counterfeit products, particularly in loose leaf markets.

Conclusion: Darjeeling tea exemplifies how geographical indications can elevate a regional product to global fame, benefiting both the local economy and the communities involved. The protection and promotion of Darjeeling tea as a GI not only preserve the unique cultural practices associated with its production but also enhance the economic wellbeing of the Darjeeling region. This case highlights the importance of stringent quality control and active legal protection to uphold the integrity and value of GI products.

6.2 Geographical Indications

6.2.2 Examples and Case Studies

6.2.2.1 Famous Geographical Indications

Roquefort Cheese (France)

- **Overview**: Roquefort is a renowned blue cheese known for its rich, complex flavors and characteristic green veins of mold. It is produced exclusively in the Roquefort-sur-Soulzon area of southern France, using milk from specially bred sheep and matured in the unique Combalou caves of the region.
- **Legal Protection**:
    - **Protected Designation**: Roquefort was one of the first cheeses to receive a controlled designation of origin (AOC) in France in 1925, and it is also protected under the European Union's Protected Designation of Origin (PDO) framework.
    - **Global Protection**: This GI status prohibits the use of the "Roquefort" name for any cheese that does not comply with the strict production criteria established by the French and EU laws, regardless of where it is produced globally.
- **Economic Impact**:

- **Market Exclusivity**: The exclusivity granted by the GI status allows Roquefort cheese to maintain a high market value and distinctiveness from other blue cheeses around the world.
- **Export Success**: Roquefort is significantly valued in international markets, especially in Europe and the United States, contributing substantially to France's economy through exports.

- **Cultural Significance**:

    - **Heritage and Traditions**: The traditional methods of cheese-making, including the use of natural cave molds to achieve its distinctive flavor and texture, are integral to the cultural heritage of the Roquefort area.
    - **Tourism and Education**: The region attracts cheese lovers and tourists who visit to learn about the unique production process, taste authentic Roquefort cheese, and explore the historic aging caves.

- **Case Study Highlights**:

    - **Quality Assurance**: Maintaining the high standards of Roquefort cheese production is crucial. The producers must adhere to strict guidelines regarding sheep breeds, milk quality, and cave-aging processes to comply with GI regulations.
    - **Economic Stability and Challenges**: While Roquefort enjoys a stable demand, it faces challenges such as climatic changes affecting pasture quality and competition from imitation products.
    - **Cultural and Environmental Sustainability**: The GI status helps preserve not only the traditional cheese-making practices but also the rural landscape and the local economy dependent on this cheese production.

Conclusion: Roquefort cheese is a prime example of how geographical indications can successfully protect and promote a regional food product on the global stage. Its GI status not only ensures the preservation of traditional production methods and local biodiversity but also supports the economic stability of the region through premium pricing and tourism. This case illustrates the benefits of GIs in maintaining cultural heritage while providing economic incentives for local producers.

6.2 Geographical Indications

6.2.2 Examples and Case Studies

6.2.2.2 Case Studies on the Impact of GIs

Benefits to Local Economies

Geographical Indications (GIs) provide substantial benefits to local economies by enhancing market visibility, ensuring premium pricing, and fostering community involvement. Here are detailed case studies that highlight these benefits:

1. **Parmigiano Reggiano (Italy):**

    - **Overview**: Known as "Parmesan," this cheese is produced in specific provinces of Italy under strict conditions defined by its GI status.
    - **Economic Impact**:

        - **Premium Pricing**: Parmigiano Reggiano commands high prices globally due to its quality and authenticity guaranteed by the GI status.
        - **Job Creation**: The industry supports thousands of jobs in rural areas, from dairy farms to local cheese production facilities.

    - **Community Benefits**:

        - **Sustainable Agriculture**: The GI criteria promote sustainable farming practices that benefit the environment and ensure the long-term viability of local agriculture.
        - **Tourism**: The region has developed a significant tourism sector based around cheese production, including factory tours and cheese-tasting events.

    - **Cultural Impact**:

        - **Preservation of Traditional Skills**: The production process that has been refined over centuries is preserved through GI status, maintaining cultural heritage.

1. **Tequila (Mexico)**:

- **Overview**: Tequila is a distilled spirit made from the blue agave plant, primarily in the area surrounding the city of Tequila and other parts of Jalisco.
- **Economic Impact**:

  - **Global Branding**: Tequila's GI status has allowed it to become a globally recognized brand, significantly boosting Mexico's export revenues.
  - **Economic Development**: The tequila industry is a major economic driver in Jalisco, providing significant employment and supporting secondary industries like bottle manufacturing and agave cultivation.

- **Community Benefits**:

  - **Infrastructure Development**: Revenue from tequila production has led to better infrastructure in production areas, including roads, schools, and healthcare facilities.
  - **Cultural Festivals**: The GI status has spurred cultural pride and annual festivals that attract tourists and celebrate the heritage of tequila making.

- **Cultural Impact**:

  - **Heritage Preservation**: The traditional methods of tequila production are preserved, showcasing Mexican culture and traditions internationally.

3. **Kona Coffee (United States, Hawaii)**:

- **Overview**: Kona coffee is cultivated on the slopes of Hualalai and Mauna Loa in the North and South Kona Districts of the Big Island of Hawaii.
- **Economic Impact**:

  - **Niche Market**: Kona coffee benefits from a GI that helps maintain its status as one of the most premium coffees on the market.
  - **Price Premium**: The GI status ensures that farmers can charge premium prices for Kona coffee, substantially higher than standard coffee prices.

- **Community Benefits**:

  - **Economic Stability for Farmers**: The premium pricing directly translates into greater economic stability for the coffee farmers in the Kona region.
  - **Local Employment**: The coffee industry creates numerous jobs in the local economy, from cultivation to hospitality.

- **Cultural Impact**:

  - **Agricultural Tradition**: Protecting Kona coffee also protects the agricultural traditions of the Hawaiian community, maintaining its unique identity and practices.

These case studies illustrate how GIs significantly contribute to local economies by creating premium markets for their products, fostering job creation, promoting sustainable practices, and preserving cultural traditions. The benefits extend beyond simple economic gains, embedding products within the cultural fabric of their regions and promoting them on a global stage.

6.2 Geographical Indications

6.2.2 Examples and Case Studies

Challenges in Enforcement and Protection

While geographical indications (GIs) offer numerous benefits, enforcing and protecting these designations, especially on an international level, presents several challenges:

- **Lack of Universal Recognition**:

- **Issue**: Not all countries recognize GIs to the same extent or under the same conditions, which can lead to inconsistencies in protection.
- **Impact**: Products that are protected under a GI in one country might be freely produced and sold under the same name in another country without any of the quality assurances or specific characteristics associated with the original GI product.

- **Misuse and Counterfeiting**:

  - **Issue**: Products that imitate GI products can be produced domestically or imported, often selling at lower prices and potentially misleading consumers.
  - **Impact**: This not only dilutes the market share of authentic products but can also damage their reputation if the imitation products are of inferior quality.

- **Cost of Regulation and Enforcement**:

  - **Issue**: Establishing and maintaining a system for monitoring and enforcing GI protections involves significant financial and administrative resources.
  - **Impact**: Especially for developing countries, the cost of such systems can be prohibitively high, limiting their ability to effectively enforce GI protections.

- **Standardization of Production Methods**:

  - **Issue**: Ensuring that all producers within a GI region adhere to the prescribed methods and standards can be challenging.
  - **Impact**: Variability in compliance can lead to inconsistencies in product quality, potentially undermining the GI's reputation.

International Disputes and Resolutions

The global nature of trade and the varying legal recognition of GIs often lead to international disputes, which are typically resolved through negotiations or through the World Trade Organization (WTO) mechanisms:

- **WTO Dispute Settlements:**

    - **Example:** A notable dispute involved the European Union and the United States over the use of names like "Parmesan" and "Feta," which the EU claimed as GIs while the US treated them as generic names.
    - **Resolution:** These disputes are often resolved through lengthy negotiations that may result in agreements to phase out the use of certain names in non-origin countries or to allow continued use under specific conditions.

- **Bilateral Agreements:**

    - **Example:** The EU has entered into several bilateral agreements with non-EU countries to mutually recognize and protect each other's GIs.
    - **Resolution:** These agreements often involve detailed lists of GIs from both parties that are recognized and protected in each other's territories, thus avoiding future disputes.

- **Challenges with New Markets:**

    - **Issue:** As global markets evolve, new disputes can arise when GI products enter new markets where their names might be considered generic.
    - **Impact:** Without international agreements or local recognition, protecting these GIs can be difficult and can hinder market expansion.

- **Cultural Differences and Perceptions:**

    - **Issue:** Different cultural understandings of what constitutes a GI and the importance of place-based names can lead to conflicts.
    - **Impact:** Products well-known as GIs in one region may be treated as generic in another, leading to international legal battles and confusion among consumers.

Strategies for Overcoming Challenges:

- **International Cooperation**: Enhancing international cooperation and dialogue through forums like the WTO and WIPO can help harmonize GI protections globally.
- **Public Awareness Campaigns**: Educating consumers about the value of GIs and the significance of authenticity can help reduce demand for counterfeit products.
- **Technological Solutions**: Using technology to track and verify the authenticity of GI products can improve enforcement and reduce fraud.

Enforcement and protection of geographical indications require ongoing international cooperation and robust legal frameworks to navigate the complex landscape of global trade and cultural differences.

CHAPTER SEVEN

NEW DEVELOPMENTS IN INTELLECTUAL PROPERTY RIGHTS

7.1 Emerging Trends in IPR

7.1.1 IPR in Biological Systems

7.1.1.1 Patenting of Genetic Material

The patenting of genetic material has emerged as a pivotal area in intellectual property law, especially as advancements in biotechnology and genetic engineering continue to accelerate. This trend raises significant legal, ethical, and practical questions about the extent to which natural and genetically modified organisms can be owned or controlled through patents.

- **Overview of Patenting Genetic Material**:
  - **Definition**: Patenting of genetic material involves claiming exclusive rights to specific sequences of DNA, methods of modifying genetic material, or the use of genetic information to produce specific outcomes, such as medical treatments or agricultural improvements.
  - **Legal Framework**: The ability to patent genetic material varies significantly by jurisdiction. In the United States, for instance, the Supreme Court has ruled that naturally occurring DNA sequences cannot be patented, whereas synthetic or cDNA (complementary DNA) can be because it is not naturally occurring.

- **Key Considerations in Patenting Genetic Material**:

  - **Novelty and Non-Obviousness**: For genetic material to be patentable, it must be demonstrably novel and non-obvious. This means the genetic sequence in question must not only be newly discovered but also must represent a distinct invention that is not a clear derivative of existing genetic knowledge.
  - **Utility**: The patent application must clearly demonstrate the practical utility of the genetic material. This could involve showing how the genetic sequence can be used to treat a disease, enhance agricultural yield, or any other practical application.

- **Ethical and Social Implications**:

  - **Access to Genetic Resources**: Patenting genetic material can restrict access to genetic resources by placing them under the control of private entities, potentially leading to ethical issues concerning equity and access, particularly in healthcare.
  - **Biodiversity and Indigenous Rights**: There are significant concerns about the impact of genetic patents on biodiversity and the rights of indigenous communities, particularly when patents are placed on genetic resources that have been used by these communities for generations.

- **Recent Developments and Judicial Decisions**:

  - **Landmark Cases**: In the U.S., the Supreme Court's decision in *Association for Molecular Pathology v. Myriad Genetics, Inc.* ruled that naturally occurring DNA cannot be patented, which has set a precedent that influences how genetic material is approached in patent law.
  - **International Perspectives**: The Nagoya Protocol on Access and Benefit-sharing provides a framework to govern the access to genetic resources and ensure fair sharing of benefits arising from their utilization, which has implications for patenting practices globally.

- **Future Outlook**:

- **Synthetic Biology and CRISPR**: Advances in synthetic biology and CRISPR (Clustered Regularly Interspaced Short Palindromic Repeats) technologies are pushing the boundaries of what can be patented. These technologies enable scientists to create and edit genetic material in ways that are likely patentable because they do not occur naturally.
- **Global Harmonization Efforts**: There is an ongoing discussion about the need for greater international harmonization of patent laws relating to genetic material, to address the global nature of biotechnology companies and the ethical implications of genetic research.

The field of patenting genetic material is one of the most dynamically evolving areas of intellectual property law, reflecting broader technological advances and their profound implications for society. As legal frameworks continue to adapt, the debate over ethical considerations and the balance between innovation and access will likely intensify, shaping the future landscape of intellectual property rights in the biological domain.

7.1 Emerging Trends in IPR

7.1.1 IPR in Biological Systems

7.1.1.1 Patenting of Genetic Material

Criteria for Patentability of Genes and Genetic Sequences

Patenting genetic material, particularly genes and genetic sequences, is governed by stringent criteria that reflect both the complexity of biology and the legal, ethical, and social issues involved. Here's a detailed look at the primary criteria used to determine the patentability of genes and genetic sequences:

- **Novelty**:

  - **Definition**: A gene or genetic sequence must be novel, meaning it has not been previously known or used in the public domain. It must represent something that is not naturally occurring in its isolated form or as part of the known genetic makeup of an organism.
  - **Assessment**: The novelty is determined by comparing the genetic sequence against known sequences stored in databases like GenBank

or EMBL, ensuring that the sequence has not been disclosed in any prior scientific literature or genetic repository.

- **Inventive Step (Non-Obviousness)**:
    - **Definition**: The gene or genetic sequence must exhibit an inventive step, which means it should not be obvious to a person skilled in the field. This criterion is crucial to prevent the patenting of genetic sequences that are ordinary extensions of existing genetic knowledge.
    - **Application**: For a genetic sequence, an inventive step might involve a new method of isolating the gene, a novel use for a known gene (such as a new therapeutic application), or a previously unknown function for a gene.
- **Utility**:
    - **Definition**: The utility criterion requires that the gene or genetic sequence has a specific, substantial, and credible utility. This means the applicant must demonstrate a real-world use for the genetic material, which goes beyond mere theoretical applications.
    - **Examples**: Utility can be demonstrated by showing how the gene or sequence can be used in medical treatments, as diagnostic tools, or for agricultural improvements. The applicant must provide evidence, such as experimental data, that supports the claimed utility.
- **Sufficiency of Disclosure**:
    - **Definition**: The patent application must disclose the gene or genetic sequence in a manner sufficiently clear and complete for it to be understood, and for the claimed utility to be replicable, by someone skilled in the art.
    - **Requirement**: This includes a detailed description of how to isolate the gene, how to replicate the genetic sequence, and how the utility is achieved. This ensures that the patent does not just monopolize knowledge but also contributes to the scientific and technological field.
- **Ethical and Legal Considerations**:

- **Human Genes:** In many jurisdictions, human genes per se are not patentable if simply isolated from the human body without modification. The ethical framework often argues that patenting pure genetic sequences, as they occur in nature, could impede scientific research and access to healthcare.
- **Synthetic or Modified Genes:** Synthetic genes, which are not naturally occurring and have been significantly altered or engineered, generally meet the patentability criteria more readily because they are considered new inventions.

The criteria for patentability of genes and genetic sequences are designed to ensure that patents in the biotechnological field foster innovation while respecting the natural origins of genetic material and addressing the potential social and ethical implications of genetic patents. As the field evolves, these criteria may be subject to further refinement to balance the interests of innovation with public welfare.

7.1 Emerging Trends in IPR

7.1.1 IPR in Biological Systems

7.1.1.2 Biotechnology Patents

Innovations in Biotechnology and Their Patenting

Biotechnology stands at the forefront of scientific innovation, significantly impacting fields such as medicine, agriculture, and environmental science. The patenting of biotechnological innovations is a critical factor in encouraging investment and development in this area. Here, we explore key aspects of biotechnology innovations and how they are patented.

- **Scope of Biotechnological Innovations:**

  - **Medical Biotechnology**: Innovations include genetic therapies, new vaccines, and biopharmaceuticals that offer solutions for treating diseases that were once considered untreatable.
  - **Agricultural Biotechnology**: Developments in genetically modified crops that resist pests and adverse weather conditions, along with biofertilizers and biopesticides, represent significant advances.

- **Industrial Biotechnology**: This involves the use of enzymes and microorganisms in the production of biofuels, bioplastics, and other sustainable materials.
- **Environmental Biotechnology**: Innovations include bioremediation techniques using organisms to clean up contaminated environments and new methods of waste management.

- **Patenting Biotechnological Innovations**:

  - **Eligibility Criteria**: Similar to other areas in genetics, biotechnological inventions must meet the criteria of novelty, inventive step, and utility. Additionally, these inventions must be describable in a way that allows a skilled practitioner to reproduce the invention without undue experimentation.
  - **Patentable Subject Matter**: Biotechnological patents often cover a wide range of subject matter, including new biological materials, processes for genetically engineering or modifying organisms, methods of using biological products, and specific uses of biotechnology in various industries.
  - **Ethical and Regulatory Considerations**: Biotechnological patents are often scrutinized for their ethical implications, especially concerning genetic modification and the impact on biodiversity. Regulatory frameworks also play a crucial role in determining what can be patented, particularly in terms of safety and impact on the environment and public health.

- **Examples of Patented Biotechnological Innovations**:

  - **CRISPR-Cas9**: This revolutionary gene-editing technology has been widely patented, with key patents held by institutions like the Broad Institute and the University of California. The patents cover various aspects of the technology, including specific applications and methods of gene editing.
  - **Golden Rice**: This genetically modified rice that produces beta-carotene, a precursor of vitamin A, is patented. It represents a significant advance in addressing vitamin A deficiency in developing countries.

   - **Oncomouse**: The first patented genetically modified animal, engineered to increase susceptibility to cancer, has been used extensively in cancer research. The patent covered the genetic modification method and the specific genetically modified mouse.

- **Challenges in Patenting Biotechnological Innovations**:

   - **Complexity of Biological Systems**: The inherent complexity of biological systems can make it challenging to meet the patent criteria of specificity and reproducibility.
   - **Overlapping Patents and 'Patent Thickets'**: Given the broad applicability of biotechnological tools and methods, overlapping patents can create dense networks of intellectual property rights, complicating the development of new products.
   - **Public Perception and Legal Challenges**: Public concerns about the ethics of genetic modification and ownership of genetic resources can lead to significant legal and societal challenges, influencing patent policies and practices.

Biotechnology patents play a pivotal role in protecting and incentivizing the significant investments required to bring biotechnological innovations from the lab to the market. The balance between promoting innovation and addressing ethical, legal, and environmental concerns is crucial in shaping the landscape of biotechnology research and its commercialization.

7.1 Emerging Trends in IPR

7.1.1 IPR in Biological Systems

Case Studies in Agricultural and Medical Biotechnology

The field of biotechnology is vast, impacting various industries significantly. Here, we explore specific case studies that highlight the impact of intellectual property rights (IPR) in agricultural and medical biotechnology, demonstrating how patents have facilitated innovation and addressed critical global challenges.

Agricultural Biotechnology: Golden Rice

- **Overview**: Golden Rice is genetically modified rice that produces beta-carotene, which the body converts into vitamin A. This rice aims to combat vitamin A deficiency (VAD), a serious health problem in over 50 countries, particularly affecting children and pregnant women.

- **Development and Patenting:**
  - **Innovators:** Developed by Dr. Ingo Potrykus of the Swiss Federal Institute of Technology and Dr. Peter Beyer of the University of Freiburg.
  - **Patent Details:** The key technology for Golden Rice (synthesis of beta-carotene in rice grains) was patented, which helped secure funding and partnerships necessary for further development and testing.
  - **Licensing Arrangements:** Golden Rice is offered under a free license to subsistence farmers by the Golden Rice Humanitarian Board.
- **Impact and Controversy:**
  - **Positive Impact:** Golden Rice has the potential to improve the health outcomes of millions at risk of VAD.
  - **Controversies:** There have been significant debates and public resistance concerning GM foods, focusing on environmental concerns, food safety, and ethical issues.

Medical Biotechnology: Humira (Adalimumab)

- **Overview:** Humira, known generically as Adalimumab, is a biologic medical product used primarily to treat autoimmune diseases such as rheumatoid arthritis, psoriasis, and inflammatory bowel disease.
- **Development and Patenting:**
  - **Innovators:** Developed by Abbott Laboratories, now AbbVie.
  - **Patent Details:** Humira has been protected by numerous patents covering the monoclonal antibody, production processes, formulations, and therapeutic uses.
  - **Patent Strategy:** AbbVie has strategically filed multiple overlapping patents to create a 'patent thicket', extending the drug's exclusivity period beyond the original patent expiration.
- **Impact and Controversy:**

- **Positive Impact**: Humira has significantly improved treatment outcomes for millions of patients worldwide.
- **Controversies**: The extensive patent coverage has led to debates over "evergreening" practices, where minor changes to a product are patented to extend the monopoly period, potentially delaying generic competition and keeping prices high.

Analysis and Lessons Learned

- **IPR's Role in Innovation**:
    - **Funding and R&D**: Patents provide a mechanism for recouping the substantial investments required in biotechnology R&D, encouraging ongoing innovation and development.
    - **Partnerships and Licensing**: Patents facilitate partnerships and licensing deals that are crucial for bringing biotechnological products to market, especially in global health contexts.
- **Balancing Innovation and Access**:
    - **Ethical and Legal Challenges**: There is a need for a balanced approach that respects intellectual property rights while ensuring affordable access to biotechnological innovations, particularly in lower-income countries.
    - **Policy Implications**: These case studies underscore the importance of robust but flexible patent laws that incentivize innovation while allowing for exceptions, such as compulsory licensing during public health crises.

These case studies in agricultural and medical biotechnology illustrate the complex interplay between innovation, IPR, and public health and safety. They highlight the necessity for policies that not only stimulate innovation and commercial activity but also address the ethical, environmental, and health implications of biotechnological advancements.

Differences Between Copyright and Patent Protection for Software

The legal landscape for protecting software is complex, involving multiple forms of intellectual property. Particularly, copyright and patent protections offer different scopes of security and cover diverse aspects of software and its applications. Understanding the nuances between these two can help developers, companies, and legal professionals effectively navigate intellectual property rights in the tech industry.

Copyright Protection for Software

- **Nature of Protection**:
    - **Copyright** protects the expression of ideas, specifically the code itself—both source code and object code. It does not protect the underlying concepts, processes, systems, or operational methods.
- **Scope and Duration**:
    - Copyright covers the literal elements of software, such as its written code and sometimes its user interface elements (to the extent that they can be considered authorial and creative). Protection is automatically granted upon creation of the work in a tangible medium and lasts for the life of the author plus 70 years in most jurisdictions.
- **Registration and Formalities**:
    - While copyright protection is automatic, registering the work with a copyright office can provide additional legal benefits, including statutory damages and attorney fees in the event of litigation.
- **Limitations**:
    - Copyright does not extend to ideas, methods of operation, or the functional aspects of software. It only protects the particular expression of those ideas.

Patent Protection for Software

- **Nature of Protection**:

- **Patents** protect new, useful, and non-obvious inventions, including processes, machines, manufacture, or compositions of matter. In software, patents might cover the unique algorithms, processes, or technical methods implemented by the software if they solve a specific technical problem in a novel way.

- **Scope and Duration:**

  - Patent protection is much broader in scope than copyright, as it covers the functional aspects of an invention. A software patent can prevent others from using the patented processes or methods, regardless of how they are implemented or expressed. The duration of a patent is generally 20 years from the filing date of the patent application.

- **Registration and Formalities:**

  - Obtaining a patent requires a detailed and often expensive process of application with the national or regional patent office, including disclosures that prove the invention's novelty, utility, and non-obviousness.

- **Limitations:**

  - The bar for patenting software is high and varies significantly between jurisdictions. For example, the European Union has stricter requirements for patenting software than the United States, often requiring that the invention have a 'technical character' or solve a 'technical problem.'

Practical Applications and Considerations

- **Strategic Use:**

  - Companies often use both copyright and patent protections in a complementary fashion to maximize the protection of their software. For instance, while the code itself is protected by copyright, the unique methods and processes can be patented.

- **Legal Challenges**:
    - The dual nature of software as both an artistic expression (copyright) and a utilitarian invention (patent) leads to ongoing legal challenges and debates, particularly concerning the overlap of these protections and their implications for innovation and competition.
- **Economic and Business Implications**:
    - Decisions on whether to seek patent protection, copyright protection, or both, often depend on the business goals, the nature of the software, and the competitive environment. Patent protection, while offering a broader scope, is more costly and difficult to obtain compared to copyright.

Understanding the distinctions between copyright and patent protection is crucial for effectively managing and safeguarding software innovations. Each type of protection offers different advantages and limitations, and the choice of protection must align with the strategic goals and operational realities of the business.

7.1 Emerging Trends in IPR

7.1.2.2 Digital and Internet-Based Innovations

Patenting in the Digital Age: Challenges and Opportunities

The digital age has revolutionized how we interact with technology, leading to a surge in innovations that blend software, hardware, and internet-based solutions. The rapid pace of digital innovation poses unique challenges and opportunities for intellectual property rights, particularly in the realm of patenting. Here's an analysis of these dynamics:

Challenges in Patenting Digital Innovations

- **Rapid Technological Change**:
    - **Issue**: The speed at which digital technology evolves often outpaces the patent system, which can be slow and cumbersome. By the time a patent is granted, the technology could be obsolete.

  - **Impact**: This misalignment can discourage inventors from seeking patents and may lead to a preference for trade secrets or rapid market deployment instead.

- **Abstract Ideas and Software Patentability**:

  - **Issue**: Patent laws vary significantly across jurisdictions regarding the patentability of software and abstract ideas. For instance, the U.S. has specific tests to determine if a software invention is merely an abstract idea, which is not patentable.
  - **Impact**: The ambiguity and complexity of these legal frameworks create uncertainty for inventors and can lead to costly litigation.

- **Non-Obviousness and Novelty**:

  - **Issue**: Demonstrating the non-obviousness and novelty of digital innovations can be challenging, especially when prior art in the digital space is vast but not always formally documented or easily accessible.
  - **Impact**: Inventors may struggle to prove that their digital innovations meet the necessary criteria for patentability, leading to rejected applications and increased costs.

Opportunities in Patenting Digital Innovations

- **Cross-Disciplinary Innovations**:

  - **Opportunity**: The convergence of digital technologies with other sectors, such as healthcare, automotive, and manufacturing, opens up new avenues for patentable inventions.
  - **Benefit**: Patents in these cross-disciplinary areas can be highly valuable, offering broad applicability and the potential for significant market exclusivity.

- **Global Market Access**:

  - **Opportunity**: Effective patenting strategies can help protect digital innovations in multiple jurisdictions, giving inventors access to global

markets.
- **Benefit**: With strategic international patent filings, businesses can protect their innovations worldwide, maximizing returns on investment and increasing competitive advantage.

- **Enhanced R&D Collaboration**:

  - **Opportunity**: Patents can facilitate R&D collaborations by clearly defining IP rights and responsibilities, encouraging partnerships between startups, universities, and large corporations.
  - **Benefit**: Such collaborations can accelerate innovation, spread risks, and combine resources and expertise to tackle complex technological challenges.

Strategies for Effective Patenting in the Digital Age

- **Proactive IP Management**:

  - **Approach**: Companies must adopt proactive IP management strategies, staying informed about legal changes and adapting their approaches to IP protection accordingly.
  - **Implementation**: Regular IP audits, strategic patent filings, and ongoing competitor and market analysis are essential.

- **Leveraging Patent Analytics**:

  - **Approach**: Use advanced patent analytics tools to identify emerging trends, potential collaborators, and competitive threats in the digital technology landscape.
  - **Implementation**: Analyzing patent landscapes can inform strategic decisions, such as where to invest in R&D and when to pursue or abandon specific patent applications.

- **Education and Training**:

  - **Approach**: Continual education and training on the latest developments in IP law and digital technology trends for all stakeholders involved in the innovation process.

- **Implementation**: Regular training sessions, workshops, and seminars can help inventors and managers understand the complexities of patenting digital innovations.

Patenting in the digital age requires a dynamic and informed approach to navigate the complexities of modern technology and its rapid evolution. By understanding the challenges and leveraging the opportunities presented by digital innovations, companies can effectively protect their intellectual property and sustain their competitive edge in the global market.

7.1 Emerging Trends in IPR

7.1.2.2 Digital and Internet-Based Innovations

Case Studies on Internet Business Methods and E-Commerce Patents

Patenting internet business methods and e-commerce strategies has been a controversial and evolving area of intellectual property law. Here, we explore some influential case studies that have shaped how such patents are viewed and enforced, offering insights into the challenges and strategic considerations involved.

Amazon's "1-Click" Patent

- **Overview**: One of the most famous examples of an internet business method patent is Amazon's "1-Click" shopping patent, officially known as U.S. Patent No. 5,960,411. Granted in 1999, this patent covered a method that allowed customers to make a purchase with a single click, using information previously stored by the system to expedite the checkout process.
- **Impact**:
    - **Business Advantage**: The "1-Click" patent gave Amazon a significant competitive edge by simplifying the online purchasing process, reportedly increasing conversion rates and customer satisfaction.
    - **Legal Controversies**: The patent was controversial, with critics arguing that it covered a broad and obvious concept, stifling innovation and competition in e-commerce.
- **Resolution**: The patent expired in 2017, leading to broader adoption of similar one-click buying options across various e-commerce platforms,

which illustrates the temporary nature of such competitive advantages in patent law.

Priceline's Reverse Auction Patent

- **Overview**: Priceline's patent for a "reverse auction" method for airline tickets allowed customers to name their price for flights, which airlines could then choose to accept or reject. This method was patented in 1998 (U.S. Patent No. 5,794,207).
- **Impact**:
  - **Innovation in Pricing Models**: The patent protected a novel approach to pricing that disrupted traditional airline ticket sales and inspired other industries to adopt similar models.
  - **Market Exclusivity**: The patent helped Priceline maintain a unique position in the online travel industry until its expiration.
- **Legal and Business Considerations**: The patent faced scrutiny and challenges, particularly regarding its breadth and the potential stifling of similar innovations. Its existence prompted discussions about the balance between protecting innovative ideas and fostering a competitive market environment.

eBay's Buy It Now® Feature

- **Overview**: eBay's Buy It Now® patent allowed online auction buyers to purchase items at a fixed price before an auction concluded. This feature bridged the gap between traditional and online auction formats, enhancing user experience by providing instant purchasing options.
- **Impact**:
  - **Enhanced User Experience**: This feature addressed the impatience or uncertainty some users felt with the auction process, providing immediate gratification and a guaranteed outcome.
  - **Legal Defense**: eBay defended this patent vigorously, notably in litigation against MercExchange, leading to a landmark Supreme Court decision (eBay Inc. v. MercExchange, L.L.C.) that altered how injunctions are issued in patent cases.

- **Resolution**: The case set a precedent that courts must apply traditional equity principles before granting injunctions in patent cases, which has implications for how internet business method patents are enforced.

Strategic Considerations

- **Navigating Legal Uncertainties**: These cases highlight the importance of navigating legal uncertainties and potential challenges when developing and patenting internet business methods.
- **Monitoring Patent Expirations**: Companies must strategically plan for the expiration of patents, as competitors can quickly adopt once-proprietary methods, diluting first-mover advantages.
- **Innovation vs. Competition**: The balance between encouraging innovation through patent protection and maintaining a competitive marketplace remains a central debate in the realm of internet business methods and e-commerce.

These case studies illustrate that while patents can provide significant competitive leverage in the digital economy, they also come with challenges that require careful legal and strategic management. As digital commerce continues to evolve, so too will the landscape of related intellectual property law, necessitating ongoing vigilance and adaptation by businesses operating in this space.

7.2 Administration of the Patent System

7.2.1 Role of Patent Offices

7.2.1.1 Functions and Responsibilities

Patent offices play a crucial role in the innovation ecosystem by administering the patent system. They serve as the regulatory bodies responsible for the examination, grant, and maintenance of patents within their jurisdiction. Here is an overview of the core functions and responsibilities of patent offices:

- **Patent Examination and Grant**:

    - **Processing Applications**: Patent offices receive and process patent applications, ensuring that all required documents and fees are submitted.

- **Examination for Compliance**: Examiners at the patent office assess applications to ensure they meet legal standards for patentability, which include novelty, non-obviousness, and utility. This process involves a thorough review of existing patents and other public disclosures (prior art) to determine if the invention is indeed new and inventive.
- **Granting Patents**: Once an application passes the examination phase, the patent office grants a patent which provides the inventor with exclusive rights to their invention for a specified period, typically 20 years.

- **Publication and Dissemination of Patent Information**:

  - **Publication**: Patent offices publish patent applications and granted patents, usually 18 months after the earliest filing date, making the information available to the public. This publication helps prevent duplication of research and allows businesses and inventors to be aware of the latest technological developments.
  - **Databases**: They maintain detailed databases that store all patent documentation, accessible to the public for search and review. These databases are critical resources for businesses, researchers, and legal experts for conducting prior art searches and legal analysis.

- **Promoting Awareness and Education**:

  - **Information and Support Services**: Patent offices provide information and support services to inventors and businesses on how to obtain and maintain patents. This often includes conducting seminars, workshops, and providing online resources to educate on the patent process and its benefits.
  - **Advocacy**: They advocate for strong intellectual property rights, emphasizing the importance of patents in promoting innovation and economic growth.

- **Policy Development and Legal Frameworks**:

- **Advisory Role**: Patent offices often advise on national policy regarding intellectual property laws. They work with legislative bodies to adapt and evolve patent laws as technology and international standards develop.
- **International Cooperation**: They collaborate with patent offices in other countries and international organizations such as the World Intellectual Property Organization (WIPO) to harmonize patent practices and policies across borders.

- **Handling Disputes and Legal Functions**:

    - **Opposition and Revocation Procedures**: After a patent is granted, third parties may challenge its validity through opposition or revocation procedures managed by the patent office. These mechanisms ensure that the patents granted maintain their integrity and deserve the monopoly status they confer.
    - **Administrative Appeals**: Patent offices also manage administrative appeals processes where applicants can contest decisions regarding their patent applications.

- **Maintenance of Patent Rights**:

    - **Renewals and Annual Fees**: They collect annual fees from patent holders to maintain the validity of granted patents. Failure to pay these fees can result in the patent lapsing.

The responsibilities of patent offices are foundational to the functioning of the patent system. They not only ensure that the rights of inventors are protected but also that the public can benefit from innovations in technology and science. By effectively managing these duties, patent offices contribute significantly to national and global economic development and technological advancement.

7.2 Administration of the Patent System

7.2.1 Role of Patent Offices

Examination and Granting of Patents

The process of examining and granting patents is a critical function of patent offices worldwide. This process ensures that only inventions that meet specific legal criteria receive patent protection. Here is a detailed look at the stages involved in the examination and granting of patents:

1. Filing the Application

- **Initial Submission**: Inventors or their representatives submit a patent application to the patent office that includes a detailed description of the invention, claims defining the scope of protection sought, drawings (if applicable), and relevant fees.
- **Formalities Check**: The patent office reviews the application to ensure that all required parts are included and properly formatted. This includes checking the applicant's information, the specification of the invention, and adherence to formal requirements.

2. Publication of Application

- **Timing**: Typically, the application is published 18 months from the filing date or the priority date (if priority is claimed from an earlier application). This publication allows the public to view the details of the invention.
- **Purpose**: Publication serves to notify the public and industry about new potential inventions and technologies. It allows third parties to file observations or objections if they believe the invention is not new or obvious.

3. Examination Process

- **Request for Examination**: In many patent systems, the examination process does not begin automatically. The applicant must request an examination within a specified period, and this often involves additional fees.
- **Search and Examination**:
    - **Search for Prior Art**: The examiner conducts a thorough search of existing technologies and patent literature to identify prior art that might be relevant to the novelty and inventive step of the claimed invention.

- **Assessment of Patentability Criteria**: The examiner evaluates the application against several criteria:
    - **Novelty**: The invention must be new, meaning it has not been previously known or used.
    - **Inventive Step (Non-obviousness)**: The invention must not be obvious to someone with knowledge and experience in the subject area.
    - **Industrial Applicability (Utility)**: The invention must be useful and have some practical application.

4. Communication with Applicant

- **Office Actions**: If the examiner finds issues with the application, they will issue an "office action" or "examination report," detailing any objections based on the findings. This might relate to the patentability of the invention, clarity of the claims, or other formal deficiencies.
- **Response from Applicant**: The applicant has an opportunity to respond to the office action, which may involve amending the claims, arguing against the objections, or providing additional data to support the invention's patentability.

5. Decision on the Application

- **Grant or Refusal**:
    - **Grant of Patent**: If the application satisfies all the patentability requirements and there are no outstanding objections, the patent office issues a patent grant. This confers exclusive rights on the patentee to exploit the invention for a limited period, usually 20 years from the filing date.
    - **Refusal**: If the examiner's objections are not overcome, the application may be refused, and the applicant can often appeal this decision or request further examination.

6. Post-Grant Procedures

- **Opposition and Maintenance**: After a patent is granted, it can be opposed by third parties within a certain period. Patent holders must also pay maintenance or renewal fees to keep the patent in force.

The examination and granting of patents are meticulously designed to balance the rights of inventors with the public interest. By ensuring that only genuine, non-obvious, and useful inventions are patented, patent offices play a crucial role in fostering innovation and promoting economic development.

7.2 Administration of the Patent System

7.2.1 Role of Patent Offices

Maintenance of Patent Databases and Records

The maintenance of patent databases and records is a fundamental responsibility of patent offices. These databases not only store detailed information about patent applications and granted patents but also serve as essential tools for public access, legal research, and the administration of intellectual property rights. Here's how patent offices manage these critical resources:

1. Collection of Data

- **Data Ingestion**: Patent offices collect data from patent applications, which include descriptions of the invention, claims, drawings, applicant information, and legal correspondence throughout the patent's life cycle.
- **Updates and Amendments**: As patents progress through various stages—from application and examination to grant and eventual expiry or renewal—updates are made to reflect current statuses, amendments, legal decisions, and renewal payments.

2. Database Structure and Accessibility

- **Digital Archives**: Modern patent offices maintain sophisticated digital archives that store vast amounts of data in structured formats, making it easy to search and retrieve information.
- **Public Accessibility**: A primary function of these databases is to provide public access. This transparency helps to avoid duplication in research and development and allows businesses and inventors to assess the

patent landscape before pursuing their own patent applications.

3. Search Facilities

- **Search Tools**: Patent databases are equipped with search tools that allow users to perform simple searches by patent number, applicant name, or keyword, as well as complex Boolean searches that combine multiple search criteria.
- **Prior Art Searches**: These databases are crucial for conducting prior art searches, which are necessary both for the examination of new patent applications and for the legal scrutiny of existing patents.

4. International Cooperation and Harmonization

- **Data Sharing**: Patent offices often participate in international data exchange agreements, such as those coordinated by the World Intellectual Property Organization (WIPO). This cooperation helps maintain consistency and accessibility of patent records across borders.
- **Harmonization of Standards**: Efforts are made to harmonize metadata standards and document formats, which facilitates the integration of global patent data and supports the work of multinational corporations and international researchers.

5. Regular Updates and Maintenance

- **System Updates**: Regular updates to the database systems are necessary to incorporate advanced data management technologies, improve user interfaces, and enhance security measures to protect sensitive information.
- **Data Integrity Checks**: Routine checks are conducted to ensure the accuracy and integrity of the data stored. This includes correcting any discrepancies and removing outdated or redundant information.

6. Enhancements and Innovations

- **Machine Learning and AI**: Some patent offices are incorporating machine learning algorithms to improve the efficiency of data processing and to enhance search functionalities, such as image-based searches for patent illustrations.

- **API Access**: Providing application programming interface (API) access to patent databases allows developers to create custom software applications that can automatically query and analyze patent data for specific purposes.

7. Educational and Analytical Resources

- **Analytical Tools**: Beyond basic search and access, many patent offices provide analytical tools that help users understand trends in patent filings, technology areas, and competitive landscapes.
- **Tutorials and Guides**: To assist users in effectively utilizing these databases, patent offices often provide tutorials, guides, and customer support.

The maintenance of comprehensive, accurate, and accessible patent databases is a critical task that supports not only the administrative functions of the patent offices but also the broader innovation ecosystem. These databases enable stakeholders from various sectors to make informed decisions and foster a culture of transparency and innovation.

7.2 Administration of the Patent System

7.2.1 Role of Patent Offices

7.2.1.2 Support and Guidance to Inventors

Providing Resources and Assistance for Patent Applications

Patent offices play an essential role in supporting and guiding inventors through the complex process of securing patent protection. This support is crucial in helping inventors navigate the legal and technical requirements of patent applications and in fostering an environment that encourages innovation. Here's how patent offices provide resources and assistance to inventors:

1. Educational Materials and Resources

- **Patent Information Centers**: Many patent offices establish patent information centers or libraries that offer a range of resources, including access to patent databases, literature on patent law, and industry publications that can help inventors understand the patent landscape in their field.

- **Online Resources and Tools**: Patent offices typically provide a comprehensive website with downloadable forms, guides on how to apply for a patent, explanations of the patent process, and tutorials on searching for prior art.
- **Publications and Manuals**: Detailed manuals on patent practice, frequently asked questions (FAQs), and brochures are made available to clarify the procedures and legal requirements for filing a patent.

2. Workshops, Seminars, and Training Programs

- **Organizing Workshops and Seminars**: Patent offices often conduct workshops, seminars, and webinars aimed at educating inventors about the patent system, recent changes in patent law, and strategies for securing comprehensive patent protection.
- **Training Programs**: Specialized training sessions may be provided, focusing on specific aspects of the patent application process, such as how to draft patent claims, how to respond to office actions, and how to manage a patent once it is granted.

3. One-on-One Assistance

- **Pre-Application Consultations**: Some patent offices offer pre-application consultation services where inventors can receive personalized advice on the patentability of their invention, the appropriateness of their application materials, and strategies for navigating the patent process.
- **Inquiry and Support Desks**: Dedicated support desks or helplines where inventors can ask questions and resolve doubts regarding their applications, either via phone, email, or in-person visits.

4. Financial Assistance Programs

- **Fee Reductions**: Reduced fees for small entities, micro-entities, or individual inventors can make it easier for them to secure patent protection without the burden of high costs.
- **Grants and Subsidies**: Some patent offices provide grants, subsidies, or vouchers that can help cover the costs of patenting, particularly for high-

potential inventions or inventors from underrepresented groups.

5. Online Filing and Management Systems

- **Electronic Filing Systems**: E-filing portals allow inventors to submit their patent applications online, reducing paperwork and speeding up the process.
- **Patent Management Dashboards**: These online tools enable inventors to track the progress of their patent applications, manage their patents post-grant, and handle renewals and other procedural matters.

6. Collaboration with Industry and Academia

- **Partnerships**: Patent offices often partner with universities, research institutions, and industry associations to provide targeted support and resources that cater to the specific needs of inventors in various sectors.
- **Innovation Promotion**: Initiatives that connect inventors with potential investors, business mentors, and commercial partners can help turn patented inventions into successful commercial products.

7.2 Administration of the Patent System

7.2.1 Role of Patent Offices

Educational and Outreach Programs

Patent offices around the world engage in educational and outreach programs designed to promote awareness and understanding of intellectual property (IP) rights, specifically focusing on the importance of patents. These programs are crucial in fostering an innovation-friendly environment that encourages individuals and businesses to protect their inventions. Here's how patent offices implement these educational initiatives:

1. Educational Workshops and Seminars

- **Objective**: To provide hands-on training and information sessions that help inventors, entrepreneurs, and students understand the patent process, from conception to commercialization.
- **Implementation**: Conducting regular workshops and seminars on various topics related to patents, such as how to file a patent application,

how to search for existing patents, understanding patent laws, and learning about the commercial aspects of patenting.

2. Online Learning Modules and Webinars

- **Objective**: To reach a broader audience including those in remote areas or international stakeholders.
- **Implementation**: Offering a range of web-based courses and live webinars that cover foundational and advanced topics in patenting. These often include interactive elements, such as Q&A sessions, to engage participants actively.

3. School and University Programs

- **Objective**: To instill an understanding of IP rights among young students and future innovators.
- **Implementation**: Partnering with educational institutions to integrate IP education into their curricula, hosting guest lectures, and organizing innovation camps or competitions that encourage students to come up with inventive solutions and learn about patents.

4. Public Awareness Campaigns

- **Objective**: To increase general public knowledge about the value of IP and its impact on daily life.
- **Implementation**: Launching multimedia campaigns using videos, infographics, and social media to explain the role of patents in promoting innovation and economic development. These campaigns often highlight case studies of successful inventors and businesses that have benefited from patents.

5. Support for Underrepresented Groups

- **Objective**: To ensure equitable access to patent resources for women, minorities, and economically disadvantaged inventors.
- **Implementation**: Developing specific programs that provide targeted assistance, mentoring, and funding opportunities to help these groups navigate the patent system and bring their inventions to market.

6. Collaboration with Industry and Professional Associations

- **Objective**: To leverage external expertise and networks to extend the reach and impact of IP education.
- **Implementation**: Forming partnerships with professional associations, industry groups, and chambers of commerce to co-host events, distribute informational materials, and facilitate networking opportunities for inventors.

7. International Cooperation

- **Objective**: To harmonize patent education across borders and share best practices internationally.
- **Implementation**: Participating in global forums and working with international organizations such as the World Intellectual Property Organization (WIPO) to develop unified educational resources and conduct joint training programs.

8. Specialized Training for IP Professionals

- **Objective**: To enhance the skills of IP professionals, including patent agents, attorneys, and corporate IP managers.
- **Implementation**: Offering advanced courses and certification programs that focus on the latest developments in patent law, case law analyses, and strategic IP management.

7.2 Administration of the Patent System

7.2.2 Regulatory Bodies and International Organizations

7.2.2.1 World Intellectual Property Organization (WIPO)

Role in Harmonizing International Patent Laws

The World Intellectual Property Organization (WIPO) is a specialized agency of the United Nations dedicated to developing a balanced and accessible international intellectual property (IP) system. WIPO plays a critical role in harmonizing international patent laws, facilitating cooperation and coordination among member states, and providing a framework for the global administration of IP rights. Here's an overview of how WIPO contributes to the harmonization of international patent laws:

1. Facilitating International Treaties and Agreements

- **Function**: WIPO oversees the negotiation and implementation of international treaties that influence patent laws across different countries. These treaties provide a common legal framework that member states can adopt and adapt to their national laws.
- **Examples**:
  - **Patent Cooperation Treaty (PCT)**: The PCT, administered by WIPO, streamlines the filing of patent applications on a global scale, allowing inventors to seek patent protection internationally for their inventions with a single patent application.
  - **Budapest Treaty**: This treaty governs the international recognition of the deposit of microorganisms for patent procedures, standardizing how biological materials are handled in patent applications.

2. Standardizing Patent Information and Documentation

- **Function**: WIPO develops and maintains systems that standardize the exchange and dissemination of patent information. This reduces barriers caused by differing national documentation and helps maintain a transparent, accessible database of global patent information.
- **Implementations**:
  - **WIPO ST.26**: Implementation of new standards like WIPO Standard ST.26, which harmonizes the format for DNA and RNA sequences listings in patent applications, ensuring consistency across national patent offices.
  - **PATENTSCOPE**: WIPO's search service, PATENTSCOPE, provides access to international Patent Cooperation Treaty (PCT) applications and patent documents of participating national and regional patent offices, facilitating easy access to a wealth of patent information.

3. Training and Capacity Building

- **Function**: WIPO conducts training programs and seminars to build capacity in understanding and implementing IP rights under international norms. This helps countries align their laws with global standards.

- **Examples**:

  - **WIPO Academy**: Offers a range of courses and training sessions to IP professionals and the public on various aspects of IP law, including patents.
  - **Technical Assistance Programs**: Provides tailored assistance to developing countries to help them comply with international IP treaties and improve their administrative capabilities.

4. Advocating for IP Policy Development

- **Function**: WIPO serves as a platform for dialogue among countries on emerging IP issues, helping to shape international IP policy in ways that foster innovation and economic development.
- **Impact**:

  - **Global IP Dialogues**: Hosts forums and discussions that address new challenges in patent law, such as the implications of digital innovation, artificial intelligence, and biotechnology.
  - **Influencing Policy Changes**: Recommendations and studies produced by WIPO often inform the policy-making process in member states, guiding them toward more uniform IP standards.

5. Dispute Resolution Services

- **Function**: WIPO provides arbitration and mediation services to resolve disputes over IP across different jurisdictions, offering an alternative to traditional court litigations.
- **Benefit**:

  - These services help parties resolve cross-border IP disputes efficiently and privately, without the complexities of varying national laws.

WIPO's role in harmonizing international patent laws is crucial for creating a more integrated and efficient global IP system. By standardizing practices, facilitating international cooperation, and providing essential resources and services, WIPO supports a patent landscape that nurtures innovation and respects the diverse interests of all stakeholders worldwide.

7.2 Administration of the Patent System

7.2.2 Regulatory Bodies and International Organizations

7.2.2.1 World Intellectual Property Organization (WIPO)

Services and Resources Provided by WIPO

The World Intellectual Property Organization (WIPO) plays a central role in the global intellectual property (IP) landscape, offering a broad array of services and resources designed to facilitate the protection and management of IP across borders. These services are crucial for individuals, businesses, and governments to navigate the complexities of IP rights effectively. Here's an overview of the key services and resources provided by WIPO:

1. Global Databases and Tools

- **PATENTSCOPE**: Provides access to international Patent Cooperation Treaty (PCT) applications and patent documents of participating national and regional patent offices. This search tool is crucial for patent research and prior art searches.
- **Global Brand Database**: Offers a free search of trademarks and brand information from multiple national and international sources, helping businesses protect their brands globally.
- **WIPO Global Design Database**: Enables the free search of industrial designs registered under the Hague System and participating national collections.
- **WIPO Sequence**: Allows users to search and retrieve DNA and amino acid sequences included in patent documentation.

2. International Registration Systems

- **PCT System**: The Patent Cooperation Treaty, administered by WIPO, simplifies the process of filing patents in up to 153 countries through a single international patent application.
- **Madrid System**: Facilitates the registration of trademarks in multiple territories with one application.

- **Hague System**: Provides a practical business solution for registering up to 100 designs in 74 contracting parties covering 92 countries, through one single international application.
- **Lisbon System**: Protects appellations of origin and geographical indications through a single registration procedure.

3. IP Law and Policy Support

- **Advisory Services**: WIPO offers legal and technical assistance to member states in developing and strengthening their IP laws in line with international standards.
- **Policy Discussions and Forums**: Hosts various global meetings and discussions to shape future IP policy, addressing new challenges such as digital transformation, artificial intelligence, and genetic resources.

4. Capacity Building and Training

- **WIPO Academy**: Provides a range of education and training programs in IP, including distance learning and face-to-face courses tailored for different audiences, from IP professionals to students.
- **Customized Workshops and Seminars**: Conducts workshops and seminars in collaboration with member states, focusing on specific IP issues relevant to the region or sector.

5. Arbitration and Mediation Services

- **WIPO Arbitration and Mediation Center**: Offers alternative dispute resolution options for resolving international commercial disputes between private parties, particularly useful in resolving cross-border IP disputes efficiently and confidentially.

6. Development and Innovation Promotion

- **IP for Development**: Focuses on integrating IP into national development plans and strategies, providing tools, funding, and resources to help developing countries use IP for economic, social, and cultural development.

- **Innovation Promotion**: Initiatives such as WIPO GREEN and WIPO Re:Search foster collaborations to address global challenges like climate change and public health through innovative IP-based solutions.

7. Technical Infrastructure Support

- **IP Office Infrastructure**: Provides technical assistance and software to modernize national IP offices, improving their processing capabilities and public access to IP services.

WIPO's comprehensive suite of services and resources supports the worldwide protection and management of intellectual property, fostering innovation and creativity for economic development and cultural enrichment globally. These services help ensure that the benefits of the IP system are accessible to all, from individual creators and inventors to large enterprises and governments.

7.2 Administration of the Patent System

7.2.2 Regulatory Bodies and International Organizations

Collaboration Between National and International Bodies

Collaboration between national and international bodies is crucial for the effective administration of intellectual property (IP) rights across different jurisdictions. This cooperation helps in harmonizing standards, sharing best practices, and facilitating the efficient processing of IP applications globally. Here's an overview of how national and international bodies collaborate in the realm of intellectual property:

1. Treaty Implementation and Harmonization

- **Function**: International treaties provide a framework for IP protection that member countries agree to implement. National IP offices collaborate with international bodies to harmonize their local laws with these international standards.
- **Examples**:
    - **World Intellectual Property Organization (WIPO)**: Facilitates the administration of multiple IP treaties like the Paris Convention, the Patent Cooperation Treaty (PCT), and the Madrid System for

trademarks.

- **World Trade Organization (WTO)**: Administers the Agreement on Trade-Related Aspects of Intellectual Property Rights (TRIPS), which sets minimum standards for many forms of intellectual property regulation as applied to nationals of other WTO Members.

2. Data Sharing and Accessibility

- **Function**: Sharing data between national and international bodies ensures that information on IP rights is accessible globally, aiding in transparency and the prevention of IP rights infringement.
- **Tools and Initiatives**:

  - **Global Databases**: Tools like WIPO's PATENTSCOPE, Global Brand Database, and others, are made possible through the collaboration of various national IP offices providing access to their patent, trademark, and design data.
  - **Common Portal Access**: Efforts to create common portals that allow simultaneous searching of multiple national and international databases improve the efficiency of prior art searches and legal research.

3. Joint Training and Capacity Building

- **Function**: To strengthen the capabilities of IP professionals worldwide and to ensure a uniform understanding of IP systems.
- **Activities**:

  - **WIPO Academy**: Offers tailored training programs that are often developed in collaboration with national IP offices, providing both online and in-person courses.
  - **Regional and International Workshops**: Regular workshops and seminars are held in collaboration with local IP offices, targeting specific regional issues and promoting best practices in IP management.

4. Development and Technical Assistance Programs

- **Function**: To assist developing countries and countries in transition to develop and strengthen their IP strategies to support economic development.
- **Programs**:

  - **IP Development Plans**: International organizations work with national governments to integrate IP into national economic development plans.
  - **Technical Assistance**: Provision of software systems for managing IP and training for the staff of national IP offices.

5. Enforcement and Legal Cooperation

- **Function**: To ensure that IP rights are enforceable across borders with the support of international cooperation.
- **Mechanisms**:

  - **Cross-Border Enforcement Initiatives**: Collaboration on enforcement issues helps in tackling global challenges like counterfeiting and piracy.
  - **Judicial and Legal Training**: Enhancing the capability of judiciary systems across countries to handle IP disputes consistently and fairly.

6. Collaborative Policy Development

- **Function**: To address emerging IP challenges and align global policy responses.
- **Focus Areas**:

  - **Digital Technologies and IP**: Addressing issues arising from digital innovations, including copyright in the digital environment, patents related to software, and more.
  - **Biotechnology and Genetics**: Harmonizing approaches to the patenting of biotechnological inventions and ensuring ethical considerations are met.

The collaboration between national and international bodies in IP administration not only strengthens the global IP system but also ensures that it remains adaptive and responsive to new challenges. These partnerships are vital for promoting innovation and creativity across borders, supporting economic growth, and ensuring that the benefits of the IP system are shared globally.

7.3 Case Studies in IPR

7.3.1 Real-World Examples

7.3.1.1 Landmark Patent Disputes

Key Cases in the Pharmaceutical Industry

The pharmaceutical industry frequently sees some of the most high-stakes and complex patent disputes, given the immense research and development costs, the potential for significant profits, and the impact on public health. These disputes often set precedents and guide patent law interpretations. Below are key landmark cases that have shaped the landscape of pharmaceutical patents.

1. Merck Co. vs. Integra Lifesciences I, Ltd.

- **Summary**: This 2005 case reached the U.S. Supreme Court, which ruled on the scope of the "safe harbor" provision of 35 U.S.C. § 271(e)(1). The provision exempts from infringement certain uses of patented inventions that are solely for uses reasonably related to the development and submission of information to the FDA.
- **Outcome**: The Supreme Court ruled in favor of Merck, stating that the use of patented compounds in preclinical studies is protected under the safe harbor provision as long as there is a reasonable basis for believing that the experiments will produce the types of information that are relevant to an IND or NDA submission to the FDA.
- **Impact**: This decision was significant for pharmaceutical companies and researchers, broadening the scope of permissible experimentation with patented compounds without facing infringement suits.

2. KSR International Co. vs. Teleflex Inc.

- **Summary**: Although not exclusively a pharmaceutical case, the 2007 Supreme Court decision in KSR International Co. vs. Teleflex Inc. had profound implications across all industries, including pharmaceuticals. The case addressed the standards for proving obviousness under United

States patent law.

- **Outcome**: The Supreme Court rejected the rigid application of the "teaching, suggestion, or motivation" test for determining obviousness and favored a more flexible approach that considers "common sense" among skilled artisans.
- **Impact**: This ruling affects pharmaceutical patents by making it more challenging to obtain patent protection for inventions that might be deemed obvious combinations of existing knowledge.

3. Association for Molecular Pathology v. Myriad Genetics

- **Summary**: This landmark 2013 U.S. Supreme Court case addressed whether human genes could be patented. Myriad Genetics held patents related to the BRCA1 and BRCA2 genes, mutations of which are associated with higher risks of breast and ovarian cancer.
- **Outcome**: The Supreme Court ruled that naturally occurring DNA sequences could not be patented merely because they had been isolated, although synthetic and cDNA (complementary DNA) sequences could be eligible for patent protection.
- **Impact**: This ruling significantly impacted the biotechnology and pharmaceutical industries by limiting the ability to patent natural genetic sequences, thus opening up more research opportunities in genomics and personalized medicine.

4. Novartis AG v. Union of India & Others

- **Summary**: This high-profile case involved Novartis' challenge to India's patent laws after its patent application for a new version of its cancer drug, Gleevec, was denied under Indian law focusing on the non-patentability of incremental inventions that do not significantly improve efficacy.
- **Outcome**: The Indian Supreme Court upheld the denial in 2013, arguing that the new version of Gleevec did not demonstrate a significant efficacy increase over the old version.
- **Impact**: This case had a profound influence on global pharmaceutical patent strategies, particularly regarding the patentability standards in emerging markets. It highlighted the tension between pharmaceutical innovation and access to medicines.

These cases exemplify the complexities and high stakes involved in pharmaceutical patent disputes. They demonstrate the balance courts must maintain between encouraging innovation through patent protection and ensuring public access to affordable medicines. Such disputes often lead to significant legal precedents that can have wide-ranging implications for the pharmaceutical industry globally.

7.3 Case Studies in IPR

7.3.1 Real-World Examples

High-Profile Technology Patent Wars

The technology sector has witnessed some of the most intense and high-stakes patent wars, involving major corporations battling over intellectual property rights associated with innovative technologies. These disputes often involve multiple jurisdictions and can affect market dynamics significantly. Here are some notable high-profile technology patent wars:

1. Apple vs. Samsung

- **Overview**: Perhaps the most famous of the modern technology patent wars, this legal battle involved Apple accusing Samsung of infringing on various patents related to the design and functionality of its smartphones and tablets.
- **Key Developments**:
  - **Initial Claims and Counterclaims**: Apple filed a lawsuit in 2011 claiming that Samsung's smartphones and tablets infringed on Apple's patents, trademarks, and user interface designs. Samsung countered with its own lawsuits alleging that Apple infringed on Samsung's patents.
  - **Verdicts and Settlements**: After several years of courtroom battles across multiple countries, the most notable verdict came in 2012 when a U.S. jury awarded Apple over $1 billion in damages, which was later reduced and followed by numerous appeals and retrials. The legal battle continued until mid-2018 when the companies settled for an undisclosed amount.
- **Impact**: This case highlighted issues regarding patent scope and the competition within the tech industry, influencing how companies

approach product design and development to avoid litigation.

2. Qualcomm vs. Apple

- **Overview**: Qualcomm and Apple have been involved in a sprawling global dispute over patents and licensing fees that impact the cost and functionality of mobile devices.
- **Key Developments**:
    - **Royalty Disputes**: Apple sued Qualcomm in January 2017, accusing it of charging unfair royalties for "technologies they have nothing to do with" and failing to pay contractual rebates. Qualcomm countersued, claiming that Apple breached and mischaracterized agreements and negotiations.
    - **Global Litigations and Settlements**: After numerous lawsuits and countersuits in various countries, the companies reached a settlement in April 2019 where Apple agreed to pay Qualcomm an undisclosed sum and entered a six-year licensing agreement.
- **Impact**: The settlement was a significant development in the mobile communications market, affecting supply chains and the future of mobile technology innovations.

3. Google vs. Oracle

- **Overview**: This landmark case involved Oracle accusing Google of copyright infringement for using Java APIs in the Android operating system without the proper license.
- **Key Developments**:
    - **Legal Battles**: Initiated in 2010, the case saw multiple court decisions, with Oracle initially claiming that Google should pay substantial damages. The core issue was whether Java APIs were copyrightable and, if so, whether Google's use constituted "fair use."
    - **Supreme Court Ruling**: In April 2021, the U.S. Supreme Court ruled in favor of Google, declaring that its use of Java APIs was fair use as it transformed the code into a new and transformative program.

- **Impact**: The decision was a significant win for software developers, reaffirming the importance of fair use provisions in software development, potentially influencing how APIs are used and shared in the tech community.

4. Nvidia vs. Samsung and Qualcomm

- **Overview**: Nvidia filed complaints against Samsung and Qualcomm in 2014, alleging that the companies infringed on its GPU patents.
- **Key Developments**:
    - **ITC Involvement and Lawsuits**: Nvidia sought to block shipments of Samsung and Qualcomm products that it claimed were using Nvidia's patented technology without permission. The International Trade Commission (ITC) initially ruled against Nvidia, which was a significant setback.
    - **Settlement**: The parties eventually settled in May 2016, with a cross-licensing agreement, the terms of which were not disclosed.
- **Impact**: This case underscored the strategic use of patent litigation in the semiconductor industry and highlighted the complexities of patent enforcement in technology involving integrated circuits and software.

These technology patent wars illustrate the complex interplay between innovation, competition, and intellectual property law. They not only affect the companies involved but also set precedents that impact industry practices, patent law interpretations, and technology development trajectories globally.

7.3 Case Studies in IPR

7.3.1 Real-World Examples

7.3.1.2 Successful Patent Commercialization

Commercializing patents effectively can transform innovative ideas into successful market products, driving business growth and contributing to economic development. Here are some notable examples of patents that have led to successful products, showcasing the potential of effective IP management and commercialization strategies.

1. The Wright Brothers' Flying Machine (Patent No. 821,393)

- **Overview**: The Wright Brothers, Orville and Wilbur, secured a patent in 1906 for their flying machine, which is considered the first practical fixed-wing aircraft.
- **Commercialization**: Though initially facing skepticism, the successful flights and demonstrations of their aircraft designs eventually led to significant contracts with both the U.S. and foreign governments, setting the foundation for the modern aviation industry.
- **Impact**: The patent not only protected their invention but also provided them the leverage needed to negotiate contracts and partnerships, thereby commercializing their technology effectively.

2. Google's PageRank Algorithm (Patent No. 6,285,999)

- **Overview**: In 2001, Larry Page, co-founder of Google, received a patent for the PageRank algorithm, which was crucial in the early development of Google's search engine.
- **Commercialization**: The patented algorithm allowed Google to produce superior search results compared to its competitors, which was integral to its rapid rise and dominance in the search engine market.
- **Impact**: This patent was critical in establishing Google's competitive advantage, leading to its IPO in 2004 and its expansion into various other technology sectors.

3. Apple's Slide-to-Unlock Feature (Patent No. 8,046,721)

- **Overview**: Granted in 2011, this patent covers the technology for unlocking a touch-screen device by sliding a finger across a specific set of points on the screen, a feature that became iconic with the iPhone.
- **Commercialization**: This feature was one of many that helped differentiate iPhone products from their competitors, contributing to the global success of Apple's mobile devices.
- **Impact**: The slide-to-unlock patent was also at the center of several patent lawsuits, underscoring its value to Apple in protecting its innovative user interface.

4. Tesla's Electric Vehicle Powertrain (Patent No. 8,078,499)

- **Overview**: Tesla Motors was granted this patent in 2011, which relates to the technology used in their electric vehicles' powertrain.
- **Commercialization**: Tesla's approach to patenting has been unique; in 2014, CEO Elon Musk announced that they would not initiate patent lawsuits against anyone who, in good faith, wanted to use their technology. This helped speed up the adoption of electric vehicle technology industry-wide.
- **Impact**: Despite the open approach, the patent portfolio has significantly contributed to Tesla's brand reputation as an innovator and leader in electric vehicle technology.

5. CRISPR Gene Editing Technology

- **Overview**: CRISPR (Clustered Regularly Interspaced Short Palindromic Repeats) technology, which has revolutionized gene editing, has been subject to multiple high-profile patents with claims from the Broad Institute and UC Berkeley.
- **Commercialization**: The technology has vast applications in medicine, agriculture, and biotechnology. Companies like Editas Medicine, CRISPR Therapeutics, and others have been founded to commercialize CRISPR technologies.
- **Impact**: Patents covering CRISPR are potentially worth billions of dollars in the biotechnology industry, making them some of the most valuable patents in modern times.

These examples illustrate how successfully patented innovations can lead to groundbreaking products that not only capture significant market share but also create entirely new markets. Effective patent commercialization involves strategic IP management, development, and sometimes litigation, underscoring the importance of a robust patent strategy in the commercial success of technological innovations.

Strategies for Leveraging Patents for Business Growth

Patents can be a powerful tool for driving business growth, providing a competitive edge, and enhancing market position. Here are key strategies businesses can employ to effectively leverage patents:

1. Protect Core Technologies

- **Rationale**: Securing patents for core technologies or products can create a unique selling proposition and prevent competitors from entering your market space.
- **Application**: Focus on obtaining robust and broad patent protection for technologies or products that are central to your business's value proposition. This ensures legal exclusivity in key areas of your business.

2. Licensing Agreements

- **Rationale**: Licensing patents can provide a significant revenue stream without the necessity of manufacturing or marketing the products yourself.
- **Application**: Develop a licensing strategy to allow other companies to use your patented technology. This can be particularly effective in markets where you do not have a presence or in industries where your technology can be applied to different products.

3. Cross-Licensing

- **Rationale**: Cross-licensing can allow businesses to bypass potential patent infringement disputes and gain access to technologies that complement their own, enhancing product offerings.
- **Application**: Engage with other firms holding patents in related fields to negotiate cross-licensing deals. This is common in high-tech industries like electronics and software, where overlapping technologies are prevalent.

4. Enhancing Brand Reputation and Attracting Investments

- **Rationale**: Patents can enhance the reputation of a business by showcasing a commitment to innovation, which can be attractive to investors and customers.
- **Application**: Publicize patent holdings in marketing materials to highlight innovation capabilities. Use a strong patent portfolio as part of the pitch to potential investors to demonstrate the protected, proprietary technology base of your business.

5. Strategic Patenting to Block Competitors

- **Rationale**: Obtaining patents on key methods and components can create barriers to entry, preventing competitors from easily replicating your products or technologies.
- **Application**: Develop a strategy that involves patenting various applications and improvements of core technologies, thus building a "patent thicket" that covers all feasible variations and uses of your technology.

6. Defensive Publication

- **Rationale**: In cases where patent protection is not the best strategy, publishing details of an invention can prevent others from obtaining a patent on it, keeping the field open.
- **Application**: Use defensive publications for inventions that are important to keep in the public domain or are not worth the cost of a patent application but for which you want to ensure no competitor can claim a patent.

7. Patents as a Tool for Negotiation

- **Rationale**: In the event of litigation, owning patents can provide leverage in negotiations, potentially leading to settlements that are favorable.
- **Application**: Use your patents as bargaining chips during negotiations or in settlement discussions if faced with litigation from other businesses.

8. Developing a Global IP Strategy

- **Rationale**: Patents are territorial; therefore, protecting your invention in key markets is crucial for global business operations.
- **Application**: Assess the primary markets for your products and secure patent protection in those countries. Consider using international patent systems like the Patent Cooperation Treaty (PCT) to manage and streamline patent filings across multiple jurisdictions.

9. Monitoring and Enforcement

- **Rationale**: Actively monitoring the market for potential infringements and enforcing patent rights are necessary to realize the full value of patents.

- **Application**: Implement a monitoring system to detect potential patent infringements, and be prepared to enforce your patents through legal actions if necessary. This demonstrates your commitment to protecting your IP and deters potential infringers.

By employing these strategies, businesses can effectively leverage their patents to not only protect innovations but also to spur business growth, enhance competitive positioning, and increase market share.

Strategies for Leveraging Patents for Business Growth

Patents can be a powerful tool for driving business growth, providing a competitive edge, and enhancing market position. Here are key strategies businesses can employ to effectively leverage patents:

1. Protect Core Technologies

- **Rationale**: Securing patents for core technologies or products can create a unique selling proposition and prevent competitors from entering your market space.
- **Application**: Focus on obtaining robust and broad patent protection for technologies or products that are central to your business's value proposition. This ensures legal exclusivity in key areas of your business.

2. Licensing Agreements

- **Rationale**: Licensing patents can provide a significant revenue stream without the necessity of manufacturing or marketing the products yourself.
- **Application**: Develop a licensing strategy to allow other companies to use your patented technology

7.3 Case Studies in IPR

7.3.2 Lessons Learned

7.3.2.1 Common Challenges and Solutions

Navigating the complex landscape of intellectual property rights, particularly patents, presents numerous challenges for businesses. Understanding these challenges and learning effective solutions can greatly aid organizations in managing their IP strategically. Below are some common challenges encountered in IP management, along with practical solutions to overcome them.

Navigating Complex Legal Landscapes

- **Challenge**: The legal frameworks governing patents vary significantly between jurisdictions, complicating the process of obtaining and enforcing IP rights internationally.
- **Solutions**:
    - **International Strategy**: Develop a clear international patent strategy that identifies key markets and tailors patent filings to the specific legal requirements and business goals in those regions.
    - **Expert Guidance**: Engage with IP lawyers and patent agents who specialize in international law and have expertise in the jurisdictions where protection is sought. Their local knowledge is invaluable.
    - **Use of Treaties**: Utilize international treaties like the Patent Cooperation Treaty (PCT) or the European Patent Convention (EPC) to streamline filings across multiple jurisdictions.

Overcoming Enforcement and Infringement Issues

- **Challenge**: Enforcing patents can be costly and complex, especially when infringement occurs across different countries.
- **Solutions**:
    - **Proactive Monitoring**: Implement regular monitoring of the market to quickly identify potential infringements. This can be done through specialized services that scan for patent breaches.
    - **Building a Legal Framework**: Establish a robust legal framework before launching products. This includes clear patent markings on products and informative materials that assert your patent rights.
    - **Litigation Readiness**: Prepare for potential litigation by setting aside resources and maintaining a litigation fund. Also, develop a relationship with a legal firm that understands your technology and

has experience in IP litigation.

- **Alternative Dispute Resolution (ADR)**: Consider using mediation or arbitration for resolving disputes as these can be less adversarial, faster, and more cost-effective than court proceedings.

Adapting to Rapid Technological Changes

- **Challenge**: Rapid innovation can render existing patents obsolete and make it challenging to protect ongoing developments.
- **Solutions**:

  - **Continuous Innovation and IP Review**: Foster a culture of continuous innovation within your organization and regularly review your IP portfolio to ensure it aligns with current technologies and market trends.
  - **Defensive Publishing**: If obtaining a patent is not practical, consider defensive publishing, which involves disclosing details of innovations publicly to prevent others from patenting similar ideas.
  - **Flexible IP Strategies**: Develop flexible strategies that can adapt to technological advancements, such as filing for utility models or design patents that may be obtained faster and offer shorter-term protection for incremental innovations.

Dealing with Patent Thickets and Blocking Patents

- **Challenge**: Navigating patent thickets and dealing with blocking patents can hinder product development and market entry.
- **Solutions**:

  - **Cross-Licensing Agreements**: Negotiate cross-licensing deals with patent holders to gain access to necessary technologies. This can be mutually beneficial and promote a cooperative environment.
  - **Purchasing or Licensing IP**: Consider purchasing or licensing patents that block your product development if cross-licensing is not an option. This direct approach can often resolve potential conflicts.
  - **Innovation Around Patents**: Encourage your R&D team to design around existing patents or innovate new solutions that do not infringe on existing patents.

The key to overcoming these common challenges in patent management is strategic planning, informed decision-making, and proactive management of IP assets. By understanding these challenges and implementing effective strategies, businesses can leverage their intellectual property to secure competitive advantages and drive long-term growth.

7.3 Case Studies in IPR

7.3.2 Lessons Learned

7.3.2.2 Best Practices for Innovators

Effective management of intellectual property (IP) is crucial for innovators looking to maximize the value and impact of their inventions. Here are some best practices for navigating the complexities of patent protection and leveraging IP for strategic advantage:

Importance of Thorough Patent Searches and Strategic Planning

- **Thorough Patent Searches**:
    - **Purpose**: Conducting comprehensive patent searches is essential not only to ensure that your invention is novel and non-obvious but also to understand the competitive landscape and potential barriers to entry.
    - **Process**: Utilize various patent databases such as USPTO, EPO, JPO, and WIPO's PATENTSCOPE. Consider hiring a professional patent searcher or using advanced AI-driven search tools to uncover relevant prior art.
    - **Benefits**: Identifies potential infringement risks, informs R&D directions to avoid existing patents, and helps refine patent applications to increase their robustness.
- **Strategic Planning**:
    - **Long-Term IP Strategy**: Develop a strategic plan that aligns IP objectives with business goals. This should include timelines for patent filings, plans for commercialization, and strategies for international patent protection.
    - **Portfolio Management**: Regularly review and manage your patent portfolio to ensure it continues to align with your business's evolving

needs and priorities. This includes decisions on renewing patents, abandoning non-core IP, or expanding into new technological areas.

- **Integration with Business Development**: Integrate IP considerations into product development, marketing, and business expansion plans to leverage IP assets fully and avoid market entry barriers.

Collaborating with Legal and Industry Experts

- **Partnering with IP Attorneys:**

  - **Selection**: Choose attorneys or legal firms that specialize in your industry and have a deep understanding of the specific technologies and legal issues involved.
  - **Collaboration**: Work closely with your legal team from the early stages of the innovation process. This ensures that all potential intellectual property rights are identified and protected from the outset. Collaborative efforts should focus on crafting robust patent applications, handling the complexities of international IP filings, and strategizing against potential infringement. Regular meetings and updates are crucial to keep the legal team aligned with the ongoing developments and adjustments in project direction. This proactive involvement can greatly mitigate risks and enhance the prospects of successful patent grants and protection.

CHAPTER EIGHT

TECHNOLOGICAL INNOVATION AND PATENTING

8.1 Technological Research and Innovation

8.1.1 From Idea to Patent

8.1.1.1 Ideation and Conceptualization

Identifying and Refining Innovative Ideas

The journey from an initial idea to a patented invention is complex and multifaceted, requiring not only creativity but also a strategic approach to development and protection. Here's how innovators can effectively navigate the ideation and conceptualization phase to lay a solid foundation for successful patenting.

Understanding the Ideation Process

- **Creative Brainstorming**: This is the initial stage where the goal is to generate a broad range of ideas without concern for feasibility or limitations. Techniques such as mind mapping, brainstorming sessions, and SCAMPER (Substitute, Combine, Adapt, Modify, Put to another use, Eliminate, Reverse) can facilitate creative thinking.
- **Problem Identification**: Start with identifying a problem that needs solving. This problem-oriented approach ensures that the idea has practical utility, enhancing its potential for commercial success and patentability.

Research and Preliminary Analysis

- **Market Research**: Investigate the current market to identify gaps and needs that your invention might fill. Understanding consumer demands and existing solutions can help refine the idea into something both innovative and commercially viable.
- **Technological Research**: Delve into existing technologies and current research to ensure that the idea is novel. This includes reviewing scientific literature, existing patents, and industry publications to avoid duplicating existing solutions.

Refining and Defining the Concept

- **Feasibility Assessment**: Evaluate the technical feasibility of the idea. This may involve preliminary experiments, prototyping, or theoretical analysis to ascertain whether the concept can be realistically implemented.
- **Iterative Refinement**: Refine the idea based on feedback from initial assessments and trials. This iterative process helps hone in on the most viable and innovative aspects of the concept.

Documenting the Invention

- **Detailed Documentation**: Keep a detailed record of the development process, including notes, sketches, and experimental results. This documentation can be crucial for patent applications and proving the provenance of the idea.
- **Confidentiality Measures**: At this stage, confidentiality is key. Use non-disclosure agreements (NDAs) when discussing the idea with potential partners, consultants, or other external parties to prevent premature disclosure that could jeopardize patent rights.

Assessing Patentability

- **Initial Patent Screening**: Conduct an initial check to determine if the idea meets basic patentability criteria: novelty, non-obviousness, and utility. This can be done in consultation with a patent attorney or through preliminary patent searches.

- **Engage with Patent Professionals**: Early engagement with IP professionals can provide valuable guidance on the patentability of the invention and the strategic steps needed for protection.

Strategic Planning for Patent Application

- **Patent Strategy Development**: Develop a comprehensive patent strategy that considers which aspects of the invention should be patented, potential markets, and how the patent fits into the broader business strategy.
- **Preparing for Application**: Plan the timing and scope of the patent application. Deciding when to file can be as crucial as the content of the application, especially in fast-moving fields where delaying can mean losing out to competitors.

8.1 Technological Research and Innovation

8.1.1 From Idea to Patent

Conceptual Frameworks and Brainstorming Techniques

Innovators can significantly benefit from structured approaches and methodologies to help navigate the ideation process. Conceptual frameworks and brainstorming techniques can facilitate the generation and refinement of ideas, providing a systematic approach to creativity and problem-solving. Here's an overview of effective frameworks and techniques that can enhance the ideation phase:

Conceptual Frameworks

1. **SCAMPER**: This technique prompts users to think about possible changes to existing products or services to create something new by applying the following manipulations: Substitute, Combine, Adapt, Modify, Put to another use, Eliminate, and Reverse.
2. **TRIZ (Theory of Inventive Problem Solving)**:

    - **Overview**: Developed by Soviet inventor Genrich Altshuller, TRIZ is a problem-solving, analysis, and forecasting tool derived from the study of patterns of invention in the global patent literature. It offers a systematic approach for understanding and solving inventive problems.

- **Application:** TRIZ provides tools and strategies such as the 40 Inventive Principles and the Contradiction Matrix to help inventors break free of psychological inertia and find innovative solutions to difficult problems.

1. **Design Thinking:**

- **Overview:** This user-centered methodology helps teams produce practical and innovative solutions by focusing on understanding the user's needs.
- **Process:** It involves five phases—Empathize, Define, Ideate, Prototype, and Test. Design thinking is particularly useful when addressing complex problems that are ill-defined or unknown.

4. **Six Thinking Hats:**

- **Overview:** Developed by Edward de Bono, this technique involves assuming different perspectives, symbolized by hats of different colors, to explore different aspects of a problem or to generate ideas in a thorough and methodical way.
- **Usage:** Each "hat" represents a different direction of thinking (optimism, judgment, emotion, data, creativity, and management), facilitating structured discussions that cover all angles of a problem.

Brainstorming Techniques

1. **Classic Brainstorming:**

- **Description:** In a group setting, participants are encouraged to think freely and suggest as many ideas as possible, fostering a non-judgmental atmosphere that values creativity and quantity over quality.
- **Tip:** Use a facilitator to guide the session and record all ideas without critique; evaluation comes later.

2. **Mind Mapping:**

- **Description**: This visual tool helps organize information, connecting related concepts around a central subject.
- **Application**: Start with a central idea and branch out with related attributes or sub-topics, using lines to connect related ideas, which helps in visualizing relationships and developing new solutions.

3. **Reverse Brainstorming**:

- **Description**: Instead of looking for solutions to a problem, participants seek ways to cause the problem. This reverse thinking can illuminate potential problems before they occur and stimulate innovative ways to prevent or solve them.
- **Application**: Once all possible ways to cause the problem are listed, reverse these actions to find potential solutions.

4. **Rapid Ideation**:

- **Description**: Participants are given a short time (usually a few minutes) to write down as many ideas as possible about a given topic or problem.
- **Usage**: This technique is useful in breaking through initial thought barriers and uncovering unexpected insights.

By integrating these conceptual frameworks and brainstorming techniques into the ideation process, innovators can enhance their creative output and develop more robust, innovative solutions that are more likely to succeed in the patent process and in the marketplace.

8.1.1.2 Research and Development (R&D)

Conducting Feasibility Studies and Experiments

Research and Development (R&D) is a critical phase in the lifecycle of any innovation, especially when transitioning from an idea to a patentable invention. Conducting thorough feasibility studies and experiments is essential to validate the practicality and novelty of an idea. Here's how to effectively manage this phase:

Feasibility Studies

1. **Purpose of Feasibility Studies**:

- **Risk Assessment**: Identify potential economic, technical, and legal risks associated with the project.
- **Resource Evaluation**: Determine if the necessary resources (time, budget, skills) are available to develop the idea into a working prototype or final product.
- **Market Viability**: Analyze the market demand, potential competition, and profitability of the invention.

2. **Components of a Feasibility Study**:

- **Technical Feasibility**: Assesses whether the current technology is capable of achieving the invention's objectives. This often involves preliminary technical experiments and proof-of-concept models.
- **Economic Feasibility**: Evaluates the cost-effectiveness of the invention, estimating production costs and potential sales to determine if the project can meet its financial goals.
- **Legal Feasibility**: Examines existing patents and regulatory requirements to ensure that the invention does not infringe on other patents and meets all compliance standards.

Conducting Experiments

1. **Experiment Planning**:

- **Objective Setting**: Clearly define what you intend to achieve or prove through the experiments.
- **Methodology Design**: Develop a structured approach for conducting experiments, including control groups, necessary equipment, and data collection methods.

2. **Implementation**:

- **Prototyping and Testing**: Build functional prototypes to test theories and improve the design based on testing outcomes. This iterative process often leads to refinements in the product design or concept.
- **Data Collection and Analysis**: Collect comprehensive data during experiments to support conclusions or further adjustments. Analyzing this data accurately is crucial for validating the invention's

functionality and effectiveness.

3. **Documentation**:

    - **Detailed Records**: Keep meticulous records of all experimental procedures, observations, and results. This documentation is crucial for patent applications and can provide evidence of the invention's development stages.
    - **Intellectual Property Considerations**: Ensure that all experimental data and related information are kept confidential to protect the intellectual property.

Iterative Development and Refinement

- **Iterative Testing**: Use the feedback from initial testing phases to make incremental improvements to the invention. This agile approach helps in refining the prototype until it meets the desired specifications and performance criteria.
- **End-user Feedback**: If possible, gather feedback from potential end-users or stakeholders to ensure the final product will meet market needs and expectations.

Evaluation and Decision Making

- **Review Findings**: Regularly review the findings from feasibility studies and experiments to make informed decisions about the continuation, modification, or termination of the project.
- **Pivot when Necessary**: Be prepared to pivot the project focus based on experimental results or external factors such as new technological advancements or changes in market demands.

The R&D phase is foundational in transforming an idea into a viable, patentable invention. Effective management of feasibility studies and experimental processes not only strengthens the potential for successful patent outcomes but also lays the groundwork for commercial success in subsequent phases.

Documenting Research Processes and Results

Documenting the research process and results is an essential step in the development of a patentable invention. This documentation not only provides a written record necessary for patent applications but also serves as valuable proof of the conception and development of the invention. Here's how innovators can effectively document their research processes and results:

1. Establish a Lab Notebook or Digital Documentation System

- **Purpose**: A lab notebook or a secure digital documentation system is vital for maintaining a chronological, detailed record of all experimental research, design iterations, and development activities related to the invention.
- **Best Practices**:
    - Use bound notebooks with consecutively numbered pages or secure, time-stamped digital entries to prevent tampering.
    - Include detailed descriptions of the research process, experimental setups, methodologies, and all changes made over time.

2. Record Detailed Descriptions of Experiments

- **What to Include**: For each experiment or test, document the purpose, date, setup (including control variables), procedures followed, materials used, data collected, and any observations or unexpected results.
- **Clarity and Detail**: Ensure that the entries are clear and detailed enough for another expert in the field to replicate the experiment and validate the results.

3. Include Sketches, Diagrams, and Photographs

- **Visual Documentation**: Supplement textual entries with sketches, diagrams, and photographs of equipment setups, prototypes, and experimental results. These visual aids can provide a clearer understanding of the invention and its development.
- **Labeling and Description**: Make sure all visual elements are well-labeled and include descriptions in the documentation that explain what each visual represents.

4. Document All Modifications and Iterations

- **Track Changes**: Record every modification, no matter how small, to the design or process of the invention. This demonstrates the progression and refinement of the idea over time.
- **Rationale for Changes**: Include explanations for why changes were made, linking them to specific experiment results or theoretical insights.

5. Securely Store and Backup Documentation

- **Physical and Digital Security**: Maintain the documentation in a secure location. If using digital formats, ensure proper cybersecurity measures are in place, including backups, encryption, and secure access controls.
- **Regular Backups**: Regularly back up digital records to prevent data loss due to hardware failures, cybersecurity incidents, or other unforeseen events.

6. Legal and Date Verification

- **Witness Signatures**: Where possible, have a witness (who understands the content but does not have a competing interest) sign off on new entries to verify the dates and content. This can provide additional legal robustness.
- **Date Every Entry**: Every entry in your documentation should be dated. If using a digital system, ensure that the date and time stamps cannot be altered.

7. Confidentiality and Disclosure Considerations

- **Controlled Access**: Limit access to the documentation to involved parties who have agreed to confidentiality, typically through non-disclosure agreements (NDAs).
- **Consider IP Implications:** Be cautious about disclosing contents publicly or in non-confidential settings until a patent application is filed, as premature disclosure can jeopardize patent rights.

Effective documentation is not only a requirement for patent filings but also a critical tool for managing the intellectual property lifecycle. It supports the legal protection of ideas, facilitates the handover to development teams, and can be crucial in defending the inventor's rights during patent enforcement or litigation.

8.1.1.3 Prototyping and Testing

Creating Prototypes and Testing for Functionality

Prototyping and testing are critical phases in the development of any new product or technology. They allow innovators to translate conceptual designs into tangible forms and to evaluate these forms for functionality, design integrity, and user interaction. Here's a detailed look at how to effectively manage these essential steps.

1. Developing the Prototype

- **Initial Prototyping**:
  - **Purpose**: The initial prototypes are typically created to transform the theoretical design into a physical or digital model. This step is crucial for understanding whether and how the design works in the real world.
  - **Approach**: Start with low-fidelity prototypes such as sketches or basic models to test basic functions and design concepts. These can be made from simpler and cheaper materials or using software simulations.
- **Iterative Design**:
  - **Process**: Based on feedback and results from initial testing, refine the prototype iteratively. This may involve multiple rounds of modifications and enhancements to improve the design, functionality, and user experience.
  - **Documentation**: Document each version of the prototype, noting changes and the reasons for these changes. This documentation will be crucial for both patent applications and future product development.

2. Testing the Prototype

- **Functional Testing**:

- **Objective**: Assess whether the prototype works as intended. Functional testing involves checking all mechanical and electronic functions to ensure they operate according to the design specifications.
- **Tools and Methods**: Use relevant tools and equipment to measure performance, durability, and compliance with technical standards.

- **User Testing**:

  - **Purpose**: Obtain feedback from potential users to gauge the usability and practicality of the prototype. User testing can provide insights into how the product is used in real-world scenarios and what improvements are needed.
  - **Methodology**: Conduct structured user tests where participants use the prototype in controlled conditions. Gather qualitative and quantitative data to inform further development.

3. Performance and Safety Evaluations

- **Testing Protocols**:

  - **Standards Compliance**: Ensure the prototype meets industry standards and regulatory requirements for safety and performance. This may involve tests such as stress testing, safety checks, and compliance certifications.
  - **Testing Environment**: Use both lab-based and field testing environments to evaluate how the prototype performs under different conditions.

4. Refinement and Finalization

- **Optimization**:

  - **Analysis**: Analyze data from all testing phases to identify areas for improvement. Make necessary adjustments to the design and materials to optimize performance, reduce costs, or enhance durability.

- **Validation**: Once adjustments are made, validate these changes with additional rounds of testing to confirm that the final design meets all required specifications and user needs.

5. Preparing for Commercialization

- **Market Fit and Scaling**:

  - **Manufacturability**: Evaluate the prototype's readiness for mass production. Consider factors like material availability, production cost, and the complexity of manufacturing processes.
  - **Pilot Production**: Before full-scale production, conduct a pilot run to identify any potential issues in the manufacturing process and to gauge market response.

6. Protecting the Invention

- **Patenting Strategy**:

  - **Provisional Application**: Consider filing a provisional patent application before entering the public testing phase to secure a filing date for your invention.
  - **Full Patent Application**: Based on the finalized prototype and after confirming the invention's novelty and functionality, prepare and file a full patent application.

Prototyping and testing not only refine the product but also build a strong foundation for the patent application by providing proof of concept and demonstrating the invention's practical application. This stage is critical for moving from concept to a market-ready product while ensuring the invention is adequately protected through patents.

Iterative Development and Refinement

Iterative development and refinement is a crucial methodology in the process of transforming an initial idea into a fully developed and market-ready product or technology. This approach allows inventors and developers to continually improve their designs based on systematic testing and feedback. Here's how this process typically unfolds:

1. Establishing a Feedback Loop

- **Continuous Feedback**: Central to iterative development is the continuous collection of feedback at every stage of the product development process. This feedback can come from a variety of sources including user testing, peer reviews, expert consultations, and performance analytics.
- **Responsive Adjustments**: Based on the feedback, adjustments are made to the design or functionality of the product. This responsive approach helps to refine the product to better meet user needs and technical requirements.

2. Prototyping Cycles

- **Rapid Prototyping**: Create quick and cost-effective prototypes to test concepts and explore different designs. These prototypes do not need to be perfect or final; their purpose is to visualize an idea and test its viability.
- **Evolution of Prototypes**: Each iteration of the prototype should evolve based on the previous testing outcomes. This might mean enhancements in design, user interface, materials used, or the underlying technology.

3. Testing and Evaluation

- **Regular Testing**: At each iteration, conduct rigorous testing tailored to the specific goals of that phase. Early iterations might focus on concept validation and basic functionality, while later tests may concentrate on reliability and user experience.
- **Objective Evaluation**: Set clear, measurable goals for each prototype iteration. Use these objectives to evaluate whether the iteration successfully addressed the issues identified in the previous round.

4. Integration of New Technologies and Trends

- **Adaptability**: Keep the development process adaptable to the integration of new technologies and market trends. This might involve incorporating new materials, software updates, or changes in user interface design prompted by evolving user expectations or technological advancements.
- **Market Alignment**: Regularly review market trends and competitor activities to ensure that the product remains relevant and competitive.

Adjust the development strategy accordingly to stay aligned with market demands.

5. Scaling from Prototype to Production

- **Scalability Testing**: Before finalizing the design, test for scalability and manufacturability. This involves assessing whether the design can be efficiently mass-produced within budget and technical constraints.
- **Pilot Runs**: Implement small-scale production runs to identify any manufacturing issues and market acceptance before full-scale production begins.

6. Documentation and IP Protection

- **Document Changes and Rationale**: Keep detailed records of each iteration, including what changes were made and why. This documentation is vital for patent applications and protecting intellectual property.
- **Protecting Iterations**: As the product evolves, consider the need for additional IP protection. File new patent applications if significant modifications impart novel functionalities or solve new problems.

7. Final Review and Launch Preparation

- **Pre-Launch Review**: Before going to market, conduct a final review of the entire development process and the end product. Ensure that the product meets all initial requirements and specifications set at the beginning of the project.
- **Market Strategy**: Develop a comprehensive go-to-market strategy that includes marketing, distribution, and post-launch support plans.

8.1.2 Innovation Process and Challenges

8.1.2.1 Overcoming Technical Barriers

Addressing Technical Challenges and Limitations

Innovation often involves navigating through a variety of technical challenges and limitations that can hinder the development and commercialization of new products or technologies. Successfully overcoming these barriers is crucial for turning innovative ideas into viable market solutions. Here's how innovators can effectively address and overcome these technical challenges:

1. Comprehensive Problem Identification

- **Deep Dive Analysis**: Begin by conducting a thorough analysis to understand the root causes of the technical challenges. This may involve a detailed examination of the existing technology, materials, processes, and environmental factors affecting the innovation.
- **Stakeholder Feedback**: Engage with end-users, industry experts, and other stakeholders to gain insights into practical challenges and usability issues that may not be apparent from internal reviews.

2. Leveraging Advanced Technologies and Research

- **Research on Emerging Technologies**: Stay updated with the latest advancements in technology that could potentially solve the technical barriers faced. This can involve integrating new materials, adopting novel engineering techniques, or applying breakthrough scientific discoveries.
- **Partnerships with Research Institutions**: Collaborate with universities, research labs, and other institutions to tap into cutting-edge research and technological resources that might not be available in-house.

3. Iterative Prototyping and Testing

- **Rapid Prototyping**: Utilize rapid prototyping tools such as 3D printing, software simulations, or CNC machining to quickly test ideas and iterate designs. This approach allows for fast failure and learning, which is essential in overcoming complex technical problems.
- **Controlled Testing Environments**: Set up experiments and pilot tests under controlled conditions to systematically evaluate different solutions and understand their impacts. This data-driven approach helps in refining the technology until it meets the desired standards.

4. Multidisciplinary Collaboration

- **Cross-functional Teams**: Form multidisciplinary teams that include engineers, scientists, designers, and business analysts to bring diverse perspectives and expertise to tackle the technical challenges. This collaboration can lead to more holistic and innovative solutions.

- **External Expertise:** If needed, consult with external experts or hire specialists with experience in specific areas that are critical for overcoming the technical barriers.

5. Utilizing Software and Analytical Tools

- **Simulation and Modeling:** Employ advanced simulation software to model how different designs or materials behave under various conditions. Simulations can help predict failures and optimize designs without the need for extensive physical testing.
- **Data Analytics:** Use data analytics to process and analyze large amounts of data collected from testing and operations. Insights gained from these analyses can drive decision-making and guide adjustments to the innovation process.

6. Risk Management and Contingency Planning

- **Risk Assessment:** Conduct regular risk assessments to anticipate potential technical failures and their implications. Understanding these risks allows for the development of strategies to mitigate them effectively.
- **Contingency Plans:** Develop contingency plans that outline steps to take if critical technical barriers are not overcome by the planned approaches. This might include pivoting the project focus, exploring alternative technologies, or adjusting project goals.

7. Intellectual Property Considerations

- **IP Protection:** As you develop new solutions to technical challenges, regularly assess the intellectual property landscape. File for patents where feasible to protect innovative solutions and maintain a competitive edge.
- **Freedom to Operate:** Ensure that the solutions developed do not infringe on existing patents or intellectual property rights of others. Conduct freedom-to-operate searches and obtain necessary licenses if required.

Collaborating with Multidisciplinary Teams

In the realm of innovation, especially when tackling complex technical projects, collaborating with multidisciplinary teams is essential. Such teams bring together diverse expertise and perspectives, enabling more comprehensive solutions to challenges that single-discipline teams might struggle to address effectively. Here's an overview of how to harness the strengths of multidisciplinary collaboration and manage potential limitations:

Benefits of Multidisciplinary Collaboration

1. **Broader Problem-Solving Capacity**: Diverse teams can approach problems from multiple angles, leading to innovative solutions that might not be apparent to specialists within a single field.
2. **Enhanced Creativity and Innovation**: The convergence of different fields often sparks creativity, as team members combine and adapt ideas from diverse disciplines, leading to breakthrough innovations.
3. **Risk Mitigation**: With experts from various backgrounds assessing a project, potential risks can be identified and mitigated more effectively, from technical challenges to market entry barriers.

Effective Strategies for Collaboration

1. **Establish Clear Communication Channels**:

    - Implement tools and practices that facilitate clear communication across different disciplines. This might include regular meetings, shared digital platforms, and communication protocols that ensure everyone understands the technical language across disciplines.

2. **Define Roles and Responsibilities**:

    - Clearly define each team member's role and responsibilities to prevent overlaps and ensure coverage of all necessary expertise areas. This clarity helps in managing the team efficiently and effectively.

3. **Foster an Inclusive Culture**:

- Encourage a team culture that values and respects different perspectives and expertise. Promoting inclusivity enhances collaboration and minimizes conflicts.

4. **Regular Integration Meetings:**

   - Conduct integration meetings where team members synthesize their findings and progress. These meetings help align the team on objectives and ensure that all aspects of the project are moving forward cohesively.

5. **Cross-Disciplinary Training:**

   - Offer opportunities for team members to learn about each other's fields. This could be through workshops, cross-training sessions, or informal knowledge-sharing meetings, which can help team members understand and appreciate each other's work better.

Managing Potential Limitations

1. **Communication Barriers:**

   - Address jargon and communication styles unique to each discipline. Encourage team members to use layman's terms when necessary and provide training on effective cross-disciplinary communication.

2. **Integration of Different Perspectives:**

   - Manage the integration of diverse perspectives by having a strong project leader or integration specialists who can align various viewpoints and approaches towards a common project goal.

3. **Balancing Contributions:**

   - Ensure that no single discipline dominates the project. Balance the input and influence of different team members to prevent bias towards any particular field of expertise.

4. **Time and Resource Management:**

    - Be mindful of the complexities involved in managing multidisciplinary projects, which may require more time and resources than single-discipline projects. Plan accordingly and ensure adequate resources are allocated to support effective collaboration.

8.1.2.2 Navigating Regulatory and Compliance Issues

Understanding Regulatory Requirements

Navigating the regulatory landscape is a critical aspect of the innovation process, particularly in industries such as pharmaceuticals, biotechnology, healthcare, and telecommunications, where products and processes are heavily regulated. Understanding and complying with these regulations not only ensures legal operation but also enhances the safety and efficacy of the innovations. Here's a guide on how innovators can effectively understand and manage regulatory requirements:

1. Identifying Relevant Regulations

- **Industry-Specific Guidelines**: Different industries are governed by specific regulatory bodies with their own set of rules. For instance, the FDA in the United States oversees food and drug safety, while the FCC regulates communications. Identify which regulatory bodies affect your industry and study their guidelines.
- **Global Considerations**: If planning to market products internationally, understand the regulatory requirements in each target market. Regulatory standards can vary widely between countries or regions (e.g., EMA in Europe, MHRA in the UK, PMDA in Japan).

2. Engaging with Regulatory Consultants

- **Expert Assistance**: Hiring experts or consultants who specialize in regulatory affairs can provide crucial insights and guidance. These professionals can help navigate complex regulations and streamline the compliance process.
- **Continuous Updates**: Regulations frequently change, and keeping abreast of these changes is crucial. Consultants can also assist in staying updated with the latest regulatory amendments and practices.

3. Early Regulatory Engagement

- **Pre-Submission Meetings**: Engage with regulatory bodies early in the development process through pre-submission meetings or preliminary consultations. This proactive approach can clarify the requirements and increase the likelihood of compliance in later stages.
- **Feedback Loops**: Use feedback from these engagements to refine product design and development strategies, ensuring alignment with regulatory expectations from the outset.

4. Compliance Testing and Validation

- **Testing Protocols**: Develop and maintain rigorous testing protocols that meet or exceed the regulatory standards for your product's safety, quality, and efficacy.
- **Third-Party Validation**: Consider using third-party labs or services to validate your compliance testing results. Independent validation can provide credibility to your data when submitting for regulatory approval.

5. Documentation and Record Keeping

- **Traceable Documentation**: Maintain detailed and traceable documentation of all research, development, and testing processes. This documentation should be organized and readily accessible for review by regulatory authorities.
- **Compliance Records**: Keep records of all compliance activities, including interactions with regulatory bodies, test results, and changes made to comply with regulatory advice. This will be invaluable during audits or inspections.

6. Training and Compliance Culture

- **Internal Training**: Conduct regular training sessions for your team on regulatory requirements and the importance of compliance. Everyone involved should understand how their role impacts regulatory compliance.
- **Compliance as Priority**: Foster a culture where compliance is seen as integral to the business process, not just a bureaucratic hurdle. This

mindset can help prevent compliance issues from arising and enhance the overall efficacy of your innovation process.

7. Preparing for Regulatory Audits

- **Audit Readiness**: Regularly review and audit your internal processes to ensure they align with the regulatory standards. Being prepared for unscheduled audits by regulatory bodies can help avoid potential fines or disruptions.

8.1.2.2 Navigating Regulatory and Compliance Issues

Ensuring Compliance with Industry Standards

Ensuring compliance with industry standards is essential for maintaining quality, safety, and efficiency in the development and distribution of new technologies. These standards often serve as benchmarks for regulatory compliance and can significantly impact the market acceptance of a product. Below is a detailed guide on how innovators can ensure their technologies meet these critical industry standards:

1. Identifying Applicable Standards

- **Industry-Specific Standards**: Each industry, whether it's telecommunications, electronics, health care, or automotive, has established its own set of standards. For example, ISO standards might apply to manufacturing processes, while IEC standards could pertain to electronic devices.
- **Standards Bodies**: Identify relevant standards bodies, such as ANSI, IEEE, and ISO, which publish and update the standards applicable to different aspects of technology and industry.

2. Integration into Product Development

- **Early Integration**: Incorporate the relevant industry standards right from the design phase of product development. This approach ensures that the final product is built to comply with these standards, reducing the need for costly redesigns.
- **Design Reviews**: Regular design reviews during the development process can help ensure ongoing compliance and address any deviations from industry standards before they become more significant issues.

3. Certification and Testing

- **Third-Party Certification**: Obtain certification from recognized third-party bodies that assess compliance with industry standards. This certification not only adds credibility to your product but also reassures customers and regulators of its compliance.
- **Routine Testing**: Implement routine testing of the product against the standards throughout the development process. This will help catch and rectify non-compliance issues early.

4. Quality Control Systems

- **Quality Management Systems (QMS)**: Establish a QMS such as ISO 9001 to oversee all areas of production and operation that could affect the quality of the final product. This system should include procedures for continuous monitoring, evaluation, and adjustments necessary to comply with the required standards.
- **Documentation**: Maintain comprehensive documentation of all compliance efforts, including test results, certification documents, and changes made to meet industry standards. This documentation will be crucial for audits and renewing certifications.

5. Staff Training and Awareness

- **Regular Training**: Provide ongoing training for all employees involved in the design, production, and quality control processes to ensure they are aware of the relevant standards and the importance of compliance.
- **Culture of Quality**: Foster a culture that values adherence to industry standards as a core aspect of the business strategy. This cultural emphasis helps in maintaining high standards of compliance routinely.

6. Continuous Improvement

- **Feedback Loops**: Establish feedback mechanisms to continually gather data on compliance and areas for improvement. Use this data to drive continuous improvements in processes and products.
- **Stay Updated**: Keep abreast of any changes to industry standards, which can occur frequently. Being proactive in updating practices in line with

new standards is vital for maintaining compliance and industry relevance.

7. Preparing for Compliance Audits

- **Internal Audits**: Conduct regular internal audits to check for compliance with industry standards. This proactive approach can help identify and correct non-compliance issues before they are flagged during external audits.
- **Audit Readiness**: Develop a strategy for dealing with audits, including quick access to necessary documentation and clear communication channels within the organization to address any auditor inquiries effectively.

8.1.2.3 Securing Funding and Resources

Identifying Funding Sources and Opportunities

Securing adequate funding and resources is a critical aspect of driving innovation from concept through to development and commercialization. Innovators need to identify various sources of funding that align with their project stages and specific needs. Here is a comprehensive guide on identifying and leveraging different funding sources for technological research and innovation:

1. Government Grants and Subsidies

- **Overview**: Many governments provide grants, subsidies, and tax incentives to support research and development activities, especially in high-tech, energy, biotech, and health care sectors.
- **How to Access**:
    - **Research Available Programs**: Look for government-funded programs such as the Small Business Innovation Research (SBIR) program in the U.S., Horizon Europe in the EU, or other similar programs depending on your location.
    - **Application Process**: Prepare a strong application highlighting the innovation, potential market impact, and alignment with national or regional economic goals.

2. Venture Capital (VC) Investment

- **Overview**: Venture capital firms provide funding in exchange for equity in the company. They are particularly interested in high-growth industries such as tech, biotech, and clean energy.
- **How to Access**:

  - **Networking**: Attend industry conferences, tech meetups, and other networking events to meet VC investors.
  - **Pitch Preparation**: Develop a compelling pitch deck that outlines your business model, market opportunity, competitive advantage, and team expertise.

3. Angel Investors

- **Overview**: Angel investors are typically high-net-worth individuals who provide capital for startups, often at earlier stages than VCs and sometimes in exchange for convertible debt or ownership equity.
- **How to Access**:

  - **Angel Networks**: Join networks that connect startups with angel investors, such as AngelList, or attend pitch events organized by local entrepreneur groups.
  - **Personal Connections**: Leverage personal networks and referrals from other entrepreneurs or business advisors.

4. Corporate Sponsorship and Partnerships

- **Overview**: Collaborations with larger corporations can provide not only funding but also valuable resources such as expertise, technology, and market access.
- **How to Access**:

  - **Industry Partnerships**: Identify potential industry partners who might benefit from your innovation. Tailor proposals to show mutual benefits.
  - **Innovation Hubs and Accelerators**: Join corporate-sponsored accelerators and hubs that offer funding, mentorship, and access to technological resources.

5. Crowdfunding

- **Overview**: Crowdfunding platforms like Kickstarter, Indiegogo, and GoFundMe can be used to raise small amounts of money from a large number of people, typically via the internet.
- **How to Access**:
  - **Campaign Creation**: Create a compelling crowdfunding campaign that includes detailed descriptions of the project, its goals, and the benefits for backers.
  - **Social Media Promotion**: Use social media and other digital marketing strategies to promote the campaign and reach a wider audience.

6. Loans and Debt Financing

- **Overview**: Traditional loans from banks or special loan programs designed for small businesses can provide essential funds for growth.
- **How to Access**:
  - **Business Credit**: Build a strong business credit score to improve your chances of securing a loan.
  - **Specialized Programs**: Look for loan programs offered through local or national government agencies that offer better terms for startups and small businesses.

7. University and Non-Profit Programs

- **Overview**: Many universities and non-profit organizations offer grants, competitions, and funding opportunities specifically for research and development.
- **How to Access**:
  - **Research Collaborations**: Collaborate with academic institutions on research projects that align with your innovation. These partnerships can often provide access to grants and other funding sources.
  - **Competitions and Awards**: Participate in innovation competitions and challenges sponsored by non-profits and educational institutions.

Conclusion

Securing funding is one of the most challenging aspects of innovation. By diversifying funding sources and strategically aligning with the right investors and programs, innovators can increase their chances of obtaining the necessary capital to bring their technological innovations to market.

8.1.2.3 Securing Funding and Resources

Managing Budgets and Resources Effectively

Effective management of budgets and resources is crucial for ensuring the successful execution and sustainability of innovative projects. Below are key strategies to help innovators manage their budgets and resources effectively:

1. Budget Planning and Forecasting

- **Overview**: Accurate budget planning and forecasting allow you to allocate resources efficiently and anticipate future financial needs.
- **How to Implement**:
  - **Detailed Budgets**: Create detailed budgets that outline all potential costs, including direct costs like materials and labor, and indirect costs such as overheads.
  - **Financial Forecasting**: Use historical data and market analysis to predict future financial conditions and adjust your budget accordingly.

2. Cost Control and Monitoring

- **Overview**: Constant monitoring of expenditures ensures that the project remains within budget and helps identify areas where costs can be reduced.
- **How to Implement**:
  - **Regular Reviews**: Conduct regular budget reviews to track spending and compare it against the forecast.
  - **Cost Reduction Strategies**: Identify less expensive alternatives and optimize resource allocation to cut costs without compromising on quality.

3. Resource Allocation

- **Overview**: Efficient resource allocation ensures that every aspect of the project receives the necessary inputs without wastage.
- **How to Implement**:
  - **Prioritization**: Allocate resources based on project priorities and deadlines.
  - **Resource Utilization Analysis**: Regularly assess how resources are used and make adjustments to maximize efficiency.

4. Financial Reporting and Transparency

- **Overview**: Transparent financial reporting builds trust with stakeholders and ensures that all financial activities are accounted for.
- **How to Implement**:
  - **Regular Financial Reports**: Prepare detailed financial reports that are easily understandable to stakeholders.
  - **Open Communication**: Maintain open lines of communication with all stakeholders about financial status and budgetary changes.

5. Managing Cash Flow

- **Overview**: Maintaining a healthy cash flow is essential for covering day-to-day expenses and keeping the project afloat.
- **How to Implement**:
  - **Cash Flow Projections**: Project your cash flow for at least the next quarter to ensure you have enough funds to cover upcoming expenses.
  - **Invoice Management**: Ensure timely billing and collection of payments to maintain a steady inflow of cash.

6. Contingency Planning

- **Overview**: Contingency funds help manage unexpected costs or financial shortfalls, reducing the risk of project delays.
- **How to Implement**:

- **Reserve Funds**: Set aside a portion of the budget as a contingency fund to cover unexpected expenses.
- **Risk Assessment**: Regularly conduct risk assessments to update and optimize the contingency plan based on potential financial risks.

7. Stakeholder Engagement

- **Overview**: Engaging stakeholders not only secures additional resources but also ensures broader support for financial and resource management strategies.
- **How to Implement**:
    - **Regular Updates**: Keep stakeholders informed about project progress and financial health through regular updates.
    - **Inclusive Decision-Making**: Involve stakeholders in key decisions, especially those affecting the project's budget or resource allocation.

8.2 International Scenario

8.2.1 Comparative Study of Patent Laws in Different Countries

8.2.1.1 Patent Law Variations

Differences in Patentability Criteria

Understanding the variations in patent laws across different countries is crucial for innovators who aim to protect their inventions globally. Patent laws vary significantly from one jurisdiction to another, particularly in terms of what constitutes patentable subject matter, the requirements for obtaining a patent, and the extent of protection it offers. Here's an overview of key differences in patentability criteria among several major jurisdictions:

1. United States

- **Criteria**: The U.S. Patent and Trademark Office (USPTO) requires that an invention be novel, non-obvious, and useful. This means the invention must not be previously disclosed anywhere in the world, must represent a significant step beyond existing technologies (non-obviousness), and must have some practical application (utility).

- **Subject Matter**: The USPTO allows patents on processes, machines, articles of manufacture, compositions of matter, and improvements thereof. Notably, the United States also permits the patenting of business methods and software, provided they meet the other statutory requirements.

2. European Union

- **Criteria**: The European Patent Office (EPO) uses similar criteria of novelty, inventive step (non-obviousness), and industrial applicability (utility). However, the EPO tends to have stricter requirements for the inventive step compared to the US.
- **Subject Matter**: The EPO does not allow patents for scientific theories, mathematical methods, aesthetic creations, schemes, rules and methods for performing mental acts, playing games or doing business, and programs for computers as such. However, technical inventions that implement business methods or software can be patented if they solve a technical problem in a novel and non-obvious way.

3. Japan

- **Criteria**: The Japan Patent Office (JPO) requires that inventions be industrially applicable, novel, and involve an inventive step. Japan's criteria closely align with those of the EPO.
- **Subject Matter**: Japan allows patents on computer software and business methods, but these must demonstrate a highly inventive step and practical application to be patentable.

4. China

- **Criteria**: Inventions must be novel, have practical applicability, and involve an inventive step. The novelty requirement in China is absolute; public disclosure anywhere in the world before the filing date can disqualify an invention.
- **Subject Matter**: China has been expanding the scope of patentable subject matter, increasingly allowing patents on software and business methods that meet the other criteria. However, similar to the EPO, such patents must include technical characteristics that represent an

improvement over existing technology.

5. India

- **Criteria**: Indian patent law requires novelty, inventive step, and industrial applicability. The inventive step requirement is stringent and often interpreted as something more than an obvious improvement by a person skilled in the art.
- **Subject Matter**: India does not allow patents for business methods, algorithms, or mathematical methods per se, though software that demonstrates a technical application in conjunction with hardware can be patented.

Implications for Innovators

- **Strategic Filing**: Innovators need to plan their patent filings strategically, taking into account the specific requirements and exclusions of each jurisdiction where they seek protection.
- **Professional Guidance**: Given the complexities and variations in international patent laws, it is advisable to seek guidance from patent attorneys who are knowledgeable about the specific laws of each target country.
- **Harmonization Efforts**: While significant differences exist, ongoing efforts by international organizations such as the World Intellectual Property Organization (WIPO) aim to harmonize aspects of patent laws globally, which may simplify the process for patent applicants in the future.

Understanding these differences is essential for global IP strategy, ensuring that innovations receive the broadest possible protection and align with business goals in different markets.

8.2.1.1 Patent Law Variations

Variations in Application Processes and Timelines

The process of applying for a patent and the associated timelines can vary significantly between different countries, affecting the strategy for international patent protection. Understanding these variations is crucial for efficiently managing patent portfolios globally. Here's a comparative look at the patent application processes and timelines in several key jurisdictions:

1. United States

- **Process**: The patent application process in the U.S. begins with filing either a provisional or non-provisional application with the U.S. Patent and Trademark Office (USPTO). A provisional application is not examined but holds the filing date for one year. A non-provisional application undergoes a substantive examination.
- **Timeline**: The overall process from filing to grant can take from 2 to 4 years, depending on the technology field and the complexity of the application. The USPTO offers Track One expedited examination for an additional fee, potentially reducing the timeline to under a year.

2. European Union

- **Process**: In the European Union, patents can be applied for through the European Patent Office (EPO) via the European Patent Convention (EPC). The process includes a search report, publication, and substantive examination. Applicants can also use the Patent Cooperation Treaty (PCT) route for an international application.
- **Timeline**: The typical duration from filing to grant is about 3 to 5 years. The EPO also provides accelerated procedures, such as PACE, for quicker examination.

3. Japan

- **Process**: In Japan, patent applications are filed with the Japan Patent Office (JPO). The process involves a request for examination, which must be filed within three years from the application filing date, followed by examination and potential grant.
- **Timeline**: The average time from application to grant is approximately 2 to 4 years. Japan offers an expedited examination process for inventions in green technology or for applicants who are senior citizens or SMEs.

4. China

- **Process**: Applications in China are submitted to the China National Intellectual Property Administration (CNIPA). The process includes a formal examination, publication, substantive examination upon request, and then grant if compliant.

- **Timeline**: The process typically takes about 3 to 5 years. China also provides a prioritized examination for certain categories of patents, which can significantly shorten the timeline.

5. India

- **Process**: The Indian patent application process involves filing with the Indian Patent Office, followed by a publication after 18 months, and a request for examination that needs to be made within 48 months from the priority date. This is followed by a substantive examination and, potentially, grant.
- **Timeline**: The timeline from filing to grant can extend up to 5 to 7 years, although efforts are being made to reduce this. India also offers an expedited examination for startups and certain other categories.

Key Considerations for Global Patent Strategy:

- **Priority Filing**: Utilize the Paris Convention priority year to synchronize multiple country filings from a single priority date.
- **PCT Route**: Consider filing a PCT application, which does not grant a patent but allows you to effectively delay entering into specific countries for up to 30 or 31 months from the earliest filing date, thus providing more time to decide where to seek patent protection based on business needs.
- **Local Legal Requirements**: Be aware of local legal requirements such as translation needs and local agent representation, which can affect both timeline and cost.

Understanding and navigating the variations in patent application processes and timelines across different jurisdictions are fundamental for creating an effective and efficient global patent strategy. This approach ensures timely and broad patent protection aligned with international business goals and market dynamics.

8.2.1.2 Case Studies of International Patent Practices

Successful International Patent Filings

Understanding the nuances of successful international patent practices can provide invaluable insights for innovators looking to protect their inventions globally. Here are several case studies that highlight effective strategies and lessons from successful international patent filings:

1. Apple Inc. – Global Strategy for Design Patents

- **Overview**: Apple has strategically used design patents to protect its innovative products, including the iconic designs of the iPhone and iPad, in multiple jurisdictions.
- **Strategy**:
    - **Filing in Key Markets**: Apple files for patents in significant markets such as the U.S., Europe, Japan, China, and South Korea simultaneously to ensure comprehensive global protection.
    - **Rapid Filing Post-Product Launch**: Apple typically files for design patents immediately after product launches, taking advantage of the grace period provisions in many countries that allow for a public disclosure of the design by the inventor within a certain period before the filing.
- **Outcome**: Apple's aggressive strategy in securing design patents has been crucial in maintaining its competitive edge and enforcing its rights against competitors, as seen in various high-profile litigation cases, such as those against Samsung.

2. Novartis AG – Navigating India's Patent Law

- **Overview**: Novartis faced significant challenges when it sought to patent its cancer drug, Glivec, in India, a country known for its stringent patent criteria regarding pharmaceuticals.
- **Challenges**:
    - **Section 3(d)**: Novartis's application was rejected under Section 3(d) of the Indian Patent Act, which prevents patenting of known substances unless they differ significantly in properties with regard to efficacy.
- **Strategy**:

- **Legal Challenge**: Novartis took the issue to the Indian courts, arguing that the interpretation of Section 3(d) was too strict and hindered pharmaceutical innovation.

- **Outcome**: The Indian Supreme Court upheld the patent office's decision. While Novartis did not succeed in obtaining a patent for Glivec, the case prompted international pharmaceutical companies to reassess their patent strategies in India.

3. Tesla Motors – Open Source Patent Strategy

- **Overview**: In 2014, Tesla Motors, led by Elon Musk, took an unconventional approach by announcing that it would not initiate patent lawsuits against anyone using its technology in good faith.
- **Strategy**:

  - **Encouraging Innovation**: Tesla's strategy aimed to encourage the adoption of electric vehicle technology and stimulate global innovation in the sector.
  - **Patent Filing**: Despite the open-source announcement, Tesla continues to file patents to document its innovations and maintain formal records of its technological advancements.

- **Outcome**: Tesla's approach has helped it build a brand associated with innovation and openness, potentially fostering wider industry collaboration and accelerating the development of electric vehicle technology.

4. Alibaba Group – E-commerce Technology Patents in China

- **Overview**: As a leader in e-commerce, Alibaba has aggressively patented its innovations in China, particularly around e-commerce, search algorithms, and cloud computing.
- **Strategy**:

  - **Massive Filing Strategy**: Alibaba files a large number of patents annually to cover all aspects of its technological developments, ensuring it remains at the forefront of e-commerce innovation.

- **Leveraging Chinese IP Law**: Understanding and utilizing the nuances of Chinese intellectual property law has allowed Alibaba to build a robust patent portfolio effectively.

- **Outcome**: Alibaba's comprehensive IP strategy has provided it with a strong defensive and offensive legal toolkit, enabling it to protect its market share and deter infringements effectively.

8.2 International Scenario

8.2.1 Comparative Study of Patent Laws in Different Countries

Challenges Faced by Inventors in Different Jurisdictions

Navigating the patent landscape across various jurisdictions presents a myriad of challenges for inventors, ranging from legal complexities to strategic and logistical issues. Understanding these challenges is crucial for developing effective strategies to secure and enforce patent rights internationally. Here are some common challenges inventors face in different jurisdictions:

1. Variability in Patentability Criteria

- **Issue**: Criteria for what constitutes patentable subject matter and the requirements for novelty, inventive step (non-obviousness), and industrial applicability (utility) vary significantly between countries.
- **Impact**: Inventors must tailor their applications to meet the specific criteria of each jurisdiction, which can complicate the preparation and filing process and increase costs.

2. Cost Implications

- **Issue**: Filing and maintaining patents across multiple jurisdictions can be prohibitively expensive. Costs include not only filing fees but also translation costs, attorney fees, and ongoing maintenance fees.
- **Impact**: Small enterprises and individual inventors may find it financially challenging to protect their inventions adequately in all desired markets.

3. Time to Grant

- **Issue**: The time from application to grant of a patent can vary widely between jurisdictions. In some countries, the process can take several years.
- **Impact**: Delays in patent issuance can hinder the ability to secure funding, enter markets, and enforce rights against infringers.

4. Legal and Regulatory Complexity

- **Issue**: Each country has its own legal system and set of rules governing patents, including how they are applied for, examined, granted, and enforced.
- **Impact**: Inventors need to navigate a complex web of legal systems, which often requires hiring local patent agents or attorneys, further increasing costs and complexity.

5. Enforcement Challenges

- **Issue**: Enforcing patents effectively in foreign jurisdictions can be difficult, particularly in countries where patent infringement is not rigorously prosecuted or where the legal processes are slow and inefficient.
- **Impact**: Inventors may struggle to protect their intellectual property from infringement, undermining the value of their patents.

6. Cultural and Language Barriers

- **Issue**: Differences in language and business practices can complicate communication and legal proceedings in foreign countries.
- **Impact**: Misunderstandings or errors in translation can lead to delays or unfavorable outcomes in the patent application and enforcement processes.

7. Changes in Law and Policy

- **Issue**: Patent laws are subject to change, and shifts in political climate or economic policy can affect the strength and scope of patent protection.
- **Impact**: Inventors must stay informed about changes in patent law and adapt their strategies accordingly, which can require additional time and

resources.

8. Local Working Requirements and Compulsory Licensing

- **Issue**: Some countries have local working requirements, where a patent holder may be compelled to manufacture the patented product locally or face compulsory licensing if the product is not being "worked" in the country.
- **Impact**: Inventors may need to set up local manufacturing or risk having their patents licensed to a third party, which can affect profitability and market control.

Strategies for Overcoming These Challenges

1. **Strategic Planning**: Develop a clear understanding of which markets are most critical for your invention and focus your resources there.
2. **Professional Assistance**: Engage experienced IP attorneys who understand the nuances of patent law in each target jurisdiction.
3. **Cost Management**: Explore cost-saving measures such as using the Patent Cooperation Treaty (PCT) for initial filings or seeking governmental and non-profit grants available for international patenting.
4. **Proactive Enforcement**: Establish partnerships with local entities and use technology such as blockchain for proof of IP ownership and management, improving enforcement capabilities.

Navigating international patent challenges requires a well-considered strategy, knowledgeable guidance, and proactive management to ensure that inventions are protected and commercialized effectively across borders.

8.2 International Scenario

8.2.2 International Cooperation on IPR

8.2.2.1 Key International Treaties and Agreements

Overview of TRIPS (Trade-Related Aspects of Intellectual Property Rights)

International cooperation on intellectual property rights (IPR) is crucial for ensuring that innovations are protected and recognized globally. One of the cornerstones of such cooperation is the establishment of international treaties and agreements that standardize the rules and enforcement mechanisms across borders. Among these, the Agreement on Trade-Related Aspects of Intellectual Property Rights (TRIPS) is particularly significant.

TRIPS Agreement Overview

- **Background**: The TRIPS Agreement is an international legal agreement between all the member nations of the World Trade Organization (WTO). It was negotiated during the Uruguay Round of the General Agreement on Tariffs and Trade (GATT) in 1994 and is administered by the WTO.
- **Purpose**: TRIPS was established to standardize the laws and practices concerning intellectual property across member countries, thereby reducing distortions in international trade and providing a clear framework for the enforcement of intellectual property rights.
- **Key Provisions**:
    - **Minimum Standards**: TRIPS sets minimum standards for the protection of various forms of intellectual property, including patents, copyrights, trademarks, geographical indications, industrial designs, and undisclosed information (trade secrets).
    - **Scope and Use**: The agreement outlines how intellectual property rights should be protected (scope) and how they can be used, licensed, or transferred (use).
    - **Enforcement**: It details the procedures and remedies that must be available so that intellectual property rights can be effectively enforced. These procedures must be fair, equitable, not unnecessarily complicated, and not entail unreasonable time limits or unwarranted delays.
    - **Dispute Resolution**: TRIPS includes mechanisms for settling disputes over intellectual property between WTO members, which are handled by the Dispute Settlement Body of the WTO.

Impact of TRIPS

- **Harmonization**: By setting minimum standards, TRIPS has helped harmonize the protection and enforcement of intellectual property across national borders, making it easier for holders of intellectual property to obtain global protection.
- **Challenges and Criticisms**:

  - **Impact on Developing Countries**: There has been ongoing debate about the impact of TRIPS on developing countries. Critics argue that TRIPS standards, particularly in the pharmaceutical sector, may limit access to affordable medicines in poorer countries by extending patent protection periods.
  - **Flexibilities**: In response, TRIPS includes certain flexibilities such as compulsory licensing and parallel importing, which allow countries to deal with public health emergencies by overriding patent rights, under specific conditions.

- **Amendments and Updates**: Since its inception, there have been amendments to TRIPS, most notably the Doha Declaration on the TRIPS Agreement and Public Health in 2001, which reaffirmed the flexibilities of member countries in circumventing patent rights for better access to essential medicines.

Role of the Paris Convention and Patent Cooperation Treaty (PCT)

International cooperation on intellectual property rights is facilitated through several key treaties, with the Paris Convention and the Patent Cooperation Treaty (PCT) being two of the most influential. These agreements help streamline the process for obtaining patent protection across multiple countries, providing a framework that supports both inventors and businesses in navigating the global patent landscape.

Paris Convention for the Protection of Industrial Property

- **Overview**: Established in 1883, the Paris Convention was one of the first intellectual property treaties. It is administered by the World Intellectual Property Organization (WIPO) and has been ratified by over 170 countries, making it one of the most widely adopted IP treaties globally.
- **Key Provisions**:

- **National Treatment**: The convention requires each contracting state to grant the same protection to nationals of other contracting states as it grants to its own nationals.
- **Right of Priority**: This is a critical aspect of the Paris Convention. It allows an applicant from a contracting state to use their first filing date in one of the member countries as the effective filing date in other member countries. This priority right is applicable for 12 months for patents and utility models, and 6 months for industrial designs and trademarks.

- **Impact**: The convention facilitates the mutual recognition of patent rights among member states, thereby significantly reducing the complexity, cost, and effort involved in obtaining patent protection in multiple jurisdictions.

Patent Cooperation Treaty (PCT)

- **Overview**: The PCT, which came into effect in 1978, builds on the principles set forth by the Paris Convention. It simplifies the process of filing patent applications on the same invention in several countries by delaying the need to file costly national phase applications.
- **Key Provisions**:

  - **Single Patent Application**: An inventor can file a single international patent application in one language, which will have the same effect as national applications filed in designated PCT member countries.
  - **International Search and Preliminary Examination**: A PCT application undergoes an international search for prior art and, optionally, a preliminary examination, which provides a report on the patentability of the invention. This process helps inventors make informed decisions about pursuing patent protection in specific countries based on the feedback received.

- **Impact**: The PCT streamlines the international patent application process, reduces costs by delaying national filings, and provides a strong basis for patent decisions with its international search report and written opinion. It currently has 153 contracting states, making it an invaluable tool for inventors seeking broad international protection for their innovations.

8.2.2.2 Collaboration Among International Patent Offices Initiatives for Harmonizing Patent Laws and Practices

Collaboration among international patent offices plays a crucial role in streamlining and harmonizing patent laws and practices, making it easier for inventors to secure and manage patents globally. Several initiatives and cooperative frameworks have been developed to reduce redundancy, simplify procedures, and create a more unified global patent system. Here are some key initiatives aimed at harmonizing patent laws and practices:

1. Patent Prosecution Highway (PPH)

- **Overview**: The Patent Prosecution Highway is a set of initiatives where participating patent offices agree to expedite the examination process for applications that have been declared patentable in another participating office. This is done on the basis that if one office has found a claim patentable, other offices can reuse this finding, significantly speeding up the process.
- **Impact**: The PPH reduces examination workload and improves patent quality by sharing information between patent offices, thereby decreasing the examination time and associated costs for applicants.

2. Cooperative Patent Classification (CPC)

- **Overview**: The Cooperative Patent Classification system is a detailed classification system for patent documents used globally. It was developed jointly by the European Patent Office (EPO) and the United States Patent and Trademark Office (USPTO) and is now used by many patent offices around the world.
- **Impact**: The CPC provides a common platform for patent documentation classification, which helps in improving the efficiency of patent searches and examination across different patent offices, thus fostering more consistent patent grants and reducing barriers to international patent applications.

3. Global Dossier

- **Overview**: The Global Dossier initiative is facilitated by the "IP5," which consists of the five largest Intellectual Property Offices in the world — the USPTO, EPO, Japan Patent Office (JPO), Korean Intellectual Property Office (KIPO), and the China National Intellectual Property Administration (CNIPA). The initiative provides a unified access point to the dossiers of patent applications, simplifying the management of international patents.
- **Impact**: This service allows patent applicants and offices to access documents and information of a patent family (applications that are related and filed in multiple countries) from a single interface, which simplifies the process of multiple filings and aids in transparency.

4. Trilateral and IP5 Cooperation

- **Overview**: The trilateral cooperation among the EPO, JPO, and USPTO, and the extension to the IP5, which includes KIPO and CNIPA, focuses on enhancing the efficiency of the global patent system. This includes efforts to harmonize practices and procedures, share best practices, and develop common tools and policies.
- **Impact**: These collaborations lead to more streamlined operations and greater consistency in patent application processing across major global economies, thereby facilitating easier and more reliable patent filings for inventors and corporations.

5. WIPO Standards

- **Overview**: The World Intellectual Property Organization (WIPO) develops and promotes standards and norms for IP rights which are adopted by its member states. These standards cover various aspects of intellectual property, including patent application filing, data exchange, documentation, and information dissemination.
- **Impact**: WIPO standards ensure that technological advancements in IP systems are shared globally, promoting interoperability and improving the efficiency of IP systems worldwide.

Benefits and Challenges of International Cooperation

International cooperation in intellectual property rights (IPR) plays a vital role in the global innovation landscape, promoting more efficient and uniform practices across borders. This cooperation provides numerous benefits but also poses significant challenges, reflecting the complex nature of aligning diverse legal systems and national interests.

Benefits of International Cooperation

1. **Streamlined Processes**: Cooperation among international patent offices can lead to more streamlined and efficient processes for filing and managing patents. Initiatives like the Patent Cooperation Treaty (PCT) simplify the filing process by allowing inventors to seek patent protection internationally through a single application.
2. **Reduced Costs**: By harmonizing patent application procedures and requirements, international cooperation can reduce the costs associated with securing and maintaining patents in multiple jurisdictions. Shared databases and classification systems, such as the Cooperative Patent Classification (CPC), help reduce the redundancy of work among patent offices, lowering costs for applicants.
3. **Enhanced Innovation**: Global standards and cooperative frameworks foster a more predictable and transparent IP environment that encourages investment in R&D. This environment supports innovation by providing clearer paths to patent protection and reducing the risks associated with international market entry.
4. **Improved IP Rights Enforcement**: Collaboration leads to better mechanisms for enforcing IP rights across borders. Initiatives like the Anti-Counterfeiting Trade Agreement (ACTA) aim to establish international standards for enforcing intellectual property rights, helping to combat counterfeiting and piracy.
5. **Increased Access to Information**: International cooperation results in more comprehensive and accessible patent databases, which provide inventors and businesses worldwide with valuable information about existing patents and technological developments. This access supports more informed research and development strategies.

Challenges of International Cooperation

1. **Diverse Legal Systems**: Aligning the varying legal systems and practices of different countries poses a significant challenge. Differences in patentability criteria, procedural requirements, and enforcement mechanisms can complicate efforts to create a unified global patent

system.

2. **Sovereignty and Policy Differences**: Countries may have conflicting national interests or policies that impact their approach to IP rights. For example, developing countries may prioritize access to medicines over pharmaceutical patent protections, leading to tensions within international frameworks like TRIPS.
3. **Complexity and Bureaucracy**: International cooperation can sometimes increase the complexity of IP systems, introducing layers of bureaucracy that may slow down the patent process. Coordinating among multiple international bodies and complying with various agreements can also be cumbersome for patent applicants.
4. **Enforcement Issues**: Despite efforts to standardize IP enforcement, practical challenges remain, particularly in ensuring that IP rights are respected across different jurisdictions. The effectiveness of enforcement still varies significantly from country to country.
5. **Technological and Operational Disparities**: Differences in the technological capabilities and operational efficiency of patent offices around the world can hinder the effectiveness of cooperative initiatives. Less developed patent systems may struggle to implement and benefit from international standards and practices.

8.2.2.3 Global Patent Strategies for Innovators

Developing Effective International Patent Strategies

For innovators looking to protect their inventions globally, crafting a well-thought-out international patent strategy is crucial. This strategy not only secures intellectual property rights across different jurisdictions but also optimizes the commercial potential of those rights worldwide. Here's a guide to developing effective international patent strategies:

1. Understanding Key Markets

- **Market Analysis**: Identify and prioritize countries where the invention has the highest commercial potential or where market entry is planned. Consider factors like market size, growth prospects, competitive landscape, and the presence of potential partners or customers.
- **Legal Environment**: Assess the strength and enforceability of IP laws in potential markets. Strong patent protection regimes are critical in high-tech, pharmaceuticals, and biotech sectors where IP is a core component of the business strategy.

2. Utilizing International Treaties

- **Patent Cooperation Treaty (PCT)**: Use the PCT to file a single international patent application that has the effect of a national application in up to 153 member countries. This approach buys time to decide in which countries to pursue national phase entry based on commercial needs, costs, and the invention's lifecycle.
- **Paris Convention**: Leverage the Paris Convention's priority right, which allows the inventor to claim a priority date based on the first filed application in one of the member countries. This is particularly useful for securing early patent rights while planning subsequent filings in other countries.

3. Balancing Costs and Benefits

- **Cost Management**: International patent filing and maintenance can be expensive. Prioritize countries based on strategic business needs, potential ROI, and the cost of obtaining and maintaining patents.
- **Portfolio Optimization**: Regularly review and streamline the international patent portfolio to focus on patents that provide strategic value and discontinue those that no longer justify their costs.

4. Strategic Filing Decisions

- **Phased Filing Strategy**: Consider a phased approach to filing, where key markets are targeted first, followed by secondary markets as business needs and financial resources allow.
- **Consider Local Requirements**: Be aware of the local filing requirements, including translation obligations and the need for local agents or representatives, which can affect timelines and costs.

5. Technology and Competitive Intelligence

- **Patent Landscaping**: Conduct patent landscape analyses to understand the competitive field and technological trends within target markets. This intelligence can guide R&D and patent filing strategies to avoid crowded fields and focus on areas with higher innovation potential.

- **Watch Services**: Implement patent watch services to monitor competitor activities and new filings in key technology areas. This will help in making informed decisions about where and when to file.

6. Managing Risks and Enforcement

- **Risk Assessment**: Evaluate the risks of patent infringement and the robustness of patent rights in different jurisdictions. Tailor the innovation and patent strategy to mitigate these risks.
- **Enforcement Plans**: Develop a clear plan for enforcing patents, including litigation, licensing agreements, and negotiations. Consider the feasibility and costs of enforcement actions in each jurisdiction.

7. Building Expert Networks

- **Collaboration with IP Professionals**: Establish relationships with experienced IP attorneys and consultants across different regions who can provide local insights and guidance on complex patent issues.
- **Industry Partnerships**: Forge alliances with local companies and research institutions that can facilitate market entry and enhance the innovator's IP strategy through joint ventures or licensing agreements.

Leveraging International Networks and Resources

For innovators and businesses operating on a global scale, effectively leveraging international networks and resources is crucial for maximizing the reach and impact of their intellectual property (IP). This approach not only enhances IP protection but also fosters innovation and market expansion. Here's how to effectively leverage international networks and resources:

1. Building Strategic Alliances

- **Industry Partnerships**: Forge relationships with international companies and research institutions that can complement your technology and market goals. These partnerships can provide local insights, access to new markets, and shared R&D resources.
- **Trade Associations and Chambers of Commerce**: Engage with these organizations, which can offer valuable networking opportunities, market intelligence, and advocacy on IP issues. They often have

branches or connections across multiple countries and can facilitate introductions to potential partners, suppliers, or customers.

2. Utilizing Global Innovation Hubs

- **Innovation Clusters**: Participate in global innovation hubs or clusters, which are geographical concentrations of interconnected businesses, suppliers, and associated institutions in a particular field. Examples include Silicon Valley for tech, Basel for pharmaceuticals, or Munich for engineering.
- **Incubators and Accelerators**: These programs can provide support in terms of office space, mentorship, and access to a network of investors and experts. Many are linked internationally, offering a gateway to global business and innovation communities.

3. Engaging with International IP Organizations

- **World Intellectual Property Organization (WIPO)**: Utilize WIPO's resources, such as the Patent Cooperation Treaty (PCT), which simplifies the process of filing patents in multiple countries. WIPO also offers various training programs, databases, and tools to support international IP activities.
- **European Patent Office (EPO) and United States Patent and Trademark Office (USPTO)**: These offices offer extensive data and search tools, seminars, and outreach programs that can be invaluable for understanding and navigating complex IP landscapes.

4. International Conferences and Trade Shows

- **Knowledge Sharing**: Attend international conferences, symposiums, and trade shows related to your industry. These events are excellent for networking, staying abreast of the latest innovations, and understanding emerging market trends.
- **Visibility and Networking**: Present your innovations and research findings at these gatherings to gain visibility and attract potential collaborators, investors, or customers.

5. Collaborative Research and Development

- **Cross-Border R&D Projects**: Participate in international R&D projects, such as those funded by the European Union's Horizon Europe program. These projects not only provide funding but also access to a consortium of international partners.
- **Government and International Grants**: Apply for grants that promote international collaboration. Many governments and international bodies offer funding specifically designed to encourage cross-border innovation.

6. Leveraging Digital Platforms and Social Media

- **Online Networking**: Utilize professional networking sites like LinkedIn to connect with international peers, join industry-specific groups, and participate in discussions. These platforms can help establish your presence in the international market.
- **Knowledge Platforms**: Engage with online platforms and forums where professionals discuss industry trends, challenges, and innovations. These interactions can provide insights and opportunities for collaboration.

7. Legal and Consultative Support

- **International Law Firms**: Work with law firms that have a presence in multiple countries or those that specialize in international IP law. They can provide crucial guidance on international patents, trademarks, compliance, and risk management.
- **Consultants and Advisors**: Hire consultants who specialize in international business expansion and IP strategy. Their expertise can help navigate different regulatory environments and cultural nuances.

www.ingramcontent.com/pod-product-compliance
Lightning Source LLC
LaVergne TN
LVHW021147160826
845679LV00024B/2077

* 9 7 9 8 8 9 4 1 5 7 2 1 4 *